DARK AMBITION

DARK AMBITION

THE SHOCKING CRIME OF DELLEN MILLARD & MARK SMICH

ANN BROCKLEHURST

VIKING

VIKING

an imprint of Penguin Canada, a division of Penguin Random House Canada Limited

Canada • USA • UK • Ireland • Australia • New Zealand • India • South Africa • China

First published 2016

www.penguinrandomhouse.ca

LIBRARY AND ARCHIVES CANADA CATALOGUING IN PUBLICATION

Brocklehurst, Ann, 1958–, author
Dark ambition : the shocking crime of Dellen Millard and Mark Smich /
Ann Brocklehurst.

Includes index.
ISBN 978-0-670-07014-5 (hardback)
ISBN 978-0-14-319826-0 (electronic)

1.Millard, Dellen. 2.Murderers—Ontario—Case studies.
3.Murder—Ontario—Case studies. 4.Murder—Investigation—
Ontario—Case studies. I.Title.

HV6535.C32O65 2016   364.152'309713   C2016-902523-3

Cover design by Five Seventeen
Cover images by Ingram Publishing/Getty Images

Printed and bound in the United States of America

10 9 8 7 6 5 4 3 2 1

Penguin
Random House
VIKING Canada

In memory of my mother,
Mildred Brocklehurst Woods

CONTENTS

TIMELINE

2011

Spring 2011
Dellen Millard becomes engaged to Jennifer Spafford, takes engagement photos at Millardair hangar at Pearson airport before engagement is abruptly broken off

June 2011
Dellen Millard and Andrew Michalski participate in Baja 500 road race

Summer 2011
Dellen Millard begins dating Christina Noudga

September 2011
Construction begins on new Millardair hangar in Waterloo

2012

March 2012
Millardair opens new Waterloo hangar

June 21, 2012
Shane Schlatman purchases the Eliminator incinerator on Millardair account

July 2–3, 2012
Laura Babcock makes eight phone calls to Dellen Millard before she disappears

November 29, 2012
Wayne Millard dies suddenly

December 14, 2012
Wayne Millard obituary published after death is deemed suicide

December 2012
Millardair cancels its transportation department certification, all employees except Shane Schlatman laid off

2013

May 5, 2013   Test drive with Igor Tumanenko

May 6, 2013   Tim Bosma disappears

May 8, 2013   Hamilton Police holds first news conference on Bosma disappearance

May 9, 2013   Sharlene Bosma makes televised appeal

May 10, 2013   Hamilton Police appeals for information on "ambition" tattoo; Millard arrested

May 11, 2013   Hamilton Police announces arrest of Millard, charged with forcible confinement and theft over $5,000

May 12, 2013   Tim Bosma's truck is found in Kleinburg driveway of Millard's mother, Madeleine Burns

May 14, 2013   Hamilton Police announces death of Tim Bosma; Millard to be charged with first-degree murder; first reports of incinerator at Millard farm

May 15, 2013   Dellen Millard appears in court to be charged with first-degree murder of Bosma

May 19, 2013   Mark Smich's sister Melissa gets married

May 22, 2013   Mark Smich is arrested

May 23, 2013   Mark Smich appears in court to be charged with first-degree murder of Bosma

December 30, 2013   *Toronto Star* publishes jailhouse interview with Dellen Millard

2014

April 10, 2014   Dellen Millard charged with first-degree murders of Laura Babcock and Wayne Millard; Mark Smich charged with first-degree murder of Laura Babcock

April 11, 2014   Christina Noudga charged as accessory after the fact in murder of Tim Bosma

August 8, 2014   Christina Noudga released from jail on bail

2016

February 1, 2016   Trial of Dellen Millard and Mark Smich begins

June 17, 2016   Dellen Millard and Mark Smich found guilty of first-degree murder of Bosma, sentenced to life imprisonment with no chance of parole until 2038

July 2016   Dellen Millard and Mark Smich appeal their first-degree murder convictions

November 14, 2016   Trial of Christina Noudga set to begin

2017

February 13, 2017   Trial of Dellen Millard and Mark Smich for murder of Laura Babcock set to begin

Fall 2017   Trial of Dellen Millard for the murder of Wayne Millard tentatively set to begin

CAST OF CHARACTERS

BOSMA FAMILY

TIM BOSMA

SHARLENE BOSMA   wife

MARY BOSMA   mother

HANK BOSMA   father

POLICE

MATT KAVANAGH   Hamilton Police, homicide detective in charge (official title re Bosma case: major case manager)

GREG RODZONIAK   Hamilton Police, lead detective on Bosma case (official title re Bosma case: primary detective)

GLENN DE CAIRE   Hamilton Police, chief

DAN KINSELLA   Hamilton Police, superintendent

GREG JACKSON   Hamilton Police, tracked cell phones, interviewed Tumanenko

PAUL HAMILTON   Hamilton Police, interviewed Millard at hangar

JOHN TSELEPAKIS   Hamilton Police, tracked cell phones, interviewed Millard

STUART OXLEY   Hamilton Police surveillance unit, tracked and arrested Millard and Smich

JENNIFER GRANATIER   Hamilton Police, tracked Christina Noudga for castoff DNA

BRENT GIBSON   Hamilton Police, escorted Bosma truck from Kleinburg to Hamilton

LAURA TROWBRIDGE   Hamilton Police, escorted Bosma truck from Hamilton to secure OPP facility

CORY WEICK   York Police, investigated Bosma truck in Kleinburg

MARK LEVANGIE   York Police, investigated Bosma truck in Kleinburg

LAURA McLELLAN   Halton Police, conducted forensic investigation of Bosma truck

DAVID BANKS	Halton Police, conducted forensic investigation of Bosma truck
BEN ADAMS	Hamilton Police, investigated Millard farm
PHILIP PECKFORD	Hamilton Police, investigated Millard farm
ANNETTE HUYS	Hamilton Police, conducted forensic investigation of Eliminator
GEORGE HIGGINS	Hamilton Police, conducted surveillance on Millard and Smich
BARRY STOLTZ	Hamilton Police, collected Super Sucker video
STEVE GRIFFIN	Waterloo Police, conducted surveillance on Millard
MIKE CARBONE	Toronto Police, took over Laura Babcock and Wayne Millard investigations

EXPERT WITNESSES

JIM FALCONER	retired OPP detective, computer forensics expert
ROBERT JONES	Waterloo Police, blood spatter expert
TRACY ROGERS	forensic anthropologist
DR. WILLIAM BARLOW	forensic dentist
DR. JOHN FERNANDES	forensic pathologist
JAMES SLOOTS	Centre of Forensic Sciences, biologist, DNA expert
ROBERT GERARD	Centre of Forensic Sciences, chemist, GSR expert
MICHAEL PLAXTON	Hamilton Police, forensic video analyst

WITNESSES

WAYNE DE BOER	Bosma tenant
IGOR TUMANENKO	went on first test drive with Millard and Smich
OMAR PALMILI	missed test drive appointment with Millard and Smich
RICK BULLMANN	Bosma neighbour
CHAZ MAIN	dirt biker who spotted Eliminator on Millard property
JAMES STIEVA	Super Sucker, employee

LAWYERS AND JUDGE

THE HONOURABLE ANDREW GOODMAN	judge
TONY LEITCH	lead Crown prosecutor
CRAIG FRASER	Crown prosecutor
BRETT MOODIE	Crown prosecutor
RAVIN PILLAY	Dellen Millard's lead lawyer
NADIR SACHAK	Dellen Millard's lawyer
DEEPAK PARADKAR	Dellen Millard's original lawyer
THOMAS DUNGEY	Mark Smich's lead lawyer
JENNIFER TREHEARNE	Mark Smich's lawyer

MILLARD FAMILY, FRIENDS, AND EMPLOYEES

MADELEINE BURNS	Dellen's mother
WAYNE MILLARD	Dellen's father
CARL MILLARD	Dellen's grandfather
ROBERT BURNS	uncle, brother of Dellen's mother
CHRISTINA NOUDGA	Dellen's girlfriend at time of Bosma's murder
LISA WHIDDEN	second girlfriend and realtor
JENNIFER SPAFFORD	ex-fiancée
ART JENNINGS	Millardair, intern, father-in-law of Shane Schlatman
SHANE SCHLATMAN	Millardair, mechanic
SPENCER HUSSEY	Millardair, employee
JAVIER VILLADA	contractor
ANDREW MICHALSKI	friend
MATT HAGERMAN	friend
AL SHARIF	Millardair, consultant
LISA WILLIAMS	Millardair, contract bookkeeper

SMICH FAMILY AND FRIENDS

MARY SMICH	Mark's mother
ANDREA SMICH	eldest sister
MELISSA SMICH	elder sister and bride
MARLENA MENESES	Mark's girlfriend
ELIZABETH MENESES	Marlena's sister
BRENDAN DALY	friend

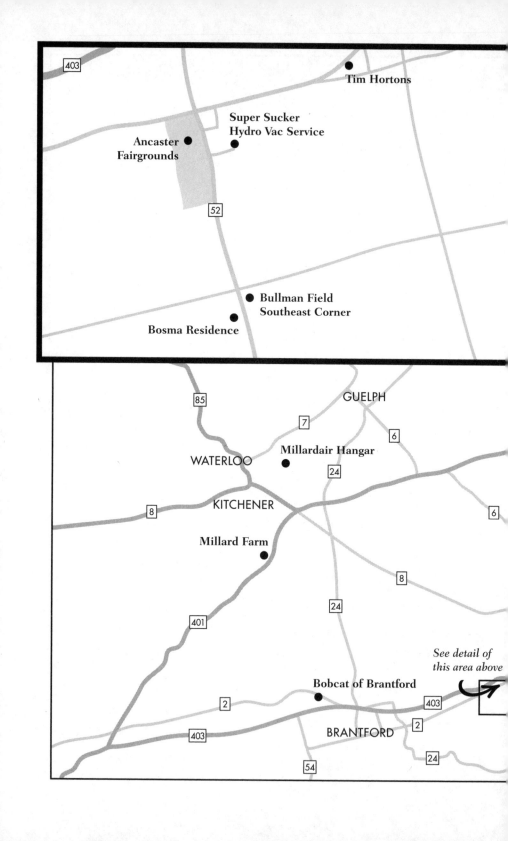

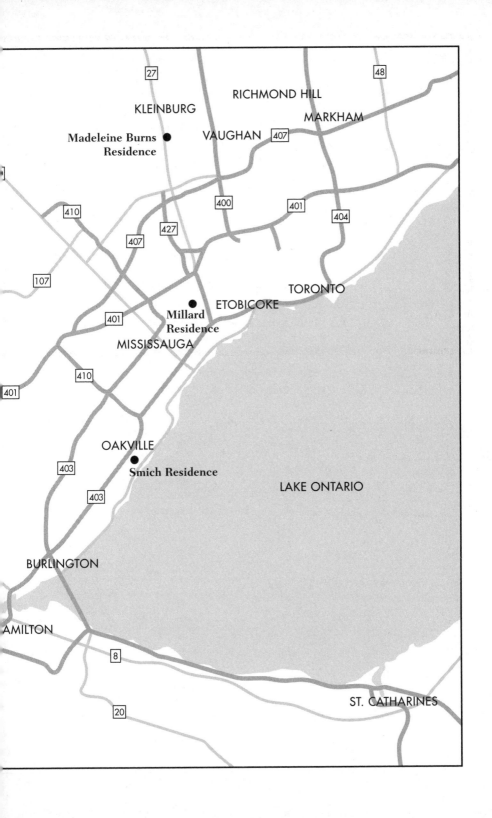

PROLOGUE

FOR SALE BY OWNER

A 2007 Dodge Power Ram 3500 Diesel 4x4 pick-up truck

170,000 kilometres – mostly highway

5.9 litre engine

Extended cab – short box

Gray cloth interior

New transmission, new brakes

Price $24,000.00

Address: Ancaster, Ontario

This is the ad posted online by Tim Bosma's wife, Sharlene, in the spring of 2013. And it is also the starting point of prosecutor Craig Fraser's opening address at the first-degree murder trial of the two men accused of Bosma's murder, Dellen Millard and Mark Smich. Fraser has turned his podium sideways so that he can face the fourteen members of the jury as he explains the case the prosecution intends to prove. His delivery is measured and dry. He is not the type of lawyer who sets off fireworks, inspires TV characters, or wins oratory awards. But for this trial, no special effects are required. Fraser's style suits the story he is telling—a story that is sensational, tragic, and almost beyond belief. And it all begins with the problems caused by that black Dodge Ram diesel.

The truck had been running up hefty repair bills, causing stress for its owners, a young family on a tight budget. A plan was put in place to sell it and replace it with a cheaper, better functioning truck, but unfortunately there weren't many prospective buyers. An earlier version of the ad that had run in April had failed to attract even one serious prospect. A man who Tim Bosma referred to as a tire kicker had emailed a few times to ask a lot of questions then never bothered to view the vehicle in person.

The first person to actually want to see the truck was a caller from Toronto who was prepared to drive one hundred kilometres to Bosma's home in Ancaster to check it out. That seemed like a good sign, so in preparation for the visit Bosma washed and waxed his truck. Then, at 7:25 on the morning of the planned appointment, he sent a text to confirm: "Good morning. It's Tim. I'm working in Hamilton today if you want to meet or do you still want to meet at my house tonight for 7 pm?" He was upset when the text went unanswered and then relieved when the man from Toronto finally called at 7:22 that evening to say he was en route to see the truck and would be there within an hour.

What happened after that would make headlines around the world. Tim Bosma left with two strangers on a test drive from which he would never return. Social media exploded with the news of his disappearance. The police requested help from the public in their search for the missing man and his truck, and their almost daily news conferences were live-streamed online and then endlessly dissected on the internet. Within days, an arrest was made, and then two weeks later another one. But the arrests didn't make things any clearer. The opposite, in fact: they made the disappearance of Tim Bosma more puzzling than ever.

The first man police arrested was Dellen Millard, a wealthy young heir to his family's aviation business who owned several million dollars' worth of properties in Toronto. On the day after he went for the test drive, he had closed on the purchase of a condo for which he was reported to have paid more than $600,000 in cash. As his lawyer and hordes of online commentators kept insisting, he could easily have afforded to buy a brand-new truck. Others pointed out that if Millard were a psychopath, devoid of empathy and seeking thrills, how much money he had was irrelevant.

The second man arrested was Mark Smich, an unemployed drug dealer who lived with his mother in her suburban middle-class home. His last arrest, a few months earlier, had been for spray-painting graffiti on a highway overpass. Until this trial, he had never inspired anywhere near the same level of interest as Millard.

ON THEIR FIRST DAY of trial, both defendants tell the court that they are pleading not guilty to first-degree murder and that they are ready to proceed.

Because of the very public nature of the early investigation into Bosma's disappearance, it has long been known that the evidence in this case is strong. Two days after Millard's arrest, Bosma's truck was found concealed inside a transport trailer parked in Millard's mother's driveway. Human remains burned beyond recognition were discovered at Millard's Southern Ontario farm. And most sinister of all, Millard was revealed to own a portable livestock incinerator, named the Eliminator, despite the fact that he kept no animals on his farm.

Fraser tells the jury that he and his two fellow prosecutors will prove that in the late evening of May 6, 2013, Tim Bosma was killed in his truck, shot by the two accused at close range, and that his body was then incinerated hours later by Millard and Smich. To make the Crown's case, there will be testimony from multiple forensic scientists, including blood-spatter and gunshot-residue experts as well as the anthropologist who examined the bones and remains found in the Eliminator. There will be video showing the Eliminator being towed to the Millardair hangar at the Region of Waterloo International Airport and then being ignited outside the hangar door—and still more video taken from the security system in the hangar. There will be extensive analysis of the cell phones used by the accused and their friends. There will be testimony from the friends and girlfriends of Millard and Smich, some of whom knew they planned to steal a truck. And there will be letters sent from jail by Millard to his girlfriend, Christina Noudga, who was charged as an accessory after the fact to Tim Bosma's murder almost a year after her boyfriend's arrest.

In his letters, Millard asks Noudga to witness tamper and get his best friend to change his statement to police. "If he knew that his words were going to get me a life sentence, he would want to change them," Millard wrote. "Show him how he can, and he will change them." He instructed Noudga to destroy his letters, but—whether for sentimental reasons or as an insurance policy or both—she defied his wishes and kept them. The very damaging letters were seized from her bedroom when it was searched upon her arrest.

Noudga's arrest occurred the same day Millard and Smich were charged with another murder, that of twenty-three-year-old Laura Babcock, on or around July 3, 2012, in the area of Toronto, ten months before Bosma's death. Millard alone was also charged with the murder, on November 29, 2012, of his father, Wayne. Although not a word will be heard about those cases at the Tim Bosma trial, the complications of prosecuting three overlapping murder cases, not to mention their multijurisdictional nature, are among the reasons it has taken almost three years for the trial for the murder of Tim Bosma to begin. From the test drive on May 6, 2013, to February 1, 2016, when Craig Fraser addresses the jury, a thousand and one days have elapsed.

Throughout this time, someone from Tim Bosma's family has attended every single court date for Dellen Millard and Mark Smich, from two-minute video appearances to the full days of pretrial motions that took place in the fall of 2015. In the face of trial delays and tedious legal arguments about evidence admissibility and the like, Tim's parents, Hank and Mary, have remained outwardly stoic—and frequently cheerful. Hank, a small, wiry man with a grey moustache, bald head, and glasses, will often approach journalists to tell them he likes an article they wrote or a TV report they did about his son. He will joke in the elevator of Hamilton's John Sopinka Courthouse about little things like where to get a coffee and make it back to court in time. Mary, a petite blonde, is more shy, but like her husband she smiles when she wishes everyone Merry Christmas on the last day of pretrial motions. The Bosmas' faith—they are active members of the

Ancaster Christian Reformed Church—has helped carry them through, as have the many friends who have accompanied them to court in the days, months, and years since Tim was taken from them.

EXCEPT FOR SOME MEMBERS of the defendants' families, a few of their friends, and the usual handful of conspiracy theorists, this is not, for the vast majority of people, a trial about guilt. It's far more about the how and the why of what happened to Tim Bosma and the very nature of evil. It's also about the dread that almost every major murder trial brings to the surface—the fear that justice will not be done. There might be a "glove doesn't fit" moment, a secret "deal with the devil." Or, in this case, one of the accused might succeed in blaming the other and walk away with no more than a few years in jail.

ONE

IT'S JUST A TRUCK

DAY 1—MONDAY, MAY 6

The two men walked up the unfinished gravel driveway to Tim and Sharlene Bosma's big new house just after 9 P.M. on May 6, 2013. The test drive, which had been arranged by phone, was originally supposed to have taken place earlier in the evening, when it would have still been light out. But the men were late getting in from Toronto, and it was almost dark when they arrived.

Although the location of Tim and Sharlene's home has often been described as country, it is more accurate to call it semi-rural. The house sits on a well-trafficked road in one of those areas that combine cornfields with transmission towers. It is not deserted, but it's also not the kind of place you stroll up to for a visit. Nor is it somewhere you walk to from the nearest bus stop—especially when you're showing up for the first time on a dark spring night. Presumably the visitors would have had to offer some kind of explanation as to how they had arrived from Toronto, one hundred kilometres to the northeast, on foot.

Exactly what they did or didn't say is one of those questions that has been the subject of speculation from the very beginning of this case. In the days after Tim Bosma disappeared, one of his friends placed an ad on Kijiji, one of the two websites where Tim had advertised his truck for sale. The idea was that someone who knew something might see the ad and provide some information. It read, "2 nights ago 3 guys came to look at [a truck] in ancaster. 2 got dropped off. And the other guy said he would be back. Our friend tim bosma took the other 2 guys for a test drive near the fairgrounds in ancaster. No one ever came back."

There are a number of variations on this story: one where the third guy goes to Tim Hortons for coffee, another where he goes to gas up, and a third where he both buys coffee and fills up on gas. The only thing known for sure about the visitors' tale is that it worked. The test drive went ahead as planned. Tim was, after all, used to dealing with strangers. It was something he did regularly as part of his job as an HVAC contractor. He was six foot one, in good shape, and easily able to take care of himself.

When he left, Tim smiled at his wife and told her he would be right back. Then he climbed into the passenger seat of his truck while the taller of the two visitors drove and the one wearing a red hoodie sat in the rear. When he didn't return at the appointed time, Sharlene called his cell phone. No answer. She tried again and probably again and again. She almost certainly called family members and best friends. And then she phoned the police.

DAY 2—TUESDAY, MAY 7

A short press release about the Tim Bosma case was issued by the Hamilton Police Service at eight o'clock the next morning. It said very briefly that Tim Bosma, age thirty-two, had gone missing. It didn't mention anything about a test drive or men from Toronto. Those details first surfaced on Facebook, where the news of the disappearance was widely shared. It was sent first to Tim and Sharlene's friends, then to their acquaintances, and pretty soon to people who had no idea who Tim Bosma was.

It didn't hurt that this man who had disappeared was easy on the eyes: blond, blue-eyed, smiling. In the photos being passed around on social media, Tim could be seen posing with his bride on their wintry wedding day. Then, ten months later, he was snapped at the hospital, a typically proud first-time father, not quite sure how to hold his new daughter, born on Christmas Day. By the time spring rolled around, however, he had morphed into a daring dad, taking the baby for tractor rides on his lap while the family's Great Dane, Ava, looked on. Inasmuch as it's possible to come to a conclusion from looking at photos, the consensus was that Tim Bosma was clearly not the type of guy to run off to Vegas or go on a bender with two strangers from out of town.

DAY 3—WEDNESDAY, MAY 8

Some thirty-six hours after Tim Bosma went missing, Staff Sergeant Matt Kavanagh of the Hamilton Police gave the first of many media briefings that would be held in this investigation.

Those news briefings, along with social media, were how people got their information about the case. Over the course of the next week, Kavanagh would become a familiar figure to those following Bosma's disappearance. Tens of thousands of viewers went online to watch live-streamed press conferences for updates and then turned to social media to discuss the developments.

In his mid-fifties, stocky, with wire-framed glasses and short-cropped, slightly receding grey hair, Kavanagh looks exactly like what he is: a cop with an Irish name in a blue-collar town. If you didn't immediately guess he was a homicide detective, you might pick gym teacher as his profession, and you'd be half right. For the more than three decades he's been with the Hamilton Police, he's also volunteered as a football coach for high school kids from tough neighbourhoods.

While Kavanagh sometimes pulls a "strict dad" act with reporters—correcting them if they get their facts wrong or repeat a question someone has already asked—he also returns phone calls and tells the press what he can, within the limits of an investigation. He occasionally lapses into cop jargon, like "attending the residence" and "interviewing the complainant," but at the same time he gives out the kind of colourful anecdotes that make a story come alive. He's happy to reveal, for example, that when the police need to have an iPhone unlocked for a murder case, an officer will take it on a plane to Apple headquarters in Cupertino, California. If it's a lesser crime and not such a big deal if the phone goes missing, they'll just send it by commercial courier.

When Kavanagh arrived at the first of the Bosma briefings (most of which can still be seen on YouTube), he apologized for being late to the handful of local reporters present and then read from a prepared statement written in standⁿacular. "This is regarding the missing person Tim. On April 28, 2013, Timothy Bosma posted his 2007 Dodg pickup truck for sale on two different websites. On Monday, May 6, a male party arranged by telephone to view the truck at Mr. Bosma's residence in Ancaster. At approximately 9:20 P.M., Mr. Bosma went for a test drive with two young males in this pickup truck. Mr. Bosma had told his spouse that the males stated they were from Toronto. Mr. Bosma has not been seen or heard from since this time."

Kavanagh provided a description of the two men in question. The one who drove the truck was white, in his mid-twenties, six foot one or two, 170 to 180 pounds. He had light to medium short brown hair and was unshaven. He wore blue jeans, a long-sleeved orange shirt, and running shoes. The second male, the one who sat in the back, was also white, in his early to mid-twenties, five foot nine or ten, small to medium build. He was wearing a red hooded sweatshirt, with the hood up mostly covering his dark hair.

The homicide unit had taken over the investigation due to what Kavanagh called "the unusual nature of the disappearance." He asked anyone with information to contact the police, and then he took questions from reporters. Like almost everyone else in town, the press had been reading about Tim Bosma's disappearance on Facebook and had heard about the third man, who had supposedly dropped the other two off.

"Is there any information about him?" a reporter asked.

Kavanagh seemed taken aback. "I'm not sure where you are getting that from," he said.

"Social media," answered the reporter.

Kavanagh said that while it was possible more people were involved, all the police had at the moment was the description of the two suspects he had provided. Sharlene Bosma had not seen any other vehicle.

"Are we to assume the suspects are back in Toronto?"

"No, we're not. The information that we had from Mr. Bosma— he relayed to his spouse that they were from the Toronto area—I can't confirm that either way, if they were from there or not."

A reporter raised the issue of why one of the city's top homicide detectives was giving a press conference about a missing persons case. "What is Hamilton Police's policy for getting the homicide squad involved?" she wanted to know.

"As I already said at the beginning of this media release, if it is an unusual missing person, then we are to be involved. And this had unusual circumstances right from the onset, so we got involved yesterday, last night."

Despite getting one of Kavanagh's trademark you're-not-listening-to-me answers, the reporter wouldn't drop the issue. "So is this a missing persons case or a murder investigation?" she asked a minute or two later.

"This is a missing persons investigation with unusual circumstances," Kavanagh said. "I think I've already spoken about that."

He had, but to be fair to the journalist, her persistent questioning reflected the widespread misconception that an adult has to be missing for twenty-four to forty-eight hours before police will take action. While this was definitely true to a greater extent in the past, current policies encourage police to assess each missing persons case individually and act accordingly.

As a result, the day after Tim Bosma went missing, Hamilton Police immediately had their search-and-rescue team and a canine unit conduct a ground search. They were assisted by officers of the Ontario Provincial Police, as they were looking not just in the area of Ancaster, where the Bosmas lived, but also westward to the small city of Brantford. The missing pickup truck was red-flagged at the border and an alert was sent out to all police agencies as well as the media. Although the truck had been advertised on both autoTRADER.ca and Kijiji, Kavanagh said there was no email path to follow or computer analysis to be done, as all contact with the prospective buyers had been by phone.

"Did he have his phone with him at the time of the disappearance?" asked a reporter.

"Yes, he did."

"Were you able to trace that, or did he make any calls from it?"

"It's been turned off. But yes, we have some data from it."

"What time was his cell phone turned off?"

"I'm not going to say that, but it was turned off."

As the news conference—which lasted just eight minutes— drew to a close, Kavanagh was asked what advice, if any, he had for people trying to sell a truck online and whether it was a dangerous thing to do.

Use common sense, he warned. Don't give out your home address. Meet somewhere in the middle of the day, not a rural location. "Obviously, these males, in the evidence we have so far, they were targeting a certain type of vehicle, and it was a Dodge Ram 3500, so if [anyone has] that type of vehicle for sale, they are to beware."

"So this truck, you think, was the target, not Bosma specifically?"

"That's correct," said Kavanagh, answering for the first time a question that would arise repeatedly during the course of the investigation and the trial.

AT THE BOSMA HOUSE, family and a crowd of friends had gathered to conduct a search for Tim. He and Sharlene were part of the Ancaster Christian Reformed Church, an institution whose members are predominantly of Dutch background and share a strong sense of community. Three years earlier, when Sharlene was pregnant and she and Tim were living in a trailer on the property, many of those same people had pitched in to help build their house. Now, even acquaintances who hadn't seen Bosma in years were joining the search parties out scouring roadside ditches and nearby fields. There were so many people looking that police became worried evidence might be disrupted or even destroyed and had to ask the volunteers to stop searching.

At that point, they returned to the Bosmas' garage, which had become a kind of informal command centre, and focused their attention on other projects. They set up a Find Tim Bosma page on Facebook and printed up Missing posters showing Bosma and his truck, and began plastering them throughout the region, everywhere from Toronto, where the test drivers supposedly lived, to Brantford, where police believed they had headed. The posters went up on lampposts, windshields, anywhere anyone could put them. Within days, they were as widespread as the Facebook posts calling for Tim's return.

As more and more people learned of Bosma's strange disappearance, it was inevitable that rumours would begin circulating, both online and off. There was talk that Bosma must have been connected to his abductors, otherwise why go off in the night with two strangers who had arrived on foot? By way of explanation, the usual theories and wild speculation cropped up. There were drugs involved. It was organized crime. Bosma was, after all, in construction, and "we all know what that means."

He and Sharlene had an awfully big home for such a young couple—maybe they had taken on too much debt. The whole situation just didn't add up. Why would anyone steal a truck that way? If you want to steal a truck, you take it with no one in it. Or if it's a carjacking, you leave the driver by the road. Nothing about this crime made any sense.

DAY 4—THURSDAY, MAY 9

On Thursday, Sharlene Bosma made an appeal to the public for information. Flanked by her mother, father, Tim's parents and his brother-in-law, she took her place in front of the microphones in the same briefing room at Hamilton Police headquarters where Detective Kavanagh had appeared the day before. She was, as anyone in her situation would be, extremely distressed. Yet on another level she was extraordinarily composed. And although she was sleep deprived, wore no makeup, and had her dark hair pulled back, she was still beautiful in the glare of the television lights. Her speech was the type of broadcast moment that makes people stop whatever they are doing to look at the television or turn up the radio. It transformed the disappearance of Tim Bosma from a quirky missing persons case into a major crime story.

With her voice shaking, Sharlene introduced herself and described Tim as her husband, partner, best friend, love of her life, and father of her two-year-old daughter. She acknowledged what everybody had been thinking since news of her husband's disappearance broke. "This does not feel like real life," she said. "This only happens on TV and in movies."

She looked down at her notes and then back up at the assembled media as she recounted her version of events, or as much of it as the police would allow. "As you know," Sharlene said, "I watched my husband drive away just after nine o'clock Monday night. He smiled at me and said he'd be right back. And I have not seen him since. You are all aware that I saw the two men who took my husband. You have already been provided a description of these two individuals. I ask you if you see anyone that closely matches this description of these men to please call the police. You've seen pictures of Tim and his truck. Please, please, if you see Tim or the truck, contact the police."

Sharlene thanked her family and the Bosmas, their friends, the churches, and all the strangers who had volunteered to be part of the search to find her husband. She said her faith in God had helped her get through the last few days.

"My husband, Tim, is a loving father to our beautiful two-year-old girl, and she needs her daddy back," Sharlene said as her voice broke and she fought back tears. "His parents need their little boy back. All of our brothers and sisters want their brother back. We look forward to being able to put our arms around Tim and to tell him how much we love him. We hope and pray that today is the last day of this nightmare."

She said that the many kids in her extended family couldn't understand what had happened to their favourite pest of an uncle and were wondering when their next water fight would be. One of them, in the way that children do, had perfectly and simply described what was going on. "Uncle Timmy has been stolen," he said.

As Sharlene became more visibly upset, Tim's mother, Mary, reached out to pat her on the back. She kept her hand there as her daughter-in-law spoke directly and angrily to the two men who had taken Tim. It was the moment that would be replayed hundreds and thousands of times, the video clip seared into everyone's minds.

"It was just a truck," she said slowly, loudly, spitting out every word. "It is just a truck.

"You don't need him, but I do, and our daughter needs her daddy back. So please, please, let him come home. We need him to come home. And may God have mercy on you."

That was the end. There were no goodbyes, no thank-yous. Sharlene and the two families simply filed out of the room while Constable Greg Slack held open the door and Detective Kavanagh followed. Slack then walked to the podium where Sharlene Bosma had just stood.

"Okay, so that concludes the briefing for today," he said to the assembled media. "That's all."

Like everyone else left in the room, he was at a complete loss for words.

THE DISAPPEARANCE OF TIM BOSMA became a discussion topic not just on the big social media sites like Facebook and Twitter but also at Websleuths.com, a forum devoted to true crime where armchair detectives "sleuth"—to use their own favourite word—missing persons and mysterious murder cases. Originally founded in 1999 to discuss the still-unsolved murder of the child beauty-pageant star JonBenét Ramsey, Websleuths now has active threads on thousands of murders in the United States, Canada, the United Kingdom, and Australia. Thanks to its popularity and longevity, it ranks high in Google search results and is a magnet for those looking for information about specific cases. And just as many people with knowledge of a crime can't resist the temptation to talk about it in real life, so too does that "loose lips" principle apply on the internet.

On at least one occasion, the actual murderer has joined in a Websleuths discussion. After the 2009 murder of Abraham Shakespeare, an illiterate Florida labourer who won $32 million in a lottery, police started investigating his financial adviser, Dorice "Dee Dee" Moore, as a suspect. Websleuths members began discussing Moore's possible involvement, and soon Moore had signed herself up as a member to defend her actions. Although she pretended to be a disinterested third party, Moore's comments betrayed insider information, and one or more sleuths reported her to police. Detectives then contacted Tricia Griffith, the owner of Websleuths, and asked her to let Moore keep posting in the hope that she would reveal more information. She did, leading to her arrest and eventual conviction for first-degree murder.

While the Moore case is the most notable one associated with Websleuths, Griffith gets several subpoenas a year from law-enforcement agencies interested in who is posting non-public details about crimes on the site. Although some members, like Moore, participate to throw people off and try to ferret out information, others just want to set the record straight, find support, or ask for advice. Websleuths encourages those with non-criminal ties to become "verified insiders" by providing forum moderators with documented proof that they are who they say they are. This private information will not be made public, but other sleuths can be satisfied that what insiders say is coming from a source who has been checked out. Likewise, members

can be verified as lawyers, doctors, police officers, and journalists. The vast majority, however, are simply true-crime fanatics
anonymously discussing cases on the internet with others who
share their fascination.

As a result of its demographic makeup, there is a low signal-to-
noise ratio on Websleuths. Posters chew over insignificant details
endlessly. Their tendency to take a fact and blow it all out of pro-
portion is exacerbated when information is scarce. In contrast,
when there is relevant material to look into, some of the sleuths
can hold their own with police and the best investigative reporters,
which is why both cops and journalists keep an eye on the site.

By the time Sharlene Bosma made her appeal, Tim's disappearance was a big enough story that several Websleuths members
were monitoring the press conference as it was streamed live
on the internet by *The Public Record*, an online Hamilton news
magazine.

"This is breaking my heart," wrote "mollymae" as she watched.
She included a sad emoticon.

"Sooooo sad and the wife speaking just makes me cry," wrote
"canadiangirl."

"I hope Tim gets home safe," wrote "LoyalSleuth."

Their sentimental reaction was not out of the ordinary. Many
Websleuths members get so wrapped up in the crimes they follow
that they even use photos of the victims as their online avatars.
Yet in spite of this, and the fact that Websleuths defines itself as
a site friendly to victims and law enforcement, an ugly strain of
commentary can emerge from members who think they know
more than anyone else. "LoyalSleuth," for example, was unwilling
to accept Detective Kavanagh's statements that Tim Bosma had
been targeted for his truck and did not know the suspects.

"Something tells me Timothy knew these people," she wrote shortly after Sharlene's appeal. "Leaving in the dark with two strangers that 'walked' to my home in the country, is too far fetched IMHO."

She and other sleuths began looking for potentially damaging information in Tim and Sharlene's past, posting links to their wedding and engagement albums, which they had discovered on the photographer's website. Within minutes, "canadiangirl" had gone through the albums and found what she believed was a clue.

"In one of these photos it looks like [Tim] may have some tattoos on his fingers," she wrote.

"You're right!" responded "LoyalSleuth," who believed the letters *SK* were tattooed on Tim's middle finger and *OK* on his index finger. "Pure assumption, but tattoos on fingers are something done in jail?" she wrote, adding that the poor quality of these tattoos supported the theory that Tim had been in custody at the time he was inked. "Identifying marks for sure," she concluded—until she looked again and noticed that the supposed jailhouse tattoos were not present in any other image of Tim.

"Photoshopped by the photographer perhaps?" suggested "canadiangirl," who was loath to see her clue get tossed.

In the end, however, she could not prevent the inevitable. Other sleuths soon pointed out that the tattooed-fingers photo on which everyone was basing their wild theories was not, in fact, a picture of Tim Bosma at all. The artsy close-up—shot from the shoulders down and showing a man buttoning his vest as he prepares for the ceremony—was of another member of the wedding party. The man "sporting the knuckle tats has a wedding ring on. TB had no wedding ring on before the ceremony," wrote "Lori McA." "AND the biggest clue it is not TB—the man pictured is wearing a dark vest. TB's vest was white/off white."

Despite this debunking, the rumours regarding Tim Bosma's tattooed fingers persisted for months. The nonexistent tattoos would be invoked time and again to prove that Tim wasn't really as squeaky clean as the media were making out, and that a regular guy with a beautiful wife and adorable baby daughter didn't just disappear off the face of the earth. The tattoo rumours fed the peculiar hope that this was not just a random crime, even if they did so at the expense of the victim's reputation and caused his family added distress.

DAY 5—FRIDAY, MAY 10

Less than twenty-four hours after Sharlene's appeal, the Hamilton Police and Detective Kavanagh called yet another press conference—this time to announce new developments in the case. They had learned that on the night Bosma went missing, at approximately 10:10 P.M., his pickup truck had been spotted in downtown Brantford. And on Thursday they had been called to an industrial area in the west end of Brantford where Bosma's cell phone had been found. The police were once again asking businesses in Brantford to check their video surveillance systems for any type of activity between 9:30 P.M. and 10:30 P.M. on Monday night. They wanted to see if they could figure out the route Bosma's truck had taken through Brantford.

The most significant information, however, came not from the phone itself but from production orders—a type of search warrant—used to obtain call information from phone companies, among other things. Police quickly discovered the phone number Tim Bosma had been called from to set up the test drive, and they soon got a production order for that phone. It turned out to be what's known as a burner phone, registered in a bogus name. The purpose of burners—which run on prepaid accounts and don't require a contract and credit card—is to avoid leaving an electronic trail. They are often replaced frequently, sometimes after just a few calls. And most important of all, they do not provide any connection to the user's real-life identity.

When police contacted the other numbers called by the burner phone, they learned that the same two men who had arrived at the Bosma home had gone for a test drive in a similar truck in Toronto on May 5, the day before. The owner of the vehicle was able to provide a description of the suspects, which not only closely matched the one given by Sharlene but added to it. Because that Sunday, the day before Bosma's test drive, had been an exceptionally warm May day, the taller of the two men had dressed for the weather in a short-sleeved T-shirt.

"On one of his wrists—the witness wasn't sure if it was the left or right—where a person wears a watch, was a tattoo of the word *ambition* framed by a box," said Kavanagh. "Police have researched this tattoo. This tattoo itself is not uncommon. Many people have the word *ambition* tattooed on their body. However, the location and the frame around it is unique. This male has not been identified as yet. There is no further description of the second male."

Kavanagh asked the public to continue providing information and then took questions from the press, the first of which was unpleasant but necessary.

"Do you think Timothy Bosma is still alive?" asked the reporter.

"We always have to hold out hope," answered Kavanagh. "That's all I can say."

Another reporter wanted to know more about the Toronto test drive. "Was it the same scenario where they met this person at his or her home, took the car for a test drive, and then brought it back? What happened?"

Kavanagh described an almost identical situation in which "two individuals walked up to this male's business not having a vehicle. The test drive was the same, the taller individual in the driver's seat, the potential victim in the passenger seat, and one male behind him."

As the reporters, by then a much bigger crowd than earlier in the week, began to interrupt each other, Kavanagh warned them to take it one at a time.

"Did he find them suspicious in any way? Did anything trigger with him that day that was unusual?"

"Yes, he did. That's all I'm going to say. Yes, he found them suspicious."

Another reporter was curious about a possible third person. "How did the two men arrive at the Toronto location? Did they drive themselves there or did somebody drop them off? Or what can you say about what happened at the Bosma residence?"

Kavanagh said that in the Toronto scenario, the witness described how two individuals walked up to his business. "He asked them how they arrived, and they said they walked there. In the Bosma case, there was no other vehicle spotted at the Bosma house. We can only presume there was a vehicle in the area."

A reporter pushed for more details on what the Toronto man found suspicious about the two visitors. "The gentleman from Toronto advertised his vehicle in the same way Mr. Bosma did: by internet. It was the same type of vehicle. It was a newer vehicle. What he found suspicious is what I've already talked about, the fact that two individuals walk up to an industrial area which is a ways from residential areas. They walk up without a vehicle. And their interest in the vehicle, he thought it was odd because of the size of the vehicle. It's more a business vehicle than a personal vehicle."

"And did he do anything to act on his suspicions? Did he cut the test drive short? Did he tell them, 'Bring me back to my business'? Did he pick up his phone and call someone?"

"No, he didn't," said Kavanagh, adding a piece of information that not all detectives would tell the media. "I think fortunately for this person, he's a very large individual. And I think that he would overpower the both of them, and I think that was his advantage."

Soon after that ominous note, the press conference ended.

DAY 6—SATURDAY, MAY 11

For the fourth day in a row, a press briefing was called at Hamilton Police headquarters. This time, it was to inform the public of an arrest in the Tim Bosma case. The news was delivered by Hamilton Police chief Glenn De Caire and force superintendent Dan Kinsella, who, even though it was a Saturday afternoon, appeared in uniform short-sleeved white shirts with badges and stripes.

The man with the "ambition" tattoo was now in custody, said Kinsella, and being charged with forcible confinement and theft over $5,000. He was Dellen Millard, twenty-seven years old, from Toronto. Kinsella declined to answer questions about whether Millard was talking, and when asked if police believed Tim Bosma was dead, he gave almost exactly the same answer Matt Kavanagh had given the day before: "There's always hope. We hold out hope."

He described the ongoing investigation as "rapid, fluid, and dynamic [and] changing minute to minute" as search warrants were being prepared and evidence gathered. During the extremely brief four-minute question period with reporters, Kinsella said police did not yet know the identity of the second suspect.

He stressed that the welfare of Tim Bosma was the top priority, and he repeatedly urged anyone with information to contact the police. "For those responsible, turn yourself in," he said as he quickly removed his papers from the podium and stood aside.

The Googling of Dellen Millard had already begun.

PETE VANDERBOOM'S MEMORIES OF the day Tim Bosma went missing begin when he said to his wife that same morning that they needed to get Tim to hook up the air conditioner in an outbuilding on their property. Vanderboom lives and runs his excavation business on a hilltop about three miles north of the Bosmas' home. The autumn before, Tim had installed a natural gas furnace in his office to replace the baseboard electric heaters that were costing a fortune. Now, he needed AC to keep the temperature down. While Vanderboom is almost ten years older than Bosma, from Burlington not Ancaster, and Canadian Dutch Reformed Church not Christian Reformed, the two men had met through business and mutual friends.

A few years earlier, Tim's mother had told Pete's wife, who she knew from the gym, that her son needed fill material for his house. Getting rid of dirt is a huge problem for excavators like Vanderboom, so he happily delivered a few loads. From time to time, Vanderboom would call Bosma to remove air conditioners

when he needed to dig around houses. The two men also socialized occasionally as part of a group that went snowmobiling in
the winter.

Vanderboom first heard that Bosma had gone missing via text
message. As soon as he could, he and a co-worker hopped in his
truck and headed over to the Bosma house. The driveway was
already packed with pickups and cars, and the garage was filled
with people.

The police had asked everyone to stick to getting the word
out about Tim's disappearance on social media and putting up
posters, but Vanderboom had other ideas. As an off-road hobby-
ist who knew the area well, he thought he could be more useful
searching back roads, the type of places someone might leave an
injured man.

For three afternoons, he and his friend drove down every farm
laneway, into every field entranceway, and along every hidden
driveway they could find between Ancaster and Brantford. At
Heron Point, they checked under a bridge near a golf course.
In other places, they got out and walked through the woods.
Spring leaves were just coming out, so they could still see well
into the distance. "A week later and everything would have been
greened over," Vanderboom recalls. "We concentrated on areas
we thought nobody else was going to be." Their best-case scenario was that they would find an injured Tim Bosma and take
him to hospital.

Later, after the police announced that Bosma had been
murdered, the unanswered questions continued to consume
Vanderboom. He wondered if Tim had somehow unknowingly crossed paths with Millard and Smich, so instead of

searching country roads, he scoured the internet looking for clues. Eventually, he had to step back. "I couldn't get this stuff out of my head, and it was driving me crazy," he said. "Maybe I just wanted it to be about more than a stupid truck."

TWO

THE CROWN'S FIRST WITNESS

Sharlene Bosma is taller in real life than she looks in the "just a truck" YouTube video, which is the opposite of how it usually works. It's far more common to find that someone you've watched on a screen is much smaller and more fragile in person. But in her black patent-leather stilettos, dark-grey pencil skirt, and turquoise blouse, Bosma towers over Detective Kavanagh as he shows her into the courtroom and points out the path she should take to the witness box.

As the trial's first witness, she will be questioned by Tony Leitch, who leads the team of three prosecutors handling this case. Leitch is a bearlike ex–football player who gives off an everyman vibe. He gets things underway with a series of personal questions, the first of which is, "Sharlene, how did you meet Tim?"

Online in November 2008, she answers. Their first date was "disastrous," but things got better fast. They married on February 13, 2010. Their daughter, who wasn't planned, arrived less than a year later. They wanted to have three children and adopt one. She hoped for a natural birth after having had a Caesarean. Three months before Tim disappeared, the couple had gone to a fertility clinic.

"What can you tell me about his character?"

"Very strong," says Sharlene, "and the patience of a saint because he was married to me."

Leitch inquires about bad habits, and Sharlene answers that her husband had quit smoking, something she had not managed.

"Gambling?" asks Leitch.

"Just poker night with the boys."

"What about drug use? Did he use drugs?"

"No."

"What about alcohol?"

"He liked his beer. He definitely had the occasional 'night,' but he didn't have a drinking problem."

"How was the state of your marriage?"

"We were in a good place," she says. "Our biggest issue was the truck, which kept breaking down, and it was costing a fortune to fix it all the time."

As he elicits more information about the black Dodge Ram, Leitch shows pictures of it on the video monitors set up in the courtroom. "I know you're not a big car person," he says to Sharlene, "but what do you know about the rims?"

"That they were all the same?" she answers quizzically, to the amusement of the courtroom gallery. It's one of several occasions when Sharlene will make people laugh. And like the punkish red highlights in her hair, it is an indication that she refuses to be typecast in the role of grieving widow. Although she has encountered what she described at her husband's memorial service as "the vilest form of evil," Sharlene can still laugh and make others laugh along with her. What happened to her husband may have changed her and her daughter's lives forever, but it seems she will not let it define them. She will not be reduced to the woman in the YouTube video. Nor will she allow Tim's daughter to become the girl whose father was murdered. Although the little girl's baby pictures have been shared all over the internet, neither Sharlene nor anyone else in the Bosma family has ever said her name in public. It has remained private.

When Leitch puts one of the Missing posters up on the courtroom screens, Sharlene tears up as she explains that Tim is smiling because he is holding his newborn nephew for the very first time. It is a difficult moment in her testimony, but not the worst. That comes when Leitch asks about how Tim was behaving before the test drive. Sharlene describes him pacing back and forth in front of the hockey game on TV. He was talking about how it was getting dark out and that it made no sense to come to see a truck so late. He got his daughter into her pyjamas and cuddled with her on the couch before Sharlene took her off to bed. When Sharlene came back downstairs, Tim asked her if he should go on the test drive, given the time of night. "Yes, you should," she said, "because we want the truck to come back."

As she tells her story to the packed courtroom, Sharlene is choking back sobs. That detail, which has never before been revealed in public, will make headlines, lead the newscasts, and be scrutinized in discussions online and off. Yet Sharlene has clearly prepared for its impact and quickly regains her composure as Leitch presses ahead to what happened when the men from Toronto arrived at her house.

Sharlene tells the prosecutor that she and her tenant, Wayne De Boer, had been out in the garage having a cigarette. It was part of a pact they had made with each other to stop smoking.

Until they could give up their habit completely, they would each have one cigarette together in the evening. As they were chatting and puffing away, Sharlene heard her husband's cell phone ring and Tim answer it. At the same time, she and Wayne heard voices and footsteps. When they looked out the open garage door, they saw two men about halfway up the driveway, approaching them in the dusk. The taller one, who Sharlene refers to as "Cell Phone Guy," was talking on his phone. When Tim came from the house into the garage, he spotted the two men and ended his call. Wayne, who will testify after Sharlene and is an articulate witness with an eye for detail, remembers hearing the distinctive sound of the visitor's flip phone clicking shut as he put it in his front jeans pocket. The only thing Wayne can't recall is if it was the left or right pocket.

No one saw or heard any kind of vehicle. Sharlene says Tim joked to the visitors that they didn't have to park in the road, that they could have left their car in the driveway. Cell Phone Guy said they had no car. A friend had dropped them off and gone to the Tim Hortons at Duff's Corners to grab a bite to eat, he explained, as he gestured to the northeast.

As Tim introduced himself and made small talk, Sharlene stepped back. "I didn't want to interfere," she tells the court. "It was Tim's truck, and I let him handle it." Leitch asks if she heard any names, if there was any physical contact. "Perhaps a handshake, but I don't remember anymore," she says.

The entire encounter was very brief. It was barely a minute before Tim pulled his truck out of the garage for the men to inspect. Both Wayne and Sharlene remember the shorter guy hanging back. His red hoodie partially hid his face and he kept his hands in the kangaroo-pouch pocket. "He seemed sketchy,"

Sharlene says. "He wouldn't look at us." After the men did a very brief inspection of the truck, they got in with Tim and started slowly down the driveway. It seemed to Sharlene as if they were testing the brakes.

As they drove off, she turned to Wayne and said, "That was weird."

To defuse the situation, Wayne indulged in a bit of black humour. "I said to Sharlene, 'That might be the last time we see Tim,'" he testifies.

The extremeness of the joke cut the tension, and soon after, the smokers headed back inside. Wayne went to his apartment in the basement, where he turned on the hockey game, while Sharlene checked on her daughter and then watched a TV show she'd recorded, the kind Tim wouldn't want to see. When the program finished, she noticed the PVR clock said 10:20 and became alarmed.

She called Tim, but it went to voice mail. Instead of leaving a message, she sent a text asking, "Where are you?" Then she texted Wayne and told him they were going to have to break their only-one-cigarette-a-night pact. They met in the garage and decided that Wayne should head to the Tim Hortons where the visitors' friend was supposed to be. When Wayne didn't see either the men or Tim's truck there, he drove to some nearby big-box stores with a well-lit parking lot, figuring that they might have wanted to take a closer look at the truck under bright lights. But the men weren't there either, so he returned to the house.

Sharlene had been speaking to Jesse, a friend who had stopped by earlier in the evening and helped Tim do some paint touch-ups on the truck and clear out his tools from its back box. She thought her husband might have gone over to Jesse's to have a beer and celebrate the truck's sale, but Jesse hadn't seen him. As a next step, Sharlene arranged to meet Jesse's girlfriend, Stephanie, at the Brassie Pub in Ancaster. She tells the court she was hoping Tim had taken the two men there to seal the deal, as in "I'll buy you beer if you buy my truck."

Up to that point, Sharlene had resisted calling the police, worried that her husband would come home and accuse her of being an "overreacting paranoid wife who just freaks out because Tim's going to be late," but Wayne convinced her to call and start the process immediately. He had spoken to his mother, who worked in a civilian capacity at a nearby police force. She told him that if a person's disappearance was out of character, there was no need to wait twenty-four hours before contacting police.

Wayne then stayed with the Bosmas' little girl while Sharlene headed to the Brassie, calling 911 on her way. The operator told her police officers would meet her at the pub. While she and Stephanie were waiting, they checked to see if there had been any activity on Tim's bank account and credit card. They even signed into his 407 Express Toll Route account on the off chance they could see if he had been on the highway. When the police arrived they talked to Sharlene and then accompanied her home. She called her mother to let her know what was going on. She also tried her husband's phone a few more times.

AS THE CROWN'S FIRST WITNESS, Sharlene Bosma was excluded from observing almost all of the pretrial proceedings, including Craig Fraser's opening address. But now that her testimony is finally done, she is free to join her family and friends, who occupy three reserved rows at the centre front of the court-room. They are directly behind the so-called "bar"—which separates the public gallery from the participants in the trial. Several times a day, the two accused men, who are not handcuffed but have special soft shackles around their ankles, shuffle directly in front of the Bosmas.

Millard and Smich sit at opposite ends of the last table on the defence side of the courtroom. Their shackled feet are hidden behind a pile of boxes placed specially to obstruct jurors' line of sight. They occasionally take notes.

Directly in front of the defendants are Smich's lawyer, Thomas Dungey, and his co-counsel, Jennifer Trehearne. In front of them and just below Justice Andrew Goodman sit Ravin Pillay, Millard's lawyer, and his co-counsel, Nadir Sachak. On the other side of the aisle are the assistant Crown attorneys: Tony Leitch, Craig Fraser, and the most junior of the three, Brett Moodie.

With ninety witnesses and four months of trial still to come, the jurors and courtroom regulars will get to know the main players well. Dungey is a shaven-headed septuagenarian with a flair for dramatic cross-examinations. Pillay, always quick to rise with an objection, is soft-spoken and detail-oriented. Sachak is the self-proclaimed Toronto city slicker who likes to chat up witnesses before moving in for the kill. And Trehearne is the legal whiz, whose work on the case revolves around complex motions as opposed to cross-examination.

Leitch is the lead prosecutor who should not be underestimated. Fraser is his trusted right-hand man. And Moodie is the junior on the team.

The judge will not play a major role in this story. His most important rulings involve the admissibility of evidence and cannot be made public until the end of Millard's and Smich's trial for the murder of Laura Babcock, which is not scheduled to take place until 2017. In the meantime, all that's reportable is an occasional comment.

The jury of eight women and six men are largely inscrutable. It's rare that they give a clue about what they are thinking.

AMONG THE DOZENS OF police officers who will testify at trial, one of the first is Detective Constable John Tselepakis, who was working the 4 P.M. to 4 A.M. shift at the Hamilton Police's Mountain Division when the missing person report for Tim Bosma came in. He was told that Bosma's wife was frantic and believed harm had been done to her husband. At 1:34 A.M. on May 7, Tselepakis sent what is known as a humanitarian or emergency request to corporate security at Bell Canada, Bosma's cell phone provider. Less than ten minutes later, at 1:43, Bell provided Tselepakis with an account of the activity on Tim Bosma's smartphone from 7 P.M. on Monday, May 6, to 1 A.M. on Tuesday, May 7. The number Tim had been called from shortly after 7 P.M., and then again just after 9 P.M., was 647-303-2279, a Toronto area code. The last two pings from Tim's cell phone came off a tower in the east end of Brantford on Monday night.

Tselepakis then contacted Wind, the service provider for the 647 number. The information he got back showed that the number was registered to a Lucas Bate. Like Bell, Wind provided a list of phone numbers called, as well as cell tower locations pinged by the phone. With a little bit of Googling, Tselepakis quickly linked one of the numbers called by the Bate phone to a

Kijiji ad for another Dodge Ram truck. By 8:30 A.M., there were already a number of leads to follow up on. Detective Kavanagh sent Sergeant Greg Jackson, a member of the homicide unit, to assist the Mountain Division.

Jackson called the number Tselepakis had found was associated with the Kijiji ad and reached Igor Tumanenko, the owner of the other Dodge Ram truck for sale. Tumanenko appeared to have valuable information, but because of his heavy accent it was difficult to get the details straight on the phone. Jackson made arrangements to visit Tumanenko's workplace in the Toronto suburb of Etobicoke that afternoon. He was accompanied by Sergeant Greg Rodzoniak, who would later become the primary detective on the Bosma investigation while Jackson eventually assumed the role of file manager in charge of all the documentation. Sitting atop this so-called investigative triangle was Detective Kavanagh, whose official title was major case manager and whose job it was to steer the investigation and oversee staffing and resources.

ALTHOUGH KAVANAGH HAD TOLD the press early on that the man who went for the first test drive was a very large individual who could easily have overpowered the suspects, Tumanenko's name was never made public. As a result, armchair detectives had no way to look him up online to decide if he really was as massive as the police had made out (and dig into every other aspect of his life). Instead, they had to content themselves with endless discussion about how the man they had nicknamed RBEG—short for Really Big Etobicoke Guy—had managed to escape the fate that met Tim Bosma. This involved much wild speculation about Tasers, chloroform, knives, and adipose tissue. Later, when it was revealed that a gun was involved—against which it would have been difficult for any potential victim to defend themselves—a grisly theory was floated on Websleuths that RBEG might have survived simply because he was too big to fit into Millard's incinerator without requiring dismemberment.

When Tumanenko is called as a witness during the first week of trial, the mystery is finally solved. He is indeed a big man, just over six foot, and in good shape, his shoulders heavily muscled under the long-sleeved grey T-shirt he wears with jeans and trainers. Despite his size, he moves quickly and lightly across the courtroom. He gives the impression of being in control, and as the court is about to learn, he is not shy about speaking his mind. He was "pissed off," he says, when the test drivers arrived late and messed up his Sunday afternoon plans. Contrary to the initial police reports, the men did not walk up to his workplace but to his apartment building in the north end of Toronto.

He was surprised that they didn't have a car but not concerned. They all shook hands. Tumanenko thinks the taller man introduced himself as Evan, which is Dellen Millard's middle name. He wore a "man bag," which Tumanenko describes as a cross between an Indiana Jones–style satchel and a smaller purse like the one carried by Zach Galifianakis's character in *The Hangover*. Despite being a Russian émigré who arrived in Canada via Israel, Tumanenko has an impressive grasp of Hollywood movie trivia along with an eye for detail. He tells the court it was the taller man who asked about his truck, saying he wanted to use it to tow race cars to Calgary.

It was also the taller guy who eventually got into the driver's seat, but not immediately. Tumanenko had planned the test drive to make the best possible sales pitch, and it began with him driving his potential customers through city streets. He turned the wheel over to the taller man just before they got on Highway 407, a toll route. When asked by prosecutor Brett Moodie why he chose that route, given the cost, Tumanenko said he wasn't one to worry about five or six dollars when selling a $32,000 truck. He figured any serious prospective buyer would want to try it out at 100 or 120 kilometres an hour.

While out on the highway, the men's conversation turned to the advantages of diesel engines. Tumanenko mentioned he had worked on Cummins engines, like the one in his truck, when he was in the Israeli army. All of a sudden, the shorter guy in the back seat—who, Tumanenko said, had been "almost invisible" and "quiet as a fish"—perked up.

"He asks me, 'What did you do in Israeli army?'" says Tumanenko, who, like many native Russian speakers, drops his articles in English. "I look at him and I tell him, 'You don't want to know what I did there.'" At that point, Tumanenko tells the court, the driver turned his head and gave the guy in the back a sharp look. He moved so fast, Tumanenko wondered if the man might have pulled a muscle in his neck.

Despite his heavy accent and occasional grammatical failings, Tumanenko is a raconteur with a way with words. His revelation about the Israeli army, he says, caused "a change of temperature, dynamic, inside of car." It also caused Tumanenko some anxiety, he testifies, because at the moment the driver looked back at his friend, he was doing 50 to 60 kilometres an hour on an exit ramp.

This is something Nadir Sachak, one of Millard's lawyers, picks up on during cross-examination when he asks Tumanenko to estimate how long the backward glance was.

"It was long enough for me," Tumanenko answers. "One second, two second, when you're driving sixty, you cannot look in the back."

"Did you say, 'Buddy, what are you doing?'"

"No. It was not so bad for me to start screaming 'Pay attention to the road,' but it was there."

"You want to describe it as a big deal, but it was not a big deal," says Sachak, who has been becoming steadily more aggressive with the witness. At one point things get so heated that Tumanenko snaps at Sachak, "Don't tell me what I don't know. I just told you exactly what happened." The judge has to intervene to set him straight on what he no doubt finds to be the curious customs of Canadian courtrooms, where the witness does not get to interrupt the lawyer, no matter how much he dislikes the questions.

Sachak requests that Tumanenko look over his police statement, made two days after the test drive. "You were being honest?" he asks.

"Yes."

"Your memory then was much better than it is today?"

"Yes and no. When detective called me and they came, second person disappeared," he says, referring to Bosma. "You become a little bit nervous."

Sachak is using Tumanenko's original police statement to try to make the point that the witness is embellishing and dramatizing what occurred. He points out to Tumanenko that all he said in his statement was that after the Israeli army comment, the two guys exchanged looks—"a glance" is how the lawyer characterizes it. Sachak says there's nothing in the statement about the events Tumanenko has just described in court—no mention of a temperature change in the truck or concern about an accident. The statement doesn't say anything about the driver adjusting his seat or moving like a mouse, another one of Tumanenko's memorable animal figures of speech.

Today is "the first time you mention anything about moving like a mouse," says Sachak.

Tumanenko answers that just because he didn't include every single detail in his original statement, it doesn't mean it didn't happen. He concedes, though, that to say the tall guy was moving in his seat like a mouse "maybe is too much."

When Sachak cuts him off at one point, Tumanenko asks, "Can I just say something?"

"No," Sachak says. "He didn't move like a mouse, and that was an exaggeration when you communicated it to the jury. Fair?"

"Fair. I said it was a kind of a pause."

A few questions later, the "ambition" tattoo comes up. Tumanenko, who has already started to catch on to lawyers and their tactics, says, "I don't remember the conversation."

"Do you recall him showing you his wrist?" asks Sachak.

"You need to understand where I come from. Tattoo language in my country is criminal language. You would no more ask someone about a tattoo than their underwear."

In certain neighbourhoods, Tumanenko adds, you could get killed over a tattoo like that. Earlier, he said that when he first spotted it, he remembered thinking, "It's very ambition to have 'ambition' on your arm."

Sachak asks Tumanenko to draw the tattoo as he remembers it. Tumanenko writes *Ambition*, capital A, the rest lowercase, with a rectangle around it. His drawing is shown to the jury.

"You've got a rectangle around the word *ambition*. It's what you saw, right?"

"What I think I saw," Tumanenko answers cautiously. It's a good response, given that Millard's tattoo, although inked in a boxy font, has no frame, and Sachak would have probably leapt on this had the witness given him an opening. Instead, Sachak asks as his final question whether Tumanenko remembers any other tattoos. He says he doesn't.

The podium is turned over to Mark Smich's lawyer, Thomas Dungey, who always cross-examines second due to the fact that his client's name is listed after Millard's on the indictment. At the beginning of Tumanenko's testimony, Dungey filed an admission, or, as it's known in legal terms, an agreed statement of facts. On behalf of his client, he admitted that Smich was present in the rear passenger seat for the May 5 test drive. He also conceded that Smich was the passenger Tumanenko had picked out of a photo lineup shown to him by Hamilton Police on May 15. As a result, Dungey has no need to hammer the witness as Sachak did. Instead, he can be nice to him and take his side. And Dungey does just that, suggesting to Tumanenko that his presence at the courthouse and the act of rereading his police statement have brought back distinct memories of the test drive in a "flash," just as he has described it. That's part of why he remembers the driver turning his head so sharply that it looked like he might have hurt his neck, isn't it? Tumanenko is happy to agree.

Smich's lawyer then asks a series of questions about whether the taller guy had tried to bargain down the price of the truck, which Tumanenko says he didn't. Dungey wants to undermine the impression Sachak tried to create that his client, Millard, was a serious potential buyer while Smich was once again the sketchy guy in the hoodie. Dungey's version is that Millard had no interest in buying a truck, just stealing one. He winds up by asking the witness if the taller man has a big ego.

"Yes," says Tumanenko, as Millard's lead lawyer, Ravin Pillay, immediately objects. The judge instructs the jury to ignore the question. Dungey thanks the witness and Tumanenko is told he is free to go. Somehow, unlike any of the other witnesses before him, he makes it out of the building without being caught on camera by any of the photographers stationed at the different sets of courthouse doors.

ALONG WITH LEADING THEM to Igor Tumanenko, without whom this case might have remained unsolved, the Lucas Bate phone also provided valuable cell tower information. The phone, a Huawei flip model, was purchased with cash at a small tech store in the west end of Toronto on March 11, 2013. The store's security video footage went back only as far as April 1. The address the buyer had provided was that of a nearby high school, Lakeshore Collegiate, in Etobicoke. There was no Lucas Bate registered there and none to be found anywhere else. Police concluded it was a bogus name.

Tracing the other calls made from what came to be known as the Bate phone, investigators reached Omar Palmili, who also had a Dodge Ram truck for sale and had been supposed to go for a test drive right after Tumanenko's. Fortunately for him, the potential buyers were late and he decided to take a nap. He slept through a call from the Bate phone and never met the man he remembers identifying himself as Ethan or Evan when they spoke.

In court, Brett Moodie asks Palmili how he feels about missing that phone call. "Back then I had my daughter, and it was shocking for me," he says and then is cut off by an objection from Ravin Pillay, which the judge upholds.

A minute or two later, Sachak walks over to the witness box to hand Palmili a copy of the police statement he made almost three years earlier. Just like Tumanenko, Palmili has told the court about details that weren't in his original statement: that the caller mumbled when he said his name and that he lowered his voice. But in contrast to Tumanenko, Palmili doesn't protest when Sachak takes him to task for these inconsistencies. From the moment he arrived in the witness box and was asked by the registrar to spit out his gum in front of the entire courtroom, things have been awkward for Palmili, who is a slim, fit-looking man wearing a grey suit and an open-collared pink shirt. It's a relief when Thomas Dungey stands up for his cross-examination and plays good cop.

"I take it you've never been involved in anything like this before," he begins.

"No," answers Palmili. He definitely hasn't.

"The reason you remember about this person mumbling, lowering his voice, is you asked him twice what his name was?"

"Yes."

"Prior to this, you had no problem."

"Correct."

"One of the reasons you remember is because you asked him his name again?"

"Yes."

"He never said to you in clear, loud English, 'My name is Dellen, my name is Millard'?"

"No."

"That's the only time he mumbles?"

"Yes, right."

Palmili is dismissed.

ON FRIDAY, MAY 10, 2013, shortly after noon, Detective Constable John Tselepakis and Detective Sergeant Paul Hamilton headed to the Waterloo area to talk to Dennis Araujo, another man with a Dodge Ram truck for sale who had been contacted with the Lucas Bate phone. Unlike Palmili and Tumanenko, Araujo never even spoke to the caller. They played telephone tag. But the police still needed an audio statement from him as a formality.

When the detectives were done and on their way back to Hamilton, they got a call from Sergeant Greg Jackson, who was finally getting results from the queries he had sent earlier that week to other police forces about the "ambition" tattoo. From two reliable police sources in Peel and Toronto, he had learned that a man by the name of Dellen Millard had a tattoo matching that description on his left forearm, carried a satchel, and lived in an area of Toronto close to a cell phone tower pinged on several occasions by the Lucas Bate phone. Jackson wanted Tselepakis and Hamilton to visit the nearby Waterloo International Airport, where Millard's family business, Millardair, had a hangar, and try to talk to the suspect.

As they entered the brand-new, red-roofed hangar, which lies far from the airport's main areas, the detectives found two men sitting in an office behind the empty reception area. "One identified himself as Mr. Millard," said Hamilton. "He made a comment to the effect of 'The suits are here.'"

Hamilton overheard Millard tell the other man in the office, "Let me put this on pause," then Millard closed the office door and came out to speak to the detectives. At one point during their conversation, Millard took a satchel out of the desk in the reception area and put it over his shoulder. "He asked us what would bring us to that particular location," said Hamilton, who answered that it was just another tip, one of many they were investigating. "I asked him if it was okay if we had a look around. He said, 'I thought you were going to say that.'"

When Hamilton inquired as to Millard's address, he gave them the address of his farm in Ayr, twenty-five kilometres southwest of the airport. As soon as they left the hangar, Hamilton reported back to the officers in charge. Then he and Tselepakis parked down the road while they waited for Waterloo Police to bring out their surveillance team.

As he finishes recounting these events, Hamilton is asked by Tony Leitch if he sees the man he met at the hangar in the court. "He's sitting at the last table in the courtroom with the white shirt on," the detective replies, as Millard raises his right hand in greeting. Hamilton appears taken aback by the gesture, as does almost everyone else, including a few members of the jury. It is one of the rare occasions they display emotion.

DETECTIVE CONSTABLE STEVE GRIFFIN of the Waterloo Police was part of the team that took over from Hamilton and Tselepakis at 3:35 P.M. that afternoon. Shortly before 4 P.M., Griffin saw a red truck with a lone white male driver, whom he described as having a thin build, exit the hangar. It was followed by a black Dodge Caravan. The vehicles drove to a bungalow-style house on nearby Maple Grove Road. The red truck went around to the back of the house and was left there. Two white males returned to the hangar in the Dodge van. The surveillance team couldn't get close enough to confirm whether Dellen Millard was one of the men. At 4:12 the Caravan drove into the hangar.

At 4:41 P.M. a blue Yukon exited the hangar and was followed by Griffin and another officer to a TD Canada Trust branch in nearby Kitchener while two more surveillance officers remained at the hangar. "The vehicle did not leave our sight," Griffin tells the court, adding that they did not know Millard was the driver until they got to the bank. "I looked in through the glass panel and saw him at the teller." The officers snapped photos of Millard returning to the Yukon while putting something in his back left pocket.

Detective Constable George Higgins of the Hamilton Police intelligence unit was headed to the hangar to take over from the Waterloo surveillance team when he got word that the target was on the move, he tells the court. He picked up his tail travelling eastbound on Highway 401 at 5:08 P.M., just before Millard turned south on Highway 6. Millard then pulled into a Petro-Canada station near Waterdown before hitting the 403 and travelling east again in the direction of Toronto. In Oakville, he stopped at a block of three high-rise apartment buildings on Speers Road, where it was later determined Mark Smich's girlfriend, Marlena Meneses, was staying with her sister. The surveillance team didn't see Millard go into the building, but they saw him come out at 7:19 P.M., after he had been out of their sight for fifty minutes. He then made his way east once more on the Queen Elizabeth Way, exiting the highway at Cawthra Road, near his Etobicoke home.

By that time, the order had come down from Detective Kavanagh to arrest Millard. At 7:30 P.M., the surveillance team boxed him in at a stop sign, surrounded his car with guns drawn, and ordered him out. He was handcuffed and searched. In his right front pocket were three black nitrile gloves and a bundle of cash totalling $350. Millard was also found to be in possession of a TD Canada Trust bank envelope containing $3,000 in fifty- and hundred-dollar bills. He was taken to Hamilton for questioning. Higgins and another officer stayed with the Yukon to wait for a tow truck. They then escorted it back to Hamilton, one officer driving in front of the tow truck and one behind. Once at their destination, they placed forensic seals on all the doors and waited for a search warrant for the vehicle.

The keys to Tim Bosma's truck were later found on Millard's key chain in the ignition.

THREE

MOTHER'S DAY

At the news briefing where they announced the arrest of Dellen Millard, Hamilton Police chief Glenn De Caire and Superintendent Dan Kinsella made no mention of a fact that would become one of the key talking points over the next few days: Dellen Millard was rich. In the media, he was variously described in breathless journalese as the wealthy heir to an aviation empire, the scion of a flying dynasty, and the well-educated CEO of Millardair, the family business.

While the money part was true, the description of Millard as well-educated was something of a stretch. He had dropped out of the Toronto French School, an exclusive private school where tuition and other expenses add up to more than $35,000 a year. At his parents' insistence, he eventually graduated from Subway Academy, which, despite its somewhat sketchy name, is an official alternative school under the auspices of the Toronto District School Board. Millard's formal academic education had stopped there.

Real estate databases revealed that Millard owned multiple properties in Toronto and its suburbs. There was his $1.2 million family home in Etobicoke; the condo in the Distillery District he had reportedly bought in cash for some $625,000, closing on the purchase the day after Tim Bosma went missing; another condo valued at half a million dollars; and a residential rental property worth more than two million. Millard's hundred-acre farm in Ayr, Ontario, had been purchased in 2011 for almost $850,000, again in cash. It didn't have any buildings on it other than a dilapidated barn, but Millard had told the real estate agent who sold it to him that he and his fiancée planned to build their dream home there. That made sense, given that the property was a convenient commute to the new Millardair hangar, which had cost an estimated eight to nine million dollars to construct and equip.

Moving the family business from Toronto's Pearson International Airport to Waterloo was a major shift in direction, an attempt to rebuild an "aviation empire" that had been dormant for years and, if the truth be known, hadn't been all that imperial even in its prime. Dellen's father, Wayne, had inherited the business from his father, Carl, when he died in 2006. At that point, Millardair planes hadn't flown in more than a decade and almost all of the company's revenues came from leasing a valuable hangar at Pearson Airport to Air Transat, a major charter carrier. Wayne wanted to reinvigorate the business to leave a legacy for his son. His idea was to open an aircraft maintenance and repair operation in Waterloo, at the centre of Canada's so-called Technology Triangle and its booming economy.

Millardair's most lucrative years for flying had been in the 1960s and 1970s, when its planes delivered auto parts to and from Detroit. It benefited strongly from the 1965 Auto Pact struck between Canada and the United States, which greatly increased cross-border trade and boosted demand for transportation services. Less profitable were Millardair's charter services, flying everyone from politicians out on the campaign trail and Toronto Symphony Orchestra musicians on a tour of the North, to racehorses and the occasional bottlenose dolphin in need of transport from Mexico to the Marine Wonderland theme park in Niagara Falls. At one time, the company experimented with providing scheduled passenger flights between Toronto and Sarnia, in Southwestern Ontario, but like everyone else in those small markets, it couldn't make the route profitable. Yet another business was training aspiring pilots, allowing them to build up the flying hours needed to get a commercial certification for different types of aircraft.

The business was founded in 1956 by Carl and Della Millard, the grandmother after whom Dellen was named. Della had died the year before he was born. She was reputed to be an astute businesswoman, while Carl was known as the colourful flying ace. By the time their only child, Wayne, was ten or eleven, he would take over piloting duties from his father while Carl wandered out of the cockpit to chat with astonished passengers. Decades later, Dellen, who was Carl's only grandchild, got the same early flight training. A family photo shows him at age two or three, an adorable little boy sporting a devilish grin, seated on Wayne's lap at the controls of a plane. By his teens, Dellen was driving cars and trucks around the airport. And on their son's fourteenth birthday, the Millards invited the press to an airfield north of Toronto, where Dellen is said to have set a somewhat obscure world record. He supposedly became the youngest pilot ever to make solo flights in both a helicopter and a fixed-wing plane on the same day.

Video footage and photos taken at the time show three generations of Millards. Carl, pushing ninety but well preserved, is beaming. Wayne, a big man with a barrel chest and ruddy face, is rushing around by the helicopter getting things organized. Dellen's mother, Madeleine Burns, who helped set up the event, is in the background. As for Dellen himself, he is an awkward and overweight adolescent with a double chin, poufy hairdo, and a voice that hasn't quite broken. He has not yet transformed himself into the slim and attractive twenty-something reporters found on Facebook in May 2013 when they went searching for information about Millard after his arrest.

While Millard himself had no personal photos posted on Facebook—his account was under the name Dee Em, of Oakville, Ontario, and had a tiny fluffy kitten in a bowl as his profile picture—his friends and family displayed a number of photos in which they had tagged him. Millard could be seen at his cousin's wedding in a suit and tie; mugging it up in headphones and a Union Jack T-shirt on a European vacation; and sporting a red mohawk while sipping a giant margarita in Mexico. The scant information on his account (he once told a friend of a friend looking to send him a Facebook invitation to a party that he had "gone off the grid") included Millard's favourite movies (*American Beauty* and *Fight Club*, among others), TV shows (*Dexter*, *The Sopranos*, and *The Office* were listed), and music (including Linkin Park, Audioslave, and a *Glee* cast album). Just two books were named—*Wizard's First Rule*, by Terry Goodkind, and *The Last Lecture*, by Randy Pausch, a Carnegie Mellon

professor diagnosed with terminal cancer who gave the epony-
mous last lecture about achieving your childhood dreams.

According to reports in the *National Post* newspaper, Dellen's
solo flights were a turning point, an accomplishment that finally
earned him some respect from his peers. Before that, he had
been seen as something of an outcast, wandering the halls of
his school provocatively eating from a box of dog biscuits and
ignoring the appalled looks of his fellow students. Although the
Toronto French School likes to see itself as a kinder, gentler
private school—geared more toward turning out future Médecins
Sans Frontières workers and bilingual diplomats than financiers
and industrialists—there are only so many parents of budding
humanitarians who can afford its fees. Wayne Millard's beat-up
pickup trucks stood out in the stream of German luxury vehicles
in the drop-off line. Charles Humphrey, the classmate who told
the *National Post* about Millard's dog biscuit habit, also recalled
that "Dellen was—and I realize I'm playing into a stereotype
here—a little marginalized, a little different. I didn't even know
the guy was so wealthy. He always looked like a bit of a hillbilly."

One of the best initial sources for information on the Millard
family was a curious obituary Dellen wrote just a few months
before the disappearance of Tim Bosma. It was for his father, who
had died on November 29, 2012, although no cause of death was
given. It began, "Wayne C. Millard has passed. He is survived by
his son Dellen Millard." Strangely, Dellen did not acknowledge the
existence of other family members, including Carl, who had been
such an influence on Wayne, and Wayne's ex-wife, Madeleine,
who was still, on paper at least, a vice president at Millardair.

Wayne and Madeleine had met at Air Canada in the mid-
1970s, when he was a pilot and she worked as a flight attendant.

By the end of the decade, the couple had left the airline to set up Canadian Wildlife Film Productions, and they joined one of the era's major animal-rights campaigns to stop the annual seal hunt in which young pups were clubbed to death for their glossy white pelts. Wayne learned to fly helicopters so that he could ferry activists and equipment to hard-to-reach locations. His dedication to that cause, readers would assume, was why Dellen's obit showed a picture of a big-eyed seal pup stranded on an ice floe next to a photo of Wayne as a dashing young pilot flashing a wry smile over his shoulder.

Dellen wrote that his father "was frugal with himself and generous to others. . . . He would answer a question with a story. He stepped carefully while advocating carefreeness. He could read and write five languages. He was patient and stubborn. He admired Christ, Gandhi and Lindbergh. He believed animal welfare was a humanitarian effort. He was a good man in a careless world. He was my father." Along with the praise and platitudes, however, there were a number of cryptic statements thrown in without context. Dellen described how his father had hoped "for a time when cooperation would be the norm and competition was only friendly" and wrote that "the only people he feared were racists."

After listing the many animal-welfare causes Wayne had supported, Dellen noted that his father's final and not-yet-launched animal-welfare mission, the Elizabeth Glass Animal Welfare Fund, named after a late ex-girlfriend of Wayne's, was accepting donations. "He believed we can make a difference in the world," Dellen's obituary ended. "With Wayne in my heart, I believe we must."

In the online guest book that accompanied the death notice, a number of friends and former colleagues paid their respects, with a few regretting that they had not been able to make it to the reception held in Wayne's honour because they had not been aware of it. Carl's sister June, an internet-savvy nonagenarian, wrote that no one had notified her of either the reception or her nephew's death. And then there was a comment from Madeleine Burns, who posted her message on New Year's Eve, 2012: "Dellen, my thoughts and prayers are with you tonight, my boy, as we embark on a new year. Your Dad's voice will always be with me, as I recall the first time I heard him say, 'This is your co pilot.' That was a long time ago. A flight to Edmonton. May all the good times sustain you and I in the times to come. I love you. Mummy xx."

DAY 7—SUNDAY, MAY 12

The vehicle towing a large transport trailer had pulled into the quiet suburban cul-de-sac in Kleinburg, Ontario, on May 9, the night before Dellen Millard was arrested. It arrived late enough that the noise and bright lights woke up at least one neighbour and distracted others from their television watching. Even after the commotion had died down and the trailer was unhitched and left in Madeleine Burns's driveway on Tinsmith Court, it was noticeable enough in the dark to catch the eye of Frank Cianfarani, who lived two doors down from Dellen Millard's mother, when he returned late from an appointment in Toronto.

Big ugly trailers were not the norm on this street of million-dollar homes with carefully landscaped lawns north of Toronto. But Burns had developed a reputation for keeping to herself during her twelve years living on the street, so no one asked her what the trailer was doing there. It wasn't until the neighbours heard the news about her son's involvement in Tim Bosma's disappearance that the possibility was raised that the trailer might be evidence as opposed to just an eyesore. Frank Cianfarani thought it was especially strange how it was backed right up against the garage, making it impossible to access or even see the trailer's rear doors. He consulted with another neighbour and together they decided they needed to call the police to come check it out.

Constable Mark Levangie of the York Regional Police rang the doorbell at Madeleine Burns's house at 1 P.M. on Mother's Day. He had been sent there to check out a trailer in connection to a missing person report. When no one answered, he did a walk around the house, looking in windows and knocking on other doors. He noted the trailer's VIN but couldn't see its licence plate because of its position against the garage doors of Burns's house. A light on the garage wall next to the trailer was broken, likely damaged when the vehicle was manoeuvred into place. The two side doors of the trailer were padlocked shut.

Levangie's partner, Cory Weick, called Hamilton Police, who told them the circumstances were urgent. They needed to find out if the missing person was inside. For this reason, they had grounds to enter the trailer without a warrant, but not the residence. Since it was impossible to access the trailer's rear doors, and neither Levangie nor Weick had bolt cutters to remove the locks on the side doors, they contacted the emergency response unit to cut the locks.

Through one of the side doors, Weick had enough space to climb up into the bed of what the officers recognized as a black Dodge Ram. Using a flashlight, he observed there was no licence plate on the truck, car parts were in the back, and nothing was underneath it. Behind it was a tarp and some other items. Weick reported that the truck's interior had been partially stripped. Because the truck was squeezed so tightly into the trailer, with just a few centimetres of clearance on either side, Weick had to climb over the top of the cab and crouch on the hood to read the VIN, located on the dash on the driver's side. The entire search, which took just a minute or two, satisfied Weick that there was no missing person inside either the trailer or the truck. Hamilton Police confirmed on the spot that the VIN belonged to Tim Bosma's truck. The trailer was found to be registered to Millardair.

After Weick emerged, Levangie closed up the trailer, placed official police seals on all three doors, and photographed the exterior. Weick requested a canvass of the entire street to see if anyone knew anything or had video of the trailer's arrival. By the end of the afternoon, they had discovered video recorded in the basement security room of a resident, who lived on a neighbouring street.

The trailer remained under guard by York Police officers until Constable Brent Gibson of the Hamilton force arrived at about 6:30 P.M. to escort it back to Hamilton. While he had two tow truck drivers with him to ensure he had the right type of hitch, no one had been notified to bring padlocks. Gibson had to use his own personal gym lock to secure the trailer's rear doors while its two side doors remained unlocked. He followed behind the trailer for the entire eighty-five-kilometre trip to the Metro Truck garage on Seaman Street in Hamilton. Once there, he placed the trailer in a locked bay surrounded by yellow crime-scene tape and padlocked the side doors. He left the garage at 9:30 P.M.

ON THAT SAME SUNDAY, at the Bosma house, as the search for Tim continued, Mary Bosma made a special Mother's Day appeal for the return of her son. Standing in Tim's garage, with the media in front of her and a row of Missing posters behind her, she spoke softly and nervously into the microphones. "Even though there's been an arrest," she said, "he still is not home with us. My heart is broken. I love him so much. We just want him home."

It was hard to watch her, so anxious and distressed, without thinking back to Sharlene's dramatic appeal. As bad as things had looked a mere three days earlier, there had still been hope. Sharlene seemed like the type of woman who, through sheer force of personality, could will her husband home and bring about the happy ending that everyone was hoping for. Now, with Dellen Millard in jail but refusing to talk, and the missing truck being pulled from his mother's driveway, that hope was undeniably dying.

Online, there was anger and frustration that the man police had in custody was not helping to find Tim Bosma. As the curious searched for information, they focused their early attention on Andrew Michalski. Four and a half years younger than Millard and a few inches shorter, Michalski pretty much fit the vague description of suspect number two. According to Facebook, he was a sports-loving, hard-partying plumber in training, whose social media pronouncements were profanity laced and vulgar.

Judging from his Facebook and Twitter accounts, Michalski appeared to idolize Dellen Millard. He faithfully chronicled his friend's activities and tweeted out comments Millard made in conversation as if they were pearls of wisdom. On one occasion, he quoted Dell Millard on Twitter as saying, "I'm either going to sleep or doing heroin." On another, he boasted that Millard's dog, Pedo, who presumably had a Twitter account in his name, had tweeted, "Turn the fucking music down Michalski." On a 2009 trip to South Beach in Miami—about which Michalski enthused, "Best weekend of my life, with Dellen!"—Andrew turned videographer, posting several videos of his adventures, including one that caught the attention of internet sleuths. Taken on Washington Avenue, South Beach's clubbing strip, it showed a gussied-up black Dodge Ram with a raised suspension, running lights atop the roof of its cab, and other modifications. "Dell and I still waiting outside and see a SICKKKKKK TRUCK!!!!!!!!!" Michalski posted to Facebook. With those online comments, and a tweet of his from February 2012—"Learn how to steal cars. #gonein60seconds," which was likely referencing a video game—Michalski had managed to convince a large portion of the internet that they had found suspect number two even if the police hadn't.

Both the mainstream media and social media sleuths were especially interested in Michalski's photographs documenting a trip he and Millard had made to the Baja 500 off-road race in Mexico in June 2011. Along with Dellen's personal mechanic, Shane Schlatman, another target of online speculation, the pair had spent months, and Millard's allotted budget of $100,000, customizing a yellow Jeep Wrangler TJ in the old Millardair hangar in Toronto. For the cross-continent journey to Baja California, the racing Jeep was placed in Millard's trailer, the same one that had just been found in Madeleine Burns's driveway. The trailer was hitched to Millard's red Dodge Ram truck, a slightly older model than Tim Bosma's, with a gas engine as opposed to diesel.

Michalski had fashioned his hair into a blue mohawk, while Millard wore a red one. The photo that would be splashed all

over the media—of Millard with his mohawk and a margarita—
was taken en route to Baja. Among other things, the photos show
the three travellers stopping at Applebee's, the San Diego Air &
Space Museum, and the Bellagio hotel in Vegas. Though the
race itself was not a success—Millard rolled out after just a few
miles—the trio all got matching "Desert Baja Racing" tattoos on
their left arms to memorialize the event.

After Millard's arrest, a long trail of comments appeared on
Facebook under one of Michalski's photos from the trip: the one
that showed Millard and Schlatman in front of a red Dodge Ram
truck pulling a trailer. Facebook users demanded Michalski tell
them where Tim Bosma was, cursed him out, and expressed
their ugly hopes he would be an eventual victim of prison rape.

While Michalski deleted his Twitter feed and temporarily took
his Facebook account private, he quickly made it public again.
Right through the trial, anyone could look at his photos and the
vitriolic comments they had provoked.

DAY 8—MONDAY, MAY 13

With Dellen Millard in custody, police forces around Southern
Ontario began exercising search warrants at his home on Maple
Gate Court in Etobicoke, his farm in Ayr, and the Millardair
hangar at Waterloo Airport. Yellow crime-scene tape went up at
various sites as media trucks and journalists arrived in droves.

Millard's Maple Gate neighbours conformed to the predictable and contradictory patterns seen when the guy next door
is arrested for doing a very bad thing. One neighbour told the
CBC that Millard seemed like a "normal kid," while another said

she always knew he was trouble and had called the police about Dellen and his friends speeding dangerously down the quiet residential cul-de-sac. When she had first moved to the street, a friend had come to visit her and mistakenly knocked on the Millards' door. Dellen's father, Wayne, had answered, looking like a dishevelled hermit, and frightened her friend. Since that time, the neighbour had ordered her kids to stay away from the Millard house and to turn down all invitations from their elderly housekeeper, who was known for inviting local children in to see the family's animal collection. When journalists peeked into the house after Dellen's arrest, they saw a mess of clothing, documents, canned goods strewn about, and a black cat.

At the new Millardair hangar in Waterloo, police officers inspected the exterior, taking photographs and blocking off the road leading to the building as they awaited a search warrant that would allow them to go inside. Airport officials made themselves scarce. Millardair, the company they had worked so hard to lure to the region, had turned into a major headache. First, after his father's sudden death, Dellen Millard had abruptly closed down the newly launched aviation maintenance business and begun seeking new tenants for the hangar. And now there was a murder investigation underway and reporters were asking questions about how much public money the airport authority had spent on runway improvements to accommodate the larger jets Wayne Millard had planned to bring in.

Things were also bleak at Millard's farm, where the media had gathered by the road in front of the barn. Police set up shop farther back on the property, erecting giant forensic tents far from journalists' prying eyes. Officers could be seen combing the fields on horseback and conducting coordinated grid searches of wooded areas by foot. Neighbours stopped by to find out what was going on and chatted with reporters. Millard was said to have driven a hard bargain when he bought the farm, which was still used to produce corn for animal feed.

On the Friday Millard was arrested, before his name had been made public, one of the neighbours had happened to be crossing the property when he noticed a strange machine he had never seen before. It was unusual enough that it caused him to stop and take a few pictures with his phone. Later, when the media showed up, copies of those photos ended up in the hands of a CBC reporter. The machine in question was a portable livestock incinerator called the Eliminator, but neighbours said there were no animals on Millard's farm.

DAY 9—TUESDAY, MAY 14

The news that everyone had been dreading came Tuesday morning. Hamilton Police chief Glenn De Caire, who had worn shirt sleeves three days earlier to announce Dellen Millard's arrest, arrived at the media briefing room in full dress uniform, an ominous sign under the circumstances. "It is with a heavy heart," he said, "that the Hamilton Police Service today announces the death of Ancaster resident Tim Bosma. A number of searches have taken place and human remains have been located. We are convinced by the totality of the evidence that these are the remains of Tim Bosma. The evidence indicates that the remains have been burned."

After offering his condolences to the Bosma family and thanking the many police forces throughout Southern Ontario who had assisted Hamilton officers, as well as the community at large, De Caire pledged, "We will continue to follow every single lead. We will work to effect the arrest of those responsible for the death of Tim Bosma."

In the afternoon, Matt Kavanagh held an investigative briefing, which began with the announcement that Dellen Millard would be charged the next day with first-degree murder. Kavanagh said that Tim Bosma had been taken to a location in the Waterloo area where his body had been burned beyond recognition and that police had warrants allowing them to continue to search two properties in the Waterloo region owned by Dellen Millard, meaning the hangar and the farm. Investigators' other priority, he stressed, was identifying and arresting the remaining suspects involved in the murder.

Anyone who's ever attended or watched a press conference on TV has probably been frustrated by the way reporters jump from topic to topic. At this particular briefing, the questions skipped around between three main areas. Journalists wanted to know about the other suspects in the case, the details of what happened to Tim Bosma, and a possible motive for the crime. When it came to the latter, many members of the media were as reluctant as the armchair sleuths to accept the lack of connection between Tim Bosma and Dellen Millard. And several of them were just as blind to how this line of inquiry can quickly turn into victim-blaming. This became evident at the start of the press conference, when one journalist barked out, "Was Bosma known to police? Does he have a criminal record?"

"You're talking the victim?" responded Kavanagh, as if to make sure he'd heard her correctly.

"Yes."

"No, he does not," said Kavanagh, who would have to deal with several more versions of this question, as well as the oft-repeated query of whether Tim Bosma was connected to Dellen Millard, to which he unequivocally answered, "There's no connection whatsoever."

As far as motive went, Kavanagh stated simply that he wished he knew and that he believed Bosma had been "targeted." Although he didn't specify, as he had at an earlier news conference, that this targeting related to the truck, it was the only inference that made sense.

A reporter asked if the first-degree murder charge meant police believed Millard had planned on killing Tim Bosma from the moment of their encounter at 9 P.M. on Monday night. Kavanagh explained that under the Criminal Code, if a victim is forcibly confined and then murdered, the charge is automatically murder in the first degree. He said that because Tim had entered his truck by his own free will but not been allowed to leave, forcible confinement was the proper charge.

Asked about other suspects, Kavanagh revealed that video evidence recovered by police showed a second vehicle following the black Dodge Ram as it left the Bosma residence. "We do not know at this time how many people were in that second vehicle, so right now we're looking for at least three, possibly more."

"Can you describe the second vehicle, the following vehicle?"

"We've had a lot of people from the different auto squads—different services we have—look at the video for us, and we can't identify it," Kavanagh said. "It looks like an SUV-type vehicle, but I don't want to be wrong about that. I'm relying on other officers to identify that vehicle for me, and that's what they give me today."

"Any indication that the second vehicle was spotted in the area of the Etobicoke incident the day before? Have you guys gone through footage from that industrial area?"

"Yes, we have. We've gone at length through the surveillance there, and no other vehicle was seen at that location."

A question or two later, Andrew Michalski came up. He had caught the eye of reporters as well as amateur sleuths. Kavanagh was asked to talk about his involvement, if any.

"Andrew had been identified; he's been interviewed; he's been cleared of having involvement."

So too had Dellen Millard's mother. "Mrs. Burns has absolutely no involvement or knowledge of this case," Kavanagh stated emphatically, when asked about the trailer in her driveway.

On the subject of how Tim Bosma had died, Kavanagh was at his least forthcoming, repeatedly stating that he could not discuss evidence that would eventually be before the court. Pretty much the only thing he would say was that police believed the victim died the night of the test drive. He declined to answer any questions about the incinerator, photos of which were now circulating on the internet.

As the news conference wrapped up, Kavanagh said that 120 officers were still working on the case, including one specially assigned to monitor social media. The public had provided a lot of tips, and police were still counting on them. "These people talk," Kavanagh said of the suspects. "They talk to other people, and we need these people to call the tip line and supply information to identify the other people involved in this crime." He guaranteed that the second suspect would be arrested.

When asked about having to break the news of Tim's death to the Bosma family, Kavanagh replied that, as the leader of the team, it had fallen to him to do that most difficult of jobs. "I'm sorry for the Bosma family," he said. "I have no idea what they're experiencing right now."

DAY 10—WEDNESDAY, MAY 15

Millard's appearance at downtown Hamilton's John Sopinka Courthouse was brief. He was charged with first-degree murder, forcible confinement, and motor vehicle theft, and was asked to indicate that he understood the charges against him. The whole procedure lasted only a few minutes and was covered by a temporary court-ordered publication ban. The purpose of the ban, which is standard practice in Canadian courts, is to protect the fairness and integrity of the case and prevent the public dissemination of information or evidence that might jeopardize the trial process. In this case, for example, the ban prevented the press from reporting the names of a long list of people who were considered potential witnesses and with whom Millard had been ordered to have no contact.

Although three sketch artists were present in court, none of them managed to capture a decent likeness of Millard. He was unshaven and unemotional, wore a wrinkled white shirt and beige pants, and, in contrast to his mohawk days, had a subdued hairstyle with short back and sides. After the brief hearing, the accused was sent back to the Hamilton-Wentworth Detention Centre, better known to locals as the notorious Barton Street jail. Its reputation is due to frequent reports of overcrowding, drug-overdose deaths, lockdowns, and various other unsavoury goings-on.

Millard's original lawyer, Deepak Paradkar, met with the press on the courthouse steps, which in Hamilton are nothing like the long, photogenic stairways leading up to historic court buildings so often seen on the news. There are just five dusty steps on Main Street, where noisy traffic speeds by. Even when reporters were pressed up close to Paradkar, with their microphones and tape recorders inches from his face, the passing trucks sometimes made it difficult to hear.

This appearance was, to put it mildly, out of the ordinary in normally tight-lipped Toronto lawyer circles. But Paradkar sees himself as more of an American-style lawyer along the lines of F. Lee Bailey and the late Johnnie Cochran, so he was happy to court the press. "I take my cues in trial preparation from the United States, and I think Canadian lawyers generally are not up to speed," he would later tell *The Hamilton Spectator*, in an interview that gave rise to a lot of tsk-tsking.

In keeping with those role models, Paradkar talked to the media regularly, from the moment it became known he was Dellen Millard's lawyer until he later left the case for reasons that have never been made public. First, he let it be known that his client would be pleading not guilty and was innocent until proven guilty before the law. Then he set about drumming home his storyline. If the dominant narrative was that this was a senseless crime about a truck, Paradkar's counter narrative was that his client didn't need to steal a truck and that his finances were fine. "He is not in debt. He owns a number of properties that are paid for," he told reporters. "Police have confirmed that he had sufficient funds to easily purchase this truck had he wished to."

Paradkar was also out to polish Millard's image as best he could. In an interview given to the CBC shortly after Millard's arrest, Paradkar said of his client, "He's a very unassuming, humble person. He's intelligent, well-educated, and financially well off, so there's no motive here." On the courthouse steps, he described Millard as "a bit of a philosopher by way of nature and background and reading," and said he was taking things one step at a time.

Asked the thorny question of whether Millard was cooperating with police, Paradkar answered that his client was exercising his constitutional right to remain silent. "The police have their information. They've been doing their investigation. They have their leads, so we're leaving it to the police."

To the surprise of reporters hungry to learn more about this mysterious crime, Paradkar didn't stop there. He went on to do something truly gasp-worthy by suggesting that Dellen Millard might have been framed. "There is a story behind this which I can't get into," he said. "Obviously, it's more than it appears to be." When pressed for details, he answered, "I can't get into the framing aspect. We're really waiting for the police investigation to be completed. There are other suspects out there . . . and once they've been apprehended, I think you'll have a fuller picture of what's going on."

The reactions to his statements were like the results of a Rorschach test as well as a harbinger of countless discussions to come. The idea that there must be something bigger going on, like a frame-up, provided a certain level of comfort to those who didn't want to believe that a thirty-two-year-old father had been killed simply for his truck. Or that another young man, who had been given all the advantages in life, could be capable of such evil.

For many people, a shadowy gang of yet-to-be-identified villains was an explanation somehow preferable to a real-life psychopath who preyed upon anyone placing an online ad. Even a far-fetched reason for Tim Bosma's death was better than no reason at all.

FOUR

FORENSICS

At the request of Hamilton Police, officers from the Halton Regional force conducted the forensic examination of Tim Bosma's truck and the trailer used to transport it. But when the team arrived at Metro Truck, where the trailer had been stored, they were not impressed with the location. The mechanics there had pulled out their cell phones and begun snapping pictures as soon as they realized they had a real-life CSI team in their midst, dusting the trailer for fingerprints and trying to get tire impressions. It was quickly arranged for the trailer to be transported to a secure Ontario Provincial Police facility in Tillsonburg, 110 kilometres to the southwest.

Constable Laura Trowbridge of the Hamilton Police was assigned to follow the trailer to Tillsonburg. All was going smoothly until shortly after 6 P.M., when she was on the 403 headed west to Brantford. As she approached the Golf Links overpass in Ancaster, the rear doors of the trailer flew open in heavy rush-hour traffic. A green-and-brown cardboard box that looked like a fruit box "sort of lifted into the air. It kind of floated out of the trailer," Trowbridge tells the court. "I assumed it was empty. It landed on the roadway toward the right side of the front of my car." She ran it over. As far as she observed, nothing else fell out.

Trowbridge, who was in an unmarked vehicle, started honking her horn at the tow truck driver, but he didn't hear her. Eventually, she got into the fast lane and directed him to pull over. The whole incident took place over a stretch of about two kilometres and lasted three minutes.

"Did you see how it opened up?" prosecutor Brett Moodie asks her.

"The lock wasn't actually securing the doors closed," Trowbridge says. Despite all the officers who had looked at the trailer, which was a key piece of evidence in a very major case, no one had noticed this. After the incident, Trowbridge and the driver had to wire the doors shut with supplies he found in his truck. While she and the trailer proceeded to Tillsonburg, Trowbridge requested that another officer come out and check for the box that had fallen out.

The rest of the ride passed without incident, and by 8 P.M. Trowbridge had left the trailer in the secure facility. Back at Hamilton Police headquarters, she was shown the box recovered by a fellow officer—it was small and white, not at all like what she had seen. Trowbridge headed out to where the incident happened and found the green-and-brown box, seized it, and took it back to the police station.

On cross-examination, Millard's lawyer, Ravin Pillay, tries, as criminal defence lawyers invariably do, to make the most of this screw-up.

"It was your job, essentially, to ensure the trailer got from Point A to the Tillsonburg detachment."

Trowbridge agrees that it was.

"You didn't take steps to ensure the doors to the trailer were closed, locked," says Pillay. "Do you know if anyone else took steps to ensure the doors were locked?"

She doesn't.

"It was a scene you needed to protect," he says. "This was a shock to you?"

"Yes, absolutely," Trowbridge says, but she was travelling about 110 kilometres an hour, so it would have been unsafe to do anything but keep going.

At some point, says Pillay, she had to take her eyes off the rear of the trailer to get the tow truck to pull over. "You don't know if anything else came out?" he asks.

Trowbridge says she doesn't think anything did. She had seen a green tarp in the trailer when the doors opened, and it was still inside after they stopped by the side of the road. It was being blown about, but it didn't drag on the ground or fall out of the trailer.

WHEN THE REAR DOORS of the trailer were opened in Tillsonburg on Wednesday, May 15, the same day Dellen Millard was charged with murder, police officers immediately saw the green tarp covering the frame of a burned-out front seat from a truck. Tim Bosma's truck was behind it, toward the front of the trailer.

Over the next three days, seven police officers and two forensic biologists would conduct an exhaustive search for evidence on the truck, the trailer, and everything within it. Hamilton Police had asked for assistance from neighbouring forces, so this was a multijurisdictional team. In charge of the identification work was Sergeant David Banks of the Halton Regional Police. His colleague Detective Constable Laura McLellan acted as the main photographer. Describing their approach to the jury, McLellan says, "We take a deep breath, look at what we have, and then make the plan."

They began by removing the seat frame and inspecting it for blood, but because it had been set on fire, there was nothing to be found beyond a corn husk stuck in a corner. Working inside the trailer, McLellan photographed the truck's exterior, including areas where it had been sanded down after the removal of its Dodge Ram and dealership emblems. The missing emblems were in the truck bed, along with the truck's headlights, tail lights, side trim, and front grille, as well as three more tarps, a roll of paper towels, and other miscellaneous items. Everything was removed, photographed, and inspected for blood and bodily fluids.

Sergeant Robert Jones, a blood-spatter expert with the Waterloo Regional Police, found multiple stains on the tarps, including one spatter stain that he said would have been created by some kind of force. He also detected signs of an attempted "cleanup" on the tarp, but, as he will tell the jury many times, removing blood is not as easy as it might seem. "You really have to scrub," he says.

To extract the truck from the trailer, the forensics team had a key cut so that Banks could lean in and straighten the truck's front wheels and have it pulled out onto a flatbed from which it was lowered to the floor. Because it had no front seats and the officers needed to preserve "the scene," they didn't have the option of driving it out. Once the truck was out, McLellan photographed everything they had been unable to see or access inside the trailer, including the interior of the Dodge Ram. The truck's windows were all rolled down except for the front passenger's window, which was partially up and broken. The glass was removed and came out intact. It was stabilized and wrapped.

With the naked eye, and then wearing orange goggles to search using a laser, the forensics officers looked for blood, finding dark-red and reddish-brown staining on the dashboard, cup holders, driver's visor, seat belts, and doors, among other places. But before they began their presumptive blood testing, the team attempted to collect gunshot residue, or GSR, which is both invisible and easy to disrupt and can therefore quickly disappear. They used a sticky dabber to lift any GSR that was present from the truck's ceiling and doors to determine whether a gun had been fired inside the vehicle.

It's impossible to test all blood from a crime scene, so the investigators selected the stains they felt would provide the most useful information. The police marked the stains they were most interested in with white circles, while the biologists from the Centre of Forensic Sciences used a distinctive gold marker. When their swabs showed a positive result for molecules associated with blood, the investigators added plus signs. Because the stripping of the interior indicated a cleanup, they especially sought out areas that the cleaners might have overlooked, including holes in the truck's floor, where they located significant stains.

Robert Jones, who began specializing in bloodstain pattern analysis in 2004, tells the jury that bloodstain patterns are predictable and reproducible. As a result, he and many other specialists in the field keep their own blood-spatter rooms to test out and verify their theories. He uses sheep's blood, which is disease free and acts in the same manner as human blood. Among the patterns he looks for are passive (blood drops), transfer (from a source to another surface), and spatter (blood dispersed by some sort of force).

On the undercarriage of Tim Bosma's truck, which was hoisted up so that investigators could get a better look, Jones discovered spatter stains, altered stains, and flow stains. Among the more than one hundred photos he includes in his presentation to the court, Jones shows pictures where forensics officers have circled in white dozens of small bloodstains on the rear wheel well and tailpipe. On photos of the back passenger step rail, he points out circular spatter stains on the chrome, as well as flow stains. "It would appear that there's been some kind of dilution effect," Jones tells the jury. "That could come from water flow from cleaning." While he can't say for sure what caused the stains on the undercarriage, they are consistent with water from a power washer or a hose hitting blood.

According to Jones, the blood source had to be below the step, which is forty-two centimetres off the ground, and somewhere in the area of the passenger door. His theory is that someone took a hose or power washer to a pool of blood on the ground, causing it to splash up underneath the truck. The hundreds of spatter spots indicated that the attempted cleanup was likely followed by a drive.

The bloodstains on the truck's interior provided less information as to what might have happened to cause what Jones calls a bloodletting event. Due to the stripped seats and carpeting, there were few patterns to work from. "I'm missing things that would give me an idea of what the mechanism was that created those stains," Jones says. "I'm missing too much inside the vehicle to say how big the event was."

All he can say is that the bloodletting event is consistent with a shooting and that the altered bloodstains inside the vehicle indicate another cleanup, which probably used water. One of his key sources of information was the glove box interior, where Jones found unaltered stains that had escaped cleanup. These small spatter stains, which likely went in through the one- to two-millimetre gap between the glove box door and the dash, "could be associated with a mist," a pattern typically caused by what Jones calls a high-energy source like a shooting. "What that would tell me is the source of blood had to be straight out in front of that crack and a little more to the passenger side," he says.

The absence of bloodstains on the driver's side of the under-carriage and their presence on the front passenger side further supports a blood source on the passenger side of the vehicle, and their absence at the rear indicates that the source of blood was located in the area of the front passenger door. These find-ings were supported when the truck was sprayed with luminol, a highly sensitive blood reagent used to detect trace amounts usually left behind after a cleanup. After spraying, the Dodge Ram glowed blue in the dark at the front passenger door, step rail, rear wheel, and rear quarter panel, as well as the driver's-side step rail, to a lesser extent, and the cargo bed.

As he finishes up his questioning of Jones, Tony Leitch offers up three hypotheticals for the witness to consider. Scene one: Leitch asks Jones if the blood situation is consistent or not with a shot from behind (meaning from the passenger in the back seat). Jones can't say, because there are too many variables and "so many dynamics involved."

Scene two: Leitch asks if a shot could have come from the

driver's seat. "Yes it could, but I lack some things that would help me out," says Jones.

Scene three: Leitch asks if there could have been two shooters. "I can't say either way with that," Jones replies. "The problem I have is I have a cleanup."

"Is there anything inconsistent with a person being shot in the passenger seat?"

No, says Jones.

DURING THEIR CROSS-EXAMINATIONS OF Jones and Banks, both defence teams ask about a shell casing for a .380 calibre bullet discovered in the back of the truck. The casing, a metal tube left behind after a gun is fired, was not present when the first photos of the truck interior were taken. It dislodged at some point after the truck was removed from the trailer but no one saw where exactly it came from—only that it ended up underneath the flipped-up back seats.

In his questioning of Banks, Nadir Sachak tries to establish that the casing must have fallen from the back seat, where Mark Smich had been, because it could not have rolled from the front without making a supposedly impossible journey over a large hump in the floor. Thomas Dungey argues that the truck had been transported all over Southern Ontario and then jerked around to get it out of the trailer in Tillsonburg. The casing could have easily moved to the back from the front seat area, he says. The only thing the two defence lawyers agree on is that the police should know where the cartridge came from—that they should have observed it right from the beginning. But Jones says he may have inadvertently dislodged the casing when he leaned into the truck looking for small bloodstains and put pressure on the rear passenger seat with his hand.

"You have no notes," Dungey says to him accusingly.

"That is correct," he replies.

"No notes whatsoever about the casing, correct?"

"No, my job was to look at bloodstains. I look at bloodstains. I don't deal with other items. If I come across something, I let other officers know," he says, adding that this is what he did.

Dungey raises his voice, trying to make Jones look careless, but it's no easy task given the detailed blood-spatter presentation he has just made and his obvious knowledge.

"The casing tells me nothing when it comes to blood pattern analysis," Jones tells Dungey. "When a casing is ejected from a gun, it can end up anywhere in the vehicle."

All of a sudden Dungey, who had not been pleased about the casing being found in the back seat area, where his client had sat, pivots. His hostility to Jones vanishes. "If a person, say the driver, points the gun, there's a good chance the casing would go flying to the back?" Dungey asks.

"It's possible," says Jones.

As Dungey starts grilling him about trajectories and what would happen if a bullet was shot from the back seat, Pillay objects. He says it's not Jones' area of expertise. Jones tells Dungey he would need a shooting reconstructionist to come up with possibilities about where the shooter was.

Dungey persists, suggesting that the driver must have shot Mr. Bosma; otherwise the front passenger window wouldn't be smashed. He asks if a shot from a Walther PPK .380, the gun the Crown believes Millard and Smich used, could go right through the neck of Mr. Bosma and then through the window. After Pillay objects again, the judge tells Smich's lawyer to move on, but Dungey's point has been made. After a few more questions about blood spatter, he wraps things up. "Thank you very much, sir," he says to Jones, who's been transformed from target to revered expert in the course of a brief cross-examination. "I appreciate it very much."

As a result of Dungey's detour, Tony Leitch makes a rare misstep during his re-examination of Jones. "Are you a shooting reconstructionist?" he asks.

"I've been trained in it, yes."

Dungey is thrilled by this unexpected answer while Leitch seems surprised by it. In hindsight it makes sense that like Jones would know about bullet trajectories. And, even though he wasn't qualified as an expert witness in the field, the jury now knows that he thinks the location of the shell casing has nothing to do with the position of the shooter. When it comes to the spent cartridge, neither defence team has any advantage.

THE FINAL TEST PERFORMED on the truck by the forensics officers was a cyanoacrylate fuming, also known as the superglue fingerprint search. Cyanoacrylate, a key ingredient in superglue, reacts with the traces of amino acids, fatty acids, and proteins found in latent fingerprints to form a sticky white substance along the ridges of the fingerprint. The resulting image can then be photographed directly or, if necessary, further enhanced. To do the fuming, the cyanoacrylate must be in its gaseous form. This is accomplished by setting alight a small amount of liquid superglue in a container—the police refer to their cyanoacrylate test kits as "hot shots"—in a sealed environment, which in this case was Tim Bosma's truck.

Laura McLellan tells the court that they found only one fingerprint as a result of the fuming. It was on the rear-view mirror and would later be matched to Dellen Millard's right thumb. Another print, which was eventually identified as being from Millard's left ring finger, was discovered when the entire exterior of the truck was dusted with grey fingerprint powder. It was on the driver's-side door to the right of the handle. These prints were two of twenty-three impressions found on twenty different items. No further information is provided as to who the rest belonged to.

CHAZ MAIN IS A bearded twenty-something wearing jeans, an untucked plaid shirt, and, his most noticeable item of apparel, snowmobile boots tied with fluorescent green laces. Given the fresh snow outside, he would almost certainly rather be spending this February day out "sledding." But thanks to his fondness for riding motorized sports vehicles on rural properties, Main discovered some key evidence in the Tim Bosma case.

Main tells the court that on Saturday, May 11, 2013, the day after Millard was arrested, he was coming over a hill on his dirt bike when he saw a flash from a camera and got waved over by a group of people he would later learn were police. They had a search warrant for Millard's farm, where Main was out riding.

"I had permission to be on the fields, so I asked what the big commotion was," says Main. He and his friend Adam, whose father owns a neighbouring property, had struck a deal with the farmer who used to lease Millard's land. In exchange for a case of beer and a bottle of Crown Royal whisky, they were free to off-road on the farm so long as they didn't do any damage to the crops. Main, who works in the concrete business in Toronto, estimated he had ridden the land more than a hundred times. He knew the farm well, but he had never met Dellen Millard, who had owned the land for two years at that point.

Sergeant Annette Huys, the officer taking photos, asked Main if he would be willing to make a statement, which he was. She directed him to Detective Constable Ben Adams, who was parked down by the barn, near the road. Main got into the back seat of Adams's unmarked police car.

"I told them about a bunch of weird activities," Main says, "a big redneck smoker in the woods and an excavator in the swamp." He had even taken pictures, because no one would believe him, he said, if he'd told them what was going on at the farm, including what he described as "people doing an engine swap in the middle of a swamp."

When Adams learned that the first time Main had seen the strange "smoker" was just the previous day, on Friday, he asked him to show police the machine, as well as the excavator and a skid-steer loader Main had reported seeing in the swamp. Main jumped back on his dirt bike and led the way, while Adams, Huys, and Sergeant Phil Peckford followed in a white four-wheel-drive police vehicle. About one hundred and fifty metres north, they reached a laneway in the middle of a treeline, an old farmers' road partially grown over at one end, where the "smoker" was parked. Main remained in the adjacent farmer's field while the police officers went to inspect the curious machine.

"We weren't quite sure what it was," Adams tells the court. "Having never seen anything like this before, we weren't sure it was safe." Peckford described it as looking like a large barbecue. Huys was taken aback by its size. The machine was some ten to eleven feet tall and mounted on a trailer with a hundred-pound propane tank affixed to it. Stencilled on the side of what it would later become clear was the burn chamber were the words THE ELIMINATOR in giant red letters. A metal tag on the device read, "Small and large animal cremators, a product of Southern Breeze Fabricators," a company based in Camilla, Georgia.

"I think I had in my mind it was going to be a smoker, from Chaz," says Huys. "We just sort of walked around it and figured out what it was. Just looking at the sheer size of it, I thought there was a real possibility someone could be inside of it." Huys looked inside a small squarish door near the base but found no signs of a body. Then she climbed up on the trailer and opened the hatch to the main chamber. There was no one inside, so the police asked Main to show them the swamp.

As the officers headed farther north, they came across two patches of cornfield that had been scorched. They also smelled an accelerant, possibly gasoline. In these two large burn circles, one of which looked as if it had recently been cleaned up, they spotted debris. (The scorch marks were not from the Eliminator, whose burn chamber interior is lined in cement, ensuring that its exterior doesn't overheat.) When they reached the swamp, the situation was as Main had described it: there was a partially buried excavator and a skid-steer, a small tractor-like vehicle more commonly referred to by the brand name Bobcat. Adams called Detective Matt Kavanagh to let him know what they had found.

Huys, who works in the Hamilton Police Service's forensics branch, returned to the Eliminator. She gently lifted out a thin piece of curved white bone from the main chamber only to find another smaller piece of bone underneath. She took photos of them from a series of different angles before carefully packing them up as evidence and returning to police headquarters. Because she needed help determining if the bones were animal or human, Huys sent the photos she had just taken to Tracy Rogers, a forensic anthropologist at the University of Toronto who consults for the Ontario Forensic Pathology Service. She was the primary forensic anthropologist during the investigation of serial killer Robert Pickton in 2002 and 2003, helping to identify the remains of women murdered on Pickton's British Columbia pig farm.

Rogers told Huys that her initial impression was that the bones were human but that she needed to see them in person. The next morning, a Sunday, Rogers arrived at the police station, where she confirmed her suspicions. On Monday, May 13, Rogers and a team of students visited the farm to examine the Eliminator and the burn circles.

WHEN ROGERS FIRST APPROACHED the incinerator, it was covered in a blue tarp. She was dressed in the white Tyvek coveralls often referred to by forensics officers and scientists as a bunny suit. Sergeant Huys pointed out the machine's bottom door, where Rogers saw some small bone fragments. Her first task was to carefully remove them so that if any more skeletal remains fell down from the main chamber she would know where they had come from.

Rogers then looked into the burn chamber to examine the seven concrete tubes traversing the width of its rectangular space. According to the plan devised with Huys, Rogers would start her recovery of remains on the right, moving tube by tube to the left until she reached the far left side, where most of the remains were caught up in a deep groove. As Rogers removed each bone fragment she would carefully hand it to Huys, who would assign it an exhibit number, photograph it, and place it in a little packet fashioned from aluminum foil and lined with paper towel so the fragile bone would not be scraped.

When all the liftable fragments on a given tube were removed, Rogers swept up any tiny remaining pieces and ash and bagged them as exhibits. She did this for tubes one to six by leaning into the incinerator, but for the final tube she became concerned that she was blocking the light and might inadvertently dislodge remains without seeing them. "With the fragile nature of bone, I needed to be closer," she tells the court. "I decided the only way was to get inside."

She and Huys shone a light up through the bottom opening and then Rogers worked inside the machine to clear out the far left side. When she needed a break, she walked over to the neighbouring field where her students were examining the burn sites, now protected by a giant forensic tent. Although the weather had turned cold and windy, they had to keep the tent sides open to let light in and not be overcome by the accelerant fumes.

Working with the police, the students set up two grids to allow them to search the area systematically. They placed pink and orange pin flags whenever they found anything in the debris and itemized their findings as exhibits, noting the location of each. Three seat-belt buckles were all recovered in one corner of a grid. Other findings included grommets, a metal spring, a large piece of burned wood, metal objects, a plastic bottle, partially melted glass, and a few coins.

Rogers continues to give the jury a detailed explanation of her work. She tells the court that the bigger of the two bones originally shown to her is the human left radius, the outer of the two bones in the forearm when the hand is extended palm upward. The curvature of the bone, displayed on the courtroom screens, is a result of fire damage, she says. She identifies the smaller bone as a human metacarpal in the palm of the hand associated with a second or third finger. Although she hasn't been able to determine if it is from the left or right hand, due to damage, she can tell it is human. Proportionally, human bones tend to be longer and thinner than animal bones, Rogers tells the jury. "Because we stand upright and don't use our upper limbs for weight bearing, the joints in humans look, as a result, very different from animals."

She explains that because bone is mostly mineral—some 70 percent—it doesn't turn to ash and disappear. The areas containing water and organic parts will burn out of bone, but the bone itself is left intact enough to recognize all the structures, even when burned at very high temperatures. (In human cremation, as it is now practised in crematoria, after the incineration phase is complete dry bone fragments are pulverized by a machine called a cremulator to process them into ashes.)

Rogers makes for a compelling witness as she stands up and points to the screen beside the witness box, explaining that the metacarpal is a good bone to use in determining whether remains are human. The rounded knuckle part with its bone curvature is very different in animals, who have to use their paws for power and speed and, as a result, have joints that lock together better than they do in humans, who do other things with these bones. The smooth head, lacking the ridge seen in animals, is one of the qualities that has allowed Rogers to determine that the bones found in the incinerator on Dellen Millard's farm are human.

As a forensic anthropologist, one of Rogers's specialties is the determination of sex and age-at-death from bones and bone fragments. In 1999, she published a key research paper on how to determine the sex of skeletal remains from looking at the distal end of the humerus, or upper arm bone, better known to non-anatomists as the funny bone. Rogers had set out to discover whether the fact that males and females have a different so-called carrying angle of the arm—approximately ten to fifteen degrees in males and twenty to twenty-five degrees in females—manifested itself in their elbow joints. She identified four morphological features of the distal humerus that could be used, with 92 percent accuracy, to determine sex when dealing with fragmentary remains.

In her examination of the Eliminator, she recovered a part of the distal humerus. Despite heat and fire damage, it was still in good enough condition to allow her to assess two of the four traits she would normally use to make a sex identification. She determined, with 75 percent accuracy, that these were the remains of a male. To assess age, Rogers inspected the head of the recovered radius bone where it meets the elbow. She found no evidence of arthritis or the telltale pitting found on older people's bones. "Can you see how nice and round and clear that surface is? That's exactly what a younger person would look like," she explains to the jury as the forearm bone is shown, once again, on courtroom screens. "I would estimate this person was under forty years of age."

In total, Rogers has identified pieces from 58 of the 206 bones in an adult human body. She has created a skeleton diagram, which shows how little remained of Tim Bosma in the incinerator. "There should have been a complete body there, and there wasn't, so it had obviously been cleaned out at some point," she says to the jury. "A lot of the remains are not there. You remember I told you bone does not disappear?"

When Rogers had gathered everything she could from the incinerator by hand, she asked the police to purchase a small handheld vacuum cleaner to help her gather up the ash and bone fragments that she couldn't get manually. "It was for the family's peace of mind that they have all the remains back," she says, as her voice catches and she appears, for a moment, about to cry. She collects herself, apologizes unnecessarily, and goes on to describe emptying the vacuum-cleaner canister into baggies.

"Everything that could be retrieved from the incinerator was retrieved."

For the Bosmas, Rogers's testimony comes at a time when trial life has begun to settle into a familiar pattern. Every morning the family and their friends—who have nicknamed themselves the Bosma Army—say a prayer in a room reserved for their use. They then file down the long sixth-floor hallway to Courtroom 600, carrying water bottles, tissue boxes, and purple pillows that say Tim Bosma Remembered. The pillows—purple was Sharlene and Tim's wedding colour—help those with bad backs sit for hours on the courtroom benches. Hank Bosma often removes his shoes.

On the day of Rogers's appearance, Hank's wife, Mary, is absent for the first time. She has chosen not to see the images of her only son's remains projected on the courtroom screens. Sharlene Bosma weeps. As Tracy Rogers leaves the courtroom, Hank follows her out. Through the glass panes in the doors, he can be seen giving her a hug in gratitude for her work.

IN A REPORT HE prepared on the Tim Bosma case on May 15, 2013, James Sloots, a forensic biologist at the Centre of Forensic Sciences, wrote that no DNA had been detected in the remains found in the Eliminator. Sloots, who had been asked by Matt Kavanagh if there was any possibility of using DNA to identify the remains, had not been optimistic. "High heat essentially destroys DNA," he tells the jury. "Before I even started, I said I don't expect to get anything from these. They didn't look like bones should look like to me. They looked highly compromised."

The incineration also left little for Dr. William Barlow, a forensic dentist and assistant professor of dentistry at the University of Toronto, to work with. All he could say after examining a tooth fragment found in the incinerator was that it was part of a root, had the appearance of a human tooth, and was most likely a lower mandibular first bicuspid. Based on the fact that it was not calcified, he believed the tooth to be from a younger person. Although Dr. Barlow obtained and examined a panoramic X-ray of Tim Bosma's teeth, there was no way for him to identify the tooth fragment as being from the victim's mouth. But he wondered if it might be possible to extract mitochondrial DNA from its pulp tissue.

Like Sloots, John Fernandes, the forensic pathologist in charge of the Bosma case, didn't hold out much hope for a DNA extraction, but he sent the tooth out for testing nonetheless. The procedure to recover mitochondrial DNA "is extraordinarily challenging to do at best of times," let alone with an incinerated tooth fragment, he tells the jury. He was disappointed but not surprised to learn the laboratory had failed at the task.

With no body, no DNA, no useful dental remains, and no finger-prints, all Dr. Fernandes had to rely on to identify the remains was the work of Dr. Barlow and Tracy Rogers. He received all the bones, fragments, and ash processed by Rogers at the scene. The total weight was just 503 grams, less than half of what normal cre-mated remains would weigh.

"When we have remains of this type, one of the first things we do is X-ray everything looking for metal, as metal will hold up," Fernandes tells the jury. They might find teeth fillings or an artificial hip, but in this case there was nothing, he says.

Prosecutor Tony Leitch asks if there is any evidence of injury to the recovered bones or of a shooting.

Fernandes says shootings do leave bone defects that are fairly typical, but the bony fragments were not sufficient to determine if a shooting had taken place.

The incineration of Tim Bosma means there are some ques-tions that will never be answered.

FIVE

SUSPECT NUMBER TWO

On May 13 at about 9:30 P.M. Matt Kavanagh phoned Sergeant Stuart Oxley, who was then with the Hamilton Police surveillance unit, to tell him he wanted officers to locate and watch Mark Smich. The target was described as five foot nine and 150 pounds with blue eyes. His date of birth was August 13, 1987. Two Oakville addresses were provided: his mother's house on Montrose Abbey Drive and an address on Speers Road associated with Smich's girlfriend, Marlena Meneses. The latter was the group of apartment buildings where Dellen Millard had stopped for about an hour before he was arrested.

The primary objective on May 14, the first day of surveillance, was to locate Smich and see where he was residing. There were five officers on the team, which began work at 7 A.M. On the first day, Smich and Meneses were identified coming and going from both Speers Road and Montrose Abbey and were photographed in a variety of locations. Smich wore a baggy grey hoodie and black pants and smoked while he talked to a young man outside a Popeyes chicken restaurant. His contact, who had a round face and glasses and rode a bike, was dressed in a camouflage jacket and matching baseball cap. When their meeting was over, Smich went into the Popeyes and got a bag of food, which he took back to the Speers Road apartment building.

On the next day, a Wednesday, officers were asked to get what is known as a DNA discard from Smich and to monitor his activity. He was first observed in the morning walking a dog. Not long after, Detective George Higgins, the same officer who had followed Millard on the day of his arrest, collected a cigarette butt tossed away by Smich. Unlike on the previous day, he was not seen in the company of Meneses and spent time skateboarding.

Although Smich had been under twenty-four-hour observation the first day, with a drugs and vice unit taking over from surveillance at 10 P.M. for the overnight shift, once it was noted that he was spending most of his time holed up inside the apartment at Speers Road, it was decided that he didn't need to be watched full-time. In general, twenty-four-hour surveillance is reserved for those considered an imminent threat to public safety. Smich's dog walking and skateboarding expeditions didn't fit the bill. There was no surveillance on Sunday, May 19, nor on Victoria Day Monday. It resumed the following Tuesday and then ended for good on Wednesday, May 22, when the call came down to arrest Smich and Meneses.

Shortly after 10 A.M., Oxley was advised that the targets were walking northbound on Dorval Drive in Oakville, with Smich straddling a BMX-type bike. They were taken down on the median in the middle of the road. Smich yelled repeatedly at Meneses, "Don't tell them anything, babe."

No one saw the arrest of Mark Smich coming. Or, to be more accurate, no one who was not a police officer or closely connected to the defendants saw it coming. Smich's arrest was a reminder to both the mainstream media and the social media detectives that no matter how public an investigation is, the police almost always have much more information than even the most dedicated reporters and true crime fanatics. In this case, despite the fact that Smich was on Millard's "no contact" list, he had never been considered a suspect in public in anywhere near the same way as Andrew Michalski and Shane Schlatman, Dellen's mechanic, had. This is mostly because—on social media, at least—Smich did not appear to be part of Millard's close group of friends.

There was only one photo of Millard and Smich together posted on Facebook, taken by Michalski in the spring of 2011. Dellen, back in his red mohawk phase, and Mark are admiring a vintage turquoise Chevy Nova from Millard's late grandfather's collection. The car is parked in the driveway of Smich's mother's house, the same house police spent the day of his arrest searching, along with the wooded area behind it.

At the time of his arrest, on May 22, 2013, Mark Smich's Facebook profile had been set to private, but information was available from the accounts of his friends and family. Just as Dellen Millard's unusual name had made reporters' and internet sleuths' work easier, so, too, did Smich's. Within minutes of the police announcement, there were already two stunning online finds. The first was a gruesome rap video in which Smich plays the role of a serial killer, and the second was a series of photos showing Smich celebrating his sister's posh wedding at a North Toronto golf club just two days before he was arrested and two weeks after Tim Bosma was murdered.

The gore video, entitled "Ghozted," begins with a close-up of a bloody cleaver followed by another close-up of a man's face with blood drops and streaks on it. The camera pulls back to show the man is slumped over and his neck is a bloody mess. Smich—dressed in a grey T-shirt, yellow pants, and rubber gloves, with a yellow surgical mask covering the lower part of his face—appears to be hacking away at the man's undershirt or arm. The Smich character then carries something away in a bucket. The set where all this takes place is covered in clear plastic sheeting, including the walls. At least two other bloodied figures appear in the video making arm motions, which look like a cross between a bad dance move and a ritualistic ceremony. Later they sit tied up in chairs. The video often appears speeded up, and there are frequent sharp cuts, giving it a jerky quality. The rap soundtrack suggests that the victims have been taken prisoner by a psycho killer. At one point, the Smich character displays what is supposed to be a human organ but is more likely animal innards.

The video was found on YouTube, where it had been posted by its director, JayDolo, who wrote in an accompanying note, "Shout Out To My Crazy Killer SAY10 aka Mark.S." He very quickly clarified that the scenes portrayed were not real after some commentators wondered online if they might be watching a snuff video. A Websleuths member called "SweetAdeline" said she would show it to her boyfriend's sister-in-law, who worked in special effects for movies, to find out if it could be real. Other sleuths—who were following the social media reaction to Smich's arrest in real time—cautioned that someone should "rip," or copy, the video. It was good advice, because the video did indeed disappear soon after.

In an effort at spin control, JayDolo posted an all-caps statement about his video: "I HAVE TAKEN IT DOWN BECAUSE THE MEDIA IS TRYING TO BLOW IT UP AS IF ITS CONNECTED TO THE

TIM BOSMA CASE. I HAVE BEEN POSTING THIS VIDEO EVERY WEEK FOR A YEAR AS I DO WITH ALL MY MUSIC—MARK IS INNOCENT UNTIL PROVEN GUILTY AND IN MY OPINION AS HIS FRIEND HE IS ONLY BEING PINPOINTED BECAUSE HE KNEW DELL. IF HE IS GUILTY THEN HE WILL SERVE HIS TIME AND ACCEPT HIS CONSEQUENCE."

This was something of an about-face for JayDolo, who, as soon as the news of Smich's arrest broke, had set up a Free Mark Smich page on Facebook, where he linked and promoted the "Ghozted" video. Either he was a very bad judge of how to generate sympathy for Smich or he was actively exploiting Smich's arrest to publicize his own music and video-production ventures. Whatever his motivation, within a matter of hours JayDolo realized that not all publicity is good publicity.

As a torrent of internet abuse rained down on JayDolo, he removed both his video and the Free Mark Smich page on Facebook. His girlfriend, Aly Stewart, a sweet-faced and successful professional model, who had been tweeting like a gangsta moll, made her Twitter account private. "Its all love SAY10. 25bid, we'll still be here for you," Aly had tweeted, using Smich's SAY10 nickname, given to him by Dellen Millard, and the slang for a life sentence of twenty-five years in Canada. "I can't believe this shit. I love u man."

Using the name James Crockett, a *Miami Vice* character, JayDolo also wrote to the many media outlets pestering him for comment. Among other things, he said the video was an "art" production made for the previous year's Halloween and it was all his idea. He confirmed that he himself was playing the victim and it was Smich in the role of the Dexter-style character, modelled on the TV serial killer. He described Mark as "the type of guy who stayed home to take care of his sick mother and dogs" and who "always helped out whoever he could." He said he hadn't seen him for the last three months.

MARK SMICH, AGE TWENTY-FIVE, had a police record for petty crime, including possession of cocaine and magic mushrooms, failure to appear in court, breach of bail terms, driving while impaired, and, most recently, painting graffiti on a highway over-pass. His father said he lived with his mother. His mother said he lived at his girlfriend's house. And his girlfriend hung up when a reporter phoned.

Compared to Dellen Millard little is known about Smich's family, but what is clear is that his problems were a long time in the making. He'd been in trouble since middle school, when his family moved from Mississauga to Oakville, partly in the hope of sorting him out, according to a former classmate. At twenty-five, he spent his days getting high and drinking in a series of base-ments and backyards. When things were going well for him, he dealt drugs and had cash to spend. But when he had no supply, he was reduced to selling single cigarettes to students at the local high school, who found him creepy. When one of his employed friends offered to get Smich a decent-paying job in construction, he turned the proposition down.

With his pasty complexion, sunken cheeks, and unflattering close-cropped haircuts, Smich looked like the druggie he was. His mother's neighbours avoided him and were none too fond of the friends and drug buyers who socialized noisily outside the house. To outward appearances at least, he was a classic black sheep. The rest of his middle-class family—divorced parents and two older sisters—were gainfully employed. His younger sister, Melissa, had, as the internet very quickly discovered, just married, although her honeymoon was about to be ruined and her wedding photos were going viral. By sheer coincidence, the photographer had unknowingly uploaded her photos to his website at almost the same time Smich was arrested. They showed Smich, an usher in the wedding party, chomping on a big cigar, mugging on the golf course, and posing awkwardly with his partner bridesmaid. He looked completely out of place among his sister's upwardly mobile friends. And the images of him celebrating sparked both outrage and incredulity.

"I know I am going to sound incredibly naïve for saying this, but HOW can someone smile and get into the festivities knowing what they've done? How can that knowledge not ruin their own lives? I'll never understand," wrote "Storme" on Websleuths.

On Twitter, there was a wave of sympathy for Melissa Smich. Not only were her wedding photos all over social media but there was also nasty speculation that she must have known her brother was involved and conspired to hide it. Reporters were tweeting at her for comment while she was away on her honeymoon. Onlookers were admonishing the journalists. "You need to have some respect. That right there is god awful journalism. So inappropriate," tweeted @RemaGouyez to a reporter at *The Hamilton Spectator*.

"I feel bad for her. Her privacy has gone out the window with her wedding pics online," wrote "flipflop" on Websleuths. There was, however, also a certain cruel irony to the unfolding events. Melissa Smich worked in marketing and had been called a "social media celebrity" by *Marketing Magazine*, which put her on their

"30 Under 30" list of young talent for 2012. Now, instead of celebrating social media, she and her family were at the centre of a
social media crisis of their own.

As it turned out, it was a Websleuths member who handled
at least part of the fallout for Melissa. "I sent an email to the
wedding photographer, they had not heard this news," wrote "flipflop." "They are removing the wedding pics."

A FORMER FRIEND OF Dellen Millard remembers being introduced to Mark Smich as far back as 2006 and having the impression that he was the weed connection. "Mark worshipped Dell,
but Dell hated him," says the friend. "Dell couldn't stand the
whole Eminem white gangsta thing that Mark had going on."
Yet despite the animosity and the fact that in those early years
Millard almost never invited Smich to gatherings or events with
his other friends, the relationship managed to endure. By 2011,
Smich was edging ever closer to the Millard inner circle. And
in 2012 he moved right to the heart of it when he and his girlfriend, Marlena Meneses, took up residence in the basement of
Wayne and Dellen Millard's house on Maple Gate Court.

Millard's habit of moving his friends into the house he shared
with his father had begun several years earlier. In 2006, when
he was twenty, he developed friendships with a group of high
school boys he met through Matthew Hagerman, grandson of
his father's housekeeper, Dina. Dina, who had originally been
hired by Dellen's grandmother and cared for her when she was
dying of cancer, had gone on to work for Wayne and look after

Dellen from the time he was a baby. She and her daughter were concerned that Dellen had no friends and prompted Matthew to spend time with him.

Given that the Millard home on Maple Gate was a teenage boy's dream, with multiple large-screen TVs, Xboxes, a swimming pool, and more, it wasn't a particularly hard sell. Matt and his friends were soon all hanging out there and, even better, at the old Millardair hangars at Pearson Airport, where Dellen kept assorted planes, vehicles, and his prized Bell helicopter, the same as the one in the opening credits of the television show *M*A*S*H*. On March 6, 2009, Millard arranged and paid for a hangar concert to celebrate the birthdays of Andrew Michalski and Mike Ciufo, another member of the gang. The concert featured the local bands Blunt Fiction and Texas, Armed to the Teeth, and, according to one friend, the bill for the event was tens of thousands of dollars. It was never clear, however, where the money to pay for it, or for anything else Dellen did, came from. "The money was just there," the friend said. In a jailhouse interview he gave to the *Toronto Star* months after he was arrested, Millard explained that he was playing to the image people had of him. "I threw some parties," he said. "I tried to make that a reality for my friends." Big events or small, he was always picking up the tab.

Although the age difference between Millard and his new friends was just four to five years, it was significant in that, when the friendships began, Millard was legally an adult with no real job or responsibilities while the friends were still in high school. What's more, when the friends turned eighteen, Millard invited them to move in with him and live in the basement, which was not a separate apartment but part of the house he shared with his father. After Millard's arrest, everyone involved in this strange arrangement was understandably reluctant to talk about it. But what is known is that Millard's buddies came from middle-class, mostly two-parent families who were ready and willing to support their sons. They had little to no contact with Wayne Millard, who was something of a recluse.

As for why Wayne allowed his home to be turned into what Millard's former friend described as a "frat house" or "drug-filled shithole," that will likely remain a mystery. Wayne is not alive to explain, and when he was, he kept to himself. Acquaintances and colleagues invariably described him as private. Dellen's father was also an alcoholic with no close friends of his own, which may explain why he was reluctant to stop his son from socializing. "Wayne just shuffled off to the bedroom, locked the door, and never said 'Get out of my house,'" said Dellen's old friend. When he had finally had enough of the freeloaders occupying his home, Wayne resorted to passive-aggressive tactics like making sure the fridge wasn't too well stocked. Eventually, word got out to the unwanted guests' parents that Wayne had had enough and wasn't willing to tolerate the strange situation any longer.

As a result, Dellen came up with a new plan. He would move his friends into his rental property in the west end of Toronto. He offered them cheap rent, and soon the gang was installed in the six-unit Tudoresque building on Riverside Drive, where they proceeded to annoy the neighbours. That situation continued until 2010, when Dellen became seriously involved with a new girlfriend and went to live with her in Oakville. It was only after they broke up in 2011 that he returned once again to his father's house and resumed his practice of moving his friends, including Mark Smich, into the basement.

During the summer of 2012, when Michalski was spending several months working in Winnipeg, he announced on Facebook his plans to return to Toronto for a long weekend. "I MISS YOU FELLAS!" he wrote. "BED DECISIONS ARE BACK!" The message tagged various basement dwellers, past and present, including Steven Kenny, Mike Ciufo, Robert Bochenek, and "Mark S.," who, like his friend Dellen, didn't use his real name on Facebook. They would all be fighting it out for beds in the Millard party pad.

NO ONE IN MILLARD'S circle of Toronto friends has ever spoken on the record about him or his lifestyle. Once it became known that he was involved in the Bosma murder, his buddies unfriended him on Facebook, deleted ill-advised Twitter accounts, and took down photos featuring Dellen Millard. The only named friend to talk to the press was Benoît Ménardo, whom Millard had met through his cousins who lived in France. Millard travelled to Europe almost every summer and stayed with his mother's younger brother, Robert Burns, his wife, Rhonda, and their six children. His cousins introduced him to their friends, who, like his buddies in Toronto, were all several years younger. Ménardo was a Facebook friend of Millard who, because he lived in France, hadn't heard about the murder. Facebook photos showed Ménardo and the Burns cousins on a trip to Canada, where Millard took his guests skydiving, helicoptering, and partying. Videos also show them in

Croatia, renting a boat to tour caves and grottoes and swimming in an area where it is explicitly prohibited. Millard is the leader, telling the crew what to do. Ménardo said it was not unusual for Millard to pay for everyone's dinner and buy them lavish gifts like Jet Skis. He had no idea what Millard did for a living.

A post-arrest storyline developed for former friends: *Yes, I used to know him*, or, *Yes, my son lived at his house, but that was a long time ago and the boys haven't seen him in ages.* People said they stopped hanging around with him once things started to get strange. They didn't know anything about what happened afterwards. They had gotten out long before the bad stuff started. And, no, they never liked Mark Smich.

This is a version of events designed to shine the most flattering light possible on those recounting it. The less flattering version is that drugs were in plentiful supply in the Millard basement from the moment he started moving his friends in. The neighbours had complained for years about activities at the Maple Gate house. And the police were called to Riverside Drive when Millard and some of his friends were found in the basement tampering with a tenant's car's engine in the middle of the night. There had always been something off about the whole setup, but it wasn't in the interest of those who were benefiting from it to see it.

AFTER SMICH'S ARREST, THE Hamilton Police kept their comments very brief. In a news conference live-streamed to tens of thousands of viewers, Superintendent Dan Kinsella told reporters that investigators were still looking for at least one more suspect but that there was no further danger to the public. Suspect number three, he said, was believed to have driven the vehicle—now identified as Dellen Millard's dark-blue GMC Yukon—that followed Tim Bosma's black Dodge Ram as it left his house for the test drive.

The next day, Thursday, May 23, Mark Smich was charged at the John Sopinka Courthouse with first-degree murder. He appeared to have a cut on his face and wore a baggy brown T-shirt and jeans. According to the reporters present, his hands were jammed in his pockets and he had to be asked twice to state his name. Smich's lawyer, Thomas Dungey, declined to talk to the press other than to say his client was pleading not guilty and that a vigorous defence was planned. Dungey's style was a study in contrasts to that of Deepak Paradkar, Millard's lawyer at the time.

While Paradkar had stood on the courthouse steps happily taking questions from the press, Dungey exited as discreetly as possible by the back door. He waved away the reporters and camera crews chasing after him. And he didn't return journalists' emails or phone calls, although sometimes his co-counsel, Jennifer Trehearne, would reply politely that they had no comment to make.

GIVEN THE OVERWHELMING AMOUNT of evidence in the early days of the Tim Bosma murder investigation, it was not hard to predict that the only viable defence strategy would be for the two accused to blame each other. In the weeks after Millard's arrest, his legal team spread the word to favoured journalists that Millard was known for picking up strays, to use their phrase.

According to his supporters he was just a generous rich guy always willing to help out less fortunate friends. It was the petty criminal Mark Smich who had dragged him into this tragedy. Not surprisingly, Smich's circle rejected this narrative, claiming their guy was the lovable stoner drug dealer corrupted by his psychopathic rich friend. Millard, the master manipulator who Mark nicknamed Dellen the Felon, had taken him on a test drive he could never have imagined.

In lawyer circles, this blame-the-co-accused strategy is known as a cutthroat defence, so called because, except on the very rare occasions when it works, the defendants end up slicing each other's throats while the prosecution gets to watch. Almost the only way a cutthroat strategy can succeed is if one of the defendants manages to convince the jury of his innocence, which invariably means taking the stand. That's why, from the first day of this trial right up until the prosecution rests its case, the question of whether Millard and Smich will testify hangs over the courtroom. Among many of the detectives, lawyers, and journalists in attendance, the feeling is that Millard the narcissist won't be able to resist, and that Smich will be forced to follow suit. The defence doesn't have to make its intentions known until the Crown has finished presenting its evidence.

Putting the defendant in the witness box is a risky proposition at the best of times, given that it subjects the accused to cross-examination and possible self-incrimination. In a cutthroat defence scenario, the stakes are even higher because the accused will not be cross-examined by just the prosecutor but by his co-accused's lawyer as well. On the other hand, given the strength of the case against Millard and Smich, an argument can be made that neither of them has anything to lose by taking the stand.

Millard is also known to be persuasive. During the lead-up to the trial, he met with at least two experienced and respected journalists, both of whom emerged from their interviews wondering if maybe he wasn't just a guy who happened to find himself in the wrong place at the wrong time. Even the police have described Millard as a "good talker." And despite his tendency to do weird things, such as wave at a homicide detective on the witness stand, on other occasions, he makes a show of respecting courthouse etiquette. He bows deeply as the jury enters and leaves the room, going well beyond the perfunctory bob performed by officers of the court.

On the downside, Millard has transformed into a jailbird after almost three years in custody. He is a far cry from the handsome, wealthy playboy described by the media after his arrest. He has lost so much weight in jail that his cheeks are sunken and there are dark circles under his eyes. His trial wardrobe is a rotation of mostly unironed shirts—plaid, striped, and plain—paired with jeans. There is no sign of the Armani or Alexander McQueen suits he once said, or perhaps joked, he might wear to court. His one big concession to the jury was cutting off the rat's tail braid he wore right up to trial. It was one of a variety of jailhouse styles—ranging from long beard to Fu Manchu moustache—that he had sported since his arrest.

Smich, in contrast, has had a makeover of a completely different kind. The once scrawny druggie has buffed up and grown out his unflattering buzz cut. His dark hair is now short, neatly parted, and gelled down. His court wardrobe consists mainly of crisp collared shirts under a selection of V-neck sweaters in charcoal grey, cobalt blue, and baby blue. In an article on the oft-overlooked co-accused of Dellen Millard, the *National Post* described Smich's look as "choirboy chic." He almost always sits ramrod straight with his eyes fixed in front of him, doing his best to ignore the long withering looks Millard frequently gives him.

Like the Bosmas, Millard and Smich were allowed to request reserved seats for their family and friends, but only Millard took up the offer and was assigned a bench to be shared with Ravin Pillay's law students. Throughout the trial, he smiles and nods at a middle-aged blond woman who frequently occupies one of his seats and often reads from a religious book during courtroom breaks. She told reporters early on that she did not wish to reveal her identity, but she was not, as many onlookers speculated, Millard's mother. The whereabouts of Madeleine Burns remains a mystery throughout the trial.

In March, however, Smich's mother and his older sister, Andrea, appear in the gallery. Smich did not request reserved seats for them, and so they line up outside the courtroom with the members of the public, who pack the largest room in the courthouse almost every day and sometimes get sent to a special overflow room with a video feed. Smich often turns and smiles at his mother and sister as they enter and leave. After photographers try to take their pictures outside the courthouse, his sister is no longer seen, but Mary Smich—a well-groomed, white-haired woman—continues to attend regularly. No one approaches her.

SIX

CAUGHT ON CAMERA

At about the same time Tim Bosma left his house with the two strangers, his neighbour Rick Bullmann was out walking his dog. Bullmann knows the time was between 9:15 and 9:30 P.M., because he is a man of routine who puts his kids to bed at 8:30 and then takes his dog out at 9:00. They usually walk along the fields atop Book Road, which intersects with Trinity Road, where the Bosmas lived some four hundred metres to the south. Bullmann had never actually met his neighbours, but he knew of them.

On the night in question, he noticed a dark-coloured pickup truck pull out of the entrance to a nearby field owned by his father. The field is rented to a farmer to store bales of hay, but in the past there had been problems with people dumping garbage there, including a truckload of drywall. It's also a spot where a car will sometimes pull over so that the driver can make a quick phone call.

Bullmann didn't find anything unexpected about the situation that night until a second vehicle drove out right after the truck—almost "simultaneously," as he describes it. He remembers the second vehicle as being bigger than a car but not as big as a truck, possibly an SUV. He watched it follow the truck, heading west on Book Road in the direction of Brantford for about five hundred yards until he lost sight of it. The next day, when members of the Bosma search party delivered flyers to his house, Bullmann thought, "Someone needs to know about this." He called the police, who arrived with sniffer dogs and combed the field but didn't find anything.

At the same time they were searching the Bullmann field, police were also checking in with local businesses that might have video surveillance. Just north of the Bullmann and Bosma residences on Trinity Road, video surveillance signs were posted at the Ancaster Fairgrounds, but when Detective Constable Barry Stoltz talked to the manager, he learned that there was, in fact, no video footage to be had. He tried Super Sucker, a hydro-excavation company located just across the road from the fairgrounds. Earlier that day, James Stieva, the marketing director, had talked to a group of people in the parking lot who informed him that they were looking for a missing person and possibly his phone. Stieva invited them to look around and mentioned that the company had video surveillance.

Although he wasn't normally in charge of the security system, in the absence of the employee who was, Stieva obtained the password and viewed the feeds, which came from four motion-sensitive cameras. By the time Constable Stoltz showed up, Stieva was able to sit him down at a computer to see video from the night before. Stoltz spotted what he believed to be a black pickup truck heading northbound closely followed by a second vehicle. The time-stamp on the computer said 18:20, but Stieva told Stoltz the system was out by three hours. The truck and the vehicle following it would have passed by at 21:20—that is, 9:20 P.M.

Police also obtained video from Bobcat of Brantford, which was on Oak Park Road, some two hundred metres south of where Tim Bosma's cell phone had been found on the property of Kemira Water Solutions, a chemical company on the outskirts of Brantford. A contractor spotted the phone, which was covered in dirt and bird droppings, while mowing the lawn. He turned it in to Liz Rozwell, a manager, who cleaned it up and then, since she wasn't familiar with Samsung phones, asked a colleague to help her plug it in and turn it on. "There was a whole bunch of dinging," Rozwell tells the court, describing the sound of texts and emails downloading.

Rozwell and her colleague didn't read the texts but went instead into the contacts and called the number labelled as "home." It was the Thursday after Bosma disappeared, and one of his sisters answered the phone. She told Rozwell not to touch anything and to call 911. Shortly after, detectives Greg Rodzoniak and Randy Kovacsik arrived. They interviewed the contractor and Rozwell, marked where the phone had been found, did a preliminary check, on foot, of Oak Park Road, and viewed Kemira's security video. It showed neither passing traffic nor the phone getting tossed. Later that day, a special search team scoured the area without much more luck. Nor did the phone yield any physical evidence due to its recent cleaning.

Only the Bobcat video offered clues as to what might have happened that night in Brantford. The video was introduced in court and explained by Michael Plaxton, a forensic video analyst with the Hamilton Police. Before moving into this new and growing field, Plaxton spent twenty-five years as a photographer with the Canadian military, which is somewhat surprising, given his grey hippie ponytail and funky retro wardrobe. He is an articulate, unflappable, and tech-savvy expert witness, called upon to interpret some very grainy videos taken in the dark.

When Plaxton first viewed the Bobcat of Brantford video, he discounted the vehicles he now believes were the Bosma truck and Millard's Yukon. He was looking for northbound traffic on Oak Park Road, passing in front of Kemira, where the cell phone had been found, and those two vehicles were travelling south. What's more, neither one had overhead cab or running lights like the Dodge Ram. But after the two vehicles pulled over at the Bobcat dealership, stopping there for some minutes, they turned around and headed north. This time, the lead vehicle had its overhead lights switched on and there was reflection from the wheels or rims, indicating they might be chrome. The headlights on the second vehicle were at the same level as the truck's tail lights, suggesting to Plaxton that it wasn't a car. "Just the proximity led me to believe it might have some significance," he tells the court.

Having decided these could indeed be the vehicles he wanted, Plaxton conducted a test. He drove from Super Sucker, where its video showed the black pickup passing at 9:20, to Bobcat, where it arrived at 9:39. Plaxton made the trip in twenty minutes, confirming that the time frame made sense.

Bobcat of Brantford had a camera that recorded audio as well as video. But it was located near an HVAC unit on the side of the building, which meant there was lots of noise and distortion on the feed. Plaxton tried to clean it up, attenuating some of the higher and lower frequencies so that he could isolate two loud booming sounds that can be heard just as the pickup and second vehicle enter the camera's range. He didn't succeed and was unable to identify the booms or their source.

Once the vehicles were pulled over and stopped for ten minutes, Plaxton saw what he described as "a lot of small lights, possibly a cigarette." As the video—which looks like a fluorescent Impressionist painting—is played and replayed in court, Plaxton points out to the jury some lights that caught his attention. "It all indicated to me some sort of activity occurring," although it was hard to figure out what, he says. No human forms are visible in the video.

At 10:26 P.M., twenty-three minutes after the vehicles departed Bobcat of Brantford, a dark truck with running lights is picked up by video cameras at Eastern Wood Preservers, just over two kilometres east of Millard's farm. It is followed by a dark SUV. They cannot be definitively identified from the video as the Bosma truck and the Millard Yukon.

At 12:19 A.M., on what was now Tuesday, May 7, the video cameras at GA Masonry show a pickup truck with running lights towing a trailer carrying a tall Eliminator-like structure as it arrives at the Millardair hangar at Waterloo Airport, followed immediately by a dark SUV. GA Masonry is located kitty corner to the hangar, approximately one hundred metres to the northeast. Its five cameras afford views of Jetliner Court, which is the street address of Millardair, and the north and east sides of the hangar.

Both vehicles park at the north end of the hangar and extinguish their lights. At 12:35, the pickup truck moves to the south end of the hangar, leaving the trailer where it is. At 12:41, the SUV also moves to the south end of the hangar. There is movement between the two vehicles, suggesting that a person is going from the pickup into the SUV. At 12:42, the SUV leaves the hangar. It returns and parks at the north end at 1:13 A.M.

At 1:33, two men and a dog can be seen in the hangar. One is tall and walks with his feet turned slightly outward like a duck. On his hip is a satchel bag. The other man is shorter and dressed in oversized clothing. The dog is Pedo, whom Millard brought home from Mexico. There is nothing in the way they behave that suggests anything out of the ordinary has just occurred.

The interior video, which has a duration of less than fifteen seconds, was taken from a camera in the northwest corner of the hangar. Originally, it had been set to pan and zoom and tilt throughout the entire building. But on April 29, the settings had been changed, as were those for the lone functioning exterior camera, which was turned toward the hangar wall. The digital video recorder with the feeds from the hangar cameras was seized from the bedroom closet of Millard's girlfriend, Christina Noudga, when she was arrested almost a year after Tim Bosma was murdered. Just as she kept the letters Millard had written her from prison, in breach of his no contact order, she also preserved the DVR.

According to the GA Masonry video, the incinerator was set alight at 1:44 A.M., when a large flame appeared above it. Plaxton explains that he identified the light as a flame because of the way it illuminated. It didn't just turn on. "It starts as a small light, then blooms into something," he tells the jury.

A few minutes later, at 1:59, the pickup truck is turned around, and at 2:30 it is driven into the hangar. At 3:23, the main lights in the hangar are turned on. At 3:54, a figure appears in the hangar doorway and moves toward the incinerator. There is a brief flare of light from the bottom of the incinerator, followed by another flare from the top. The figure returns to the hangar. At 5:30 A.M., the pickup truck is moved out of the hangar and parked at its south end. A person can be seen walking away from the truck to the north end of the hangar. The door is closed. At 5:38, two figures can be seen walking toward the south end of the hangar. At 5:55, the pickup truck is backed up to the loading door on the west side of the hangar. At 6:05, it's moved to the north end of the hangar. At 6:08, the SUV pulls the incinerator into the hangar. At 7:02, the SUV leaves the hangar. Because it is now light out, it can be definitively identified as a dark-blue Yukon with no hubcaps—or the Chevy Tahoe version of the vehicle, which is the same SUV but with a different name and manufacturer.

AS WELL AS ANALYZING video to guide the jury through the movements of Tim Bosma's truck and Dellen Millard's Yukon on the night of May 6 and morning of May 7, Michael Plaxton explains some serious CSI-style work he carried out as part of the Bosma investigation. He used a technique called reverse projection photogrammetry to establish that it was indeed Millard's Yukon that drove first past Super Sucker and then, by implication, past all the other video cameras.

Reverse projection photogrammetry is the science of determining the size of objects within photos or video. Among other things, it can be used to include or exclude a suspect based on his or her height, but in this case it was used to measure Millard's Yukon by taking it back to the scene at Super Sucker and rephotographing it through the company's surveillance system. The new video obtained is then overlapped with the original video to analyze similarities and differences.

The recreation took place on June 12, 2013, five weeks and two days after the disappearance of Tim Bosma. To duplicate lighting positions and establish as closely as possible the conditions when the original video was filmed, Plaxton obtained sunset times from the National Research Council and timed his video recording accordingly. There were some conditions he couldn't control, however. June 12 was a little more overcast and therefore darker than he would have preferred, and since May 6, the bushes and weeds outside Super Sucker had grown appreciably.

Orange fluorescent marks were applied to the Yukon to aid with the matching process as a police officer drove the vehicle back and forth for Plaxton, who was inside Super Sucker talking to him on a cell phone. "I'm speaking to him and telling him to move the car an inch forward, an inch back," Plaxton tells the jury. "Speed was a problem. I had him drive through the field of view at seventy, eighty, ninety" kilometres an hour. Because Plaxton needed the video frames to match, he had hooked up his system to Super Sucker's so that he could see the recording from May 6 and the live feed together. The end product is his gradual overlap of the two videos.

"Are you looking for differences or similarities or some combination of both?" Tony Leitch asks Plaxton.

"Police have presented me with their hypothesis. We believe this is the blue Yukon belonging to Mr. Millard. Can we disprove it? I did an overlay for the period of time the SUV is seen proceeding south and then proceeding north."

The overlay showing the initial image of the vehicle heading south on May 6 is shown to the jury as it is replaced in 10 percent increments with the June 12 image.

"What is your opinion as to whether there are any discernible differences?" asks Leitch.

"I saw no difference. In my opinion, there are no differences between the vehicles."

As the image is overlaid, the two vehicles match precisely.

When the same experiment is carried out for the vehicle heading northbound, some thirty-five minutes later, as it did on May 6, there are some inconsistencies. The brake lights are not activated on June 12 and a significant amount of foliage has grown up, obscuring a bright patch on the road that was seen in the original video. While there are slight inconsistencies and differences, Plaxton tells Leitch they are explainable.

"What's your opinion of similarity or differences between the two vehicles heading north in the original and recreated videos?" the prosecutor asks.

"I formed the opinion these two vehicles are similar in shape and size. I can't say they are the same vehicle, but I am of the opinion they are the same or a similar make and model," Plaxton says. "We know the vehicle used on the twelfth of June is a GMC Yukon. More likely than not, the unknown vehicle seen on the sixth of May is either a Yukon or a Chevy Tahoe." A further identifying feature was that the vehicle in the original Super Sucker video had no hubcaps, just like Millard's Yukon.

Yet another characteristic that can be used to identify vehicles is their headlights, which are often unique, due to changes to the suspension, damage to the front end, and misalignment. "Over time and rough usage, we do tend to see some differences," says Plaxton. "The best point of view is from up above if possible."

Reverse projection photogrammetry could not be done on the Bosma truck because it was both undriveable and, as a crime scene, unavailable. However, based on its chrome rims, chrome running boards, and overhead running lights, Plaxton says it appears consistent with the vehicle in the Super Sucker video, although he doesn't have enough detail to tell if it's the same truck.

"Is there anything inconsistent with the Bosma vehicle?" Leitch asks.

"No," says Plaxton.

IT IS A STANDARD tactic of defence lawyers to try to undermine the credibility of police and expert witnesses. And this approach is seen regularly during *Regina v. Millard and Smich*, where a total of ninety witnesses testify, including more than thirty police officers and more than a dozen expert witnesses like Michael Plaxton, many of whom are affiliated with law enforcement. Ravin Pillay provides multiple examples when he questions witnesses about the Super Sucker video.

Millard's lawyer begins by lambasting Constable Barry Stoltz for failing to take a picture of his watch or cell phone clock next to the Super Sucker video system clock, which was out by three hours. Although Stoltz had talked to Super Sucker's James Stieva about the time discrepancy, checked his own cell phone, and written up the three-hour time lag in his notes, he had not followed the best practices used by those who regularly deal in forensic video. Because so many security videos are off by minutes and often hours, time verification matters a great deal. Analysts like Plaxton try to get pictures to illustrate the time variation or call the National Research Council's atomic clock to get the precise time. Stoltz hadn't done either.

"This was the biggest case, highest profile case, you've been involved in," Pillay says to the police officer.

"Yes."

"Is it fair to say that your notes of May 7 are detailed?"

"Yes."

"They chronicle your activities?"

"I try to make as complete notes as possible, but sometimes I make omissions. I am human. Sometimes I make mistakes."

"There's nothing about checking the [video] time-stamp against your cell phone."

"Those words? No."

"Anything about you making sure?"

"I made note that the video is three hours behind."

Pillay says that the first time Stoltz ever mentioned having checked his cell phone was earlier in the week, when he met with prosecutors for witness preparation. He asks why Stoltz didn't take a photo of his watch with the video time-stamp.

"I didn't have a watch at that time," says Stoltz.

"Precision is critical, right?"

Stoltz says Stieva told him the video was three hours out and that he confirmed it. Pillay is hinting that he didn't bother to confirm it, just took Stieva's word, and that there was no cell phone check or it would be in Stoltz's notes.

"You did not record *how* you did it," Pillay says. "You're certain it was out exactly three hours?"

"Within the minute."

"And you have that recollection three years later?"

"Yes."

"I'm going to suggest that you have no notes because you didn't do it. Agree or disagree?"

"I disagree."

When Pillay tells him he has nothing to back up his version of events, Stoltz, who has been a wishy-washy witness until this point, finally responds with authority. "You have my testimony, sir, and my note it was three hours behind."

Pillay then questions James Stieva, the Super Sucker manager, about how he knew the security video system was three hours off. Stieva is a good-natured guy who doesn't appear at all intimidated by testifying in court.

"Is it fair to say your memory is not perfect?" Pillay asks.

"Fair."

"You're not the security person?"

"No."

"You just happened to be there, so you took it upon yourself to attend to this?"

"Yes."

"You knew, prior to viewing it, the time-stamp was out."

"I knew upon my first viewing . . . I noticed the time was different."

He doesn't know for how long it had been out, or how it became off—if it was incrementally over time or all at once. "I know that it was quite close to three hours," he says. "I could not guarantee that to the minute it was three hours."

"You didn't call the National Research Council and check against the atomic clock?"

"I did not," he replies, clearly puzzled as to how anyone could expect such a thing.

After a few more questions about how he can be sure about the three-hour time difference, Stieva tells Pillay, "I'm a stickler for time. I'm always on time. I never show up late." As a gift, he says, his wife gave him an eight-hundred-dollar Swiss Military watch.

When it's his turn for cross-examination, Mark Smich's lawyer, Thomas Dungey, asks Stieva, "What time does your watch say?"

"Four minutes after eleven."

"From what I can see," says Dungey, as he eyes the clock on the courtroom wall along with everybody else, "it's 11:06, so you're a couple of minutes off."

"Or that clock is," says Stieva, to laughter in the courtroom.

A reporter who is live-tweeting the trial checks her cell phone's time and tells her Twitter followers it's 11:05.

After Constable Stoltz had left Super Sucker, and before Stieva knew Michael Plaxton would be stopping by to check things out further, Stieva did something in keeping with his fondness for exact times and corrected the clock on the video security system. That meant Plaxton had to rely on Stieva's and Stoltz's information.

After grilling Stoltz and Stieva, Pillay goes after Plaxton. "You didn't do anything to try and verify the time-stamp?" Pillay asks.

"There was nothing I could have done to verify that." (Plaxton testified earlier that he had checked sunset times, but while that helped with determining hours, it didn't aid in calculating minutes.)

Having beaten the three-hour time difference to death, Pillay moves on to his main line of cross-examination, which is a lot more interesting. It is about another truck that can be seen in the feeds from Super Sucker but was never shown to the court during Plaxton's direct examination. The truck travels north at 9:05 P.M. and then south at 9:15. The vehicle Pillay is referring to has all three characteristics of the Bosma truck: running lights, chrome rims, and chrome running boards. Plaxton agrees with Pillay that he can't say it's not the same vehicle.

"That segment was not directed to you by anyone prior to today, the investigators didn't tell you about that segment," Pillay suggests as he shows the video of the truck headed north at 9:05 P.M.

Plaxton contradicts him. "Yes, I would have seen that segment."

"You didn't include it in your report. You missed that."

While it is true that Plaxton didn't include it in his report, he has just said that he had indeed seen the truck.

Pillay plays another piece of Super Sucker video. It shows a truck like the Bosma one, only this time it's headed south on Trinity Road. "That's another segment you were not directed to view, not in your report, not in your examination in chief" by the Crown, says Pillay. "The first time you're providing evidence about that is now."

Plaxton agrees, but neither he nor Tony Leitch, who conducted the direct examination, seems surprised or fazed by this video of what could be the Bosma truck heading north at 9:05 and south at 9:15.

In contrast, the audience, including the journalists covering the trial, is completely confused. While the prosecution must disclose to the defence all the evidence against the accused, it is not obliged to present every single piece of evidence in court. It gets to pick and choose the facts and witnesses that best make its case. Leitch didn't use the videos Pillay showed, but Millard's lawyer was free to ask Plaxton about them.

As observers tried to make sense of the 9:05 and 9:15 truck sightings, two theories emerged: one, that it was a different truck ("Everybody pimps out their truck these days," says a police officer who worked on the case); and two, the theory that it was indeed the Bosma truck. After leaving the house, it could have headed north on Trinity Road, past Super Sucker at 9:05 for what appeared to be a regular test drive. The truck would not have pulled directly into the Book Road field where Millard and Smich had stashed the Yukon before heading to the Bosmas' on foot. Instead, Millard would have driven their victim somewhere north on Trinity Road, and either he or Smich or both of them could have shot Tim Bosma in the truck. Then they would have driven back past Super Sucker at 9:15 and returned to the field to pick up the Yukon at just about the time Rick Bullmann was walking his dog. Smich would have gotten out of the pickup and into the Yukon. According to the witness, the vehicles he saw headed east down Book Road and not north up Trinity. If Bullmann's memory is correct, they would have had to turn around on Book Road at some point and come back. If his memory is incorrect, they may have just headed straight up Trinity Road. This would explain why no glass from the shattered passenger window or anything else was found in the field. If what happened there was simply a pickup of the Yukon, as opposed to a murder, it would be far easier to leave no evidence.

There is, however, a timing problem with this theory. Extremely precise cell phone records put Millard and Smich in the Bosmas' driveway at 9:05, which means the Super Sucker video would have had to be out by more than three hours. That would explain why Pillay was so persistent in his questioning of Stieva and Stoltz.

In the end, though, the Crown does not have to prove where or at what time Tim Bosma was killed. Only his killers know that. The task of the prosecutors is to prove that Millard and Smich are guilty of first-degree murder. While TV and movie dramas can tie up all the loose ends, in real-life investigations and trials, there are always questions that linger.

SEVEN

THREE GENERATIONS

When Dellen Millard's grandfather Carl died at age ninety-two in 2006, he left the family business to his only child, Wayne. Even though Millardair had requested cancellation of its key operational licences in the nineties and was no longer in the flying business, Carl still enjoyed coming into his shag-carpeted office, checking out the planes, and reading flight magazines. Visitors said that entering the wooden, wartime-era Millardair hangars was like stepping into a time machine. Despite having patented a number of inventions in his time (some of them with Wayne, and ranging from an aircraft takeoff velocity indicator system to removable wing covers for large aircraft), Carl refused to get a company computer. His office administrator, Hilda, who was a former Millardair stewardess, worked on a manual type-writer, insisting that, unlike newfangled twenty-first-century technology, it still worked when the power went out. Millardair's only concession to the post–telephone communications era was a fax machine.

Not surprisingly, the airport authority no longer had much use for Millardair. Officials wanted the old hangars torn down. They also informed Wayne that they did not intend to renew the twenty-five-year lease, expiring in 2011, on the newer hangar Carl had built on airport land in 1986. Given that Wayne was almost seventy and Dellen had never expressed any interest in the family aviation business, it would have made sense to wind the company down, but Wayne was a romantic with a love of flying, planes, and Millardair. He didn't want to let things go. In the years between his father's death and the lease expiry, he tried hard to convince several other airport businesses to collaborate on an aircraft maintenance operation at Pearson Airport. While none of the possible ventures panned out, Wayne's lawyers did succeed in negotiating a $2 million payment from airport authorities, who originally hadn't wanted to give him a cent in compensation for the terminated lease.

At the same time, there was interest in Millardair from the Region of Waterloo International Airport in Ontario's booming Technology Triangle. Waterloo Airport "practically begged us to build a hangar at an area of their airport they want to develop and offered unheard-of conditions for a lease—which we are signing onto this month," Wayne wrote in an email to a friend sent in August 2011. He explained that he was partnering with three top maintenance people he knew from his flying days with the discount airline Canada 3000 to open an MRO (maintenance, repair, and overhaul) facility to do heavy maintenance on small airliners. Wayne included in the email a picture of the land being prepared for the new hangar, on which construction was about to begin that month. He expressed his hope that it would be finished over the winter. "It's going to be 50,000 square feet—212 x 243' with a 60' high taildoor, good for 2 [Airbus] 320s or [Boeing] 737s, or 1 [Boeing] 757 or [Airbus] 310."

This was a huge, multimillion-dollar project, unlike anything Wayne had ever done. Although he had worked for Millardair off and on over the decades—flying cargo, training junior pilots, and handling some administrative tasks, mostly on a part-time basis—the company had always been Carl Millard's baby. Carl had been reluctant to give more control of Millardair to his son, which aggravated an already difficult personal relationship. Wayne had never forgiven his father for separating from his mother, Della, when he was a teenager; meanwhile, Carl didn't know how to cope with his son's drinking. At one point, the pair didn't speak for years.

Carl did not learn that Wayne had married or that Madeleine was having a baby until he got a call at his Toronto airport office. A former employee recalls that he hurried straight to the hospital to meet his first and only grandchild. While the birth helped Carl smooth things over with Wayne temporarily, he never warmed to his new daughter-in-law, who, according to friends and employees, he regarded as a gold digger.

While the Millard family was always very private, Millardair pilots gossiped among themselves about where its money had originated. A popular theory was that Della had some family money that she had invested wisely in real estate and stocks, and that the wealth likely wasn't generated solely by Millardair's operations. Former Millardair employees always stress that much of the credit for running the business should go to Della Millard, who continued to work with Carl long after the two split up.

When Carl died, Wayne bought a full page in *The Globe and Mail* for his obituary, illustrated with photos of his mother, father, and planes, to tell the story of Carl's life. His father's birth, on November 28, 1913, "was only 10 years after the Wright Brothers' first flight," Wayne wrote. "Their invention of the 'flying machine' and Carl's path through life were going to intersect." The sight one day of a big red monoplane thundering overhead inspired the fifteen-year-old Carl to fly, a goal he pursued steadfastly in the decade to come. Despite the onset of the Great Depression and the fact that he had dropped out of school in Grade 8, Carl succeeded in rebuilding an abandoned gristmill and earning enough money to buy a wrecked 26-horsepower Aeronca C-2, which he refurbished in his father's barn. It was an extension of the skills he had learned changing the main bearings in the Model T Ford he had used to drive milk cans from the family farm to the cheese factory.

Unfortunately, having spent all his money on the plane itself, Carl had nothing left over for flying lessons. He had to practise taxiing, at ever-higher speeds, in the family cow pasture. His father, Earl, who didn't have the aviation bug, yelled at him during one session: "Why don't you keep going? Can't it fly?" Carl accepted the challenge, and soon the C-2 was airborne. Returning to earth, however, proved more difficult. The airplane landed in a nose-over that resulted in a broken prop. Flying lessons couldn't be avoided any longer. Carl signed up with Captain Tom Williams, a First World War ace, who lived nearby. "The way to afford the enormous expense of advance lessons leading to the commercial license was found by rebuilding another aircraft, a Reid Rambler open-cockpit biplane, and using it for barnstorming at country fairs, aerobatic displays and passenger hopping," Wayne wrote. Even Earl eventually agreed to go up with Carl for a bird's-eye view of his farm.

In 1937, while delivering a load of feed to the Tavistock Mills, Carl met Della Mitchell, who ran the accounting and bookkeeping office for the firm. They married in 1939, and not long after, Carl became the forty-sixth pilot to be hired by Trans-Canada Airlines (the predecessor to Air Canada), where he would work for fifteen years before he and Della started their first aviation company, Millard Auto Aero Marine Ltd. The business distributed Steelcraft boats as well as Beech, Fleet, and Bellanca aircraft, and was run out of the Millards' tiny bungalow in the Yonge and Eglinton neighbourhood of Toronto.

Millardair, the company for which Carl is best known, was formed in 1963 and gradually grew to a fleet of twenty aircraft and forty employees dedicated to charter flying, both passengers and freight. Aircraft included various Pipers and Beeches, Douglas DC-3, Douglas C-117, Douglas DC-4, Cessna Citation, and Hansa Jet. "Millardair was known to be a good place for beginning pilots and apprentice mechanics to start a career, as Carl was known to have lots of faith and interest in seeing the next generation come along," wrote Wayne. "Literally hundreds of pilots and mechanics started their career at Millardair. Many regularly dropped in to chat with Carl about the good old days, and let him know they appreciated the confidence he put in them."

While Wayne was correct that Carl was deeply admired by many pilots who began their careers at Millardair before moving on to bigger and better things, like any larger-than-life figure, he also had his detractors. Some pilots bitterly resented how he had charged them for training while they built up the flying hours they needed to move on. And as much as Carl was admired for challenging some of the sillier aspects of the federal government's transportation bureaucracy, in other cases he was seen as needlessly obstreperous.

According to Wayne's obituary, this ornery streak is what caused his father to leave his one-room schoolhouse in Grade 8, when the "school marm" took a dislike to young Carl. "Another boy, the school prankster, had loaded all the students' bench seats with cap pistol sparkers so that when the seats were slammed down to start the morning class there erupted a halluva lot of noise and smoke," Wayne wrote. "Carl's delight at the incident annoyed the school marm, and she tried to threaten Carl into revealing the culprit, but she ran up against a boy with principles whose attitude was, 'If you want to catch somebody, do it yourself, you're not going to use me.'"

Carl was determined to give his son some of the advantages in life that he himself had lacked. Wayne was sent to board at Upper Canada College, a private school in Toronto known for turning out captains of industry, financiers, lawyers, and politicians. Its alumni include four mayors of Toronto, four Ontario premiers, and seven provincial chief justices, as well as assorted Rhodes scholars, Olympic medallists, and recipients of the Order of Canada. Although Wayne didn't remember his alma mater fondly enough to send his own son there, for a while at least, regular updates of his progress through life appeared in *Old Times*, the school's alumni magazine. In 1964, *Old Times* reported that Wayne Millard, a member of the class of 1961, had been named chief pilot at Millardair. Two years later, it announced, "Wayne Millard has passed the examinations of the Airline Transport Board in London and is now authorized to fly chartered British Airlines." A few months after that, it reported Wayne had been hired by Air Canada, where he worked until he was fired from his first officer's job for wearing his hair below his shirt collar in 1973.

An arbitration board eventually ruled that the regulation was not legally enforceable and ordered that Wayne, who had inherited his father's penchant for challenging authority, be reinstated with $20,000 in back pay. But he quickly went looking for another battle, which he found in the airline's rules about long versus short shirtsleeves. "He just liked getting up management's nose," a fellow pilot wrote on an airline message board in 2010. "I don't think CALPA [Canadian Air Line Pilots Association] was willing to go to bat for that one. Anyway, he resigned shortly afterward. As he said, 'I couldn't see the point in staying.' I know how that feels."

In Carl's obituary, Wayne described and his father and mother as "alpha personalities" and "perfectionists" whose vibrant business partnership made for a lively marriage. The aviation community referred to them as Carl and Dell, the Dynamic Duo," he wrote, ignoring the fact that his parents' marriage had broken up decades before Della's death.

This ability to shut his eyes to reality also manifested itself in Wayne's relationship with his son. He seemed unable to accept that Dellen had no interest in the family company, telling the *Toronto Star* after Carl died that his son might revive Millardair as a helicopter business. For some reason, Wayne was determined that Dellen should do what he had not—take over and run a revitalized Millardair—while Wayne would continue to go about his eccentric pursuits. These included Skyping about saving elephants with an African woman who liked to be addressed as "Your Royal Highness," trying to learn multiple foreign languages, and tracing his family's genealogy to see if he could confirm

Carl's claim that the Millards were descended from the Mohawk leader Joseph Brant.

Just before the demolition of the old hangars at Pearson Airport began, Wayne invited former colleagues to stop one last time and take any mementos they might want. He spoke of the new venture in Waterloo as Dellen's project, something that would both ensure his son's future and allow the Millardair name to live on. While Wayne was far from blind to the risk involved—noting in an email to a friend in August 2011 that "the unknown in all this downwind sailing is whether we will get the customers we need"—he also believed that fate was on his side.

He may well have been inspired by the gamble his father had taken in 1960, when Carl had bought the old hangars and transported them in one piece to another part of the airfield. "Most said it couldn't be done, that it would all come apart and collapse like a bunch of toothpicks," wrote Wayne. No one would insure the move, which was necessitated by the construction of the airport's new Terminal One. According to Wayne, it put the Millard family's entire life savings at risk.

Like his father, Dellen had a sentimental attachment to the old hangar facilities—just not for aviation purposes. He liked to invite friends there to party, work on cars, and ogle his helicopter and his family's planes. When Dellen got engaged, just before the hangars were torn down, he arranged for the engagement photo shoot to take place there. Among other things, the photos show Dellen and his fiancée, Jennifer Spafford, kissing in the hangar rafters, posing with his grandfather's classic white Thunderbird, which leaves a trail of special effects fog, and making faces through the window of his Bell helicopter. Spafford, a ballet teacher, sports a variety of hairstyles and at least six different outfits, including pink satin toe shoes as she poses atop a Jeep. Millard has his hair gelled into a slight mohawk (brown, not red), a few days' worth of stubble, and several changes of clothes. The photo shoot was orchestrated by Millard, down to every last detail. He even carved up a pair of brand-new jeans with a large knife to get the ripped jean look he wanted.

BY THE TIME MILLARD collected the CD of the engagement photos from the photographer, just a few weeks later, however, the wedding had been called off. According to a police source, Spafford discovered that Millard had been cheating on her with eighteen-year-old Christina Noudga. Distraught, she moved out of the Oakville house they had bought together in her name and into a condo owned by Millard near his mother's house, where she said she paid rent.

The break-up was one of a number of events that make 2011 a key year in Dellen Millard's life. It was the year that Noudga became his girlfriend, the year that Mark Smich began to play a major role, and the year that Wayne Millard decided it was time for his twenty-five-year-old son to do something he had never done before and get an actual job.

AN OLD FRIEND OF Madeleine Burns's family says young Dellen was like the cartoon character Dennis the Menace— spoiled, clever, and with a tendency to get himself into trouble. He remembers Dellen offering a bunch of tulips to his grandmother, Madge Burns, who wasn't especially pleased that they had been picked without permission from her own garden. As a boy, he could take his bike apart and put it back together, and he always had plenty of money in his pocket. He was allowed to drive cars around the airport at a young age, and like his father before him he learned to fly as an adolescent. He took frequent vacations down south and had his own horse, which was kept on a property owned by Madeleine after she and Wayne split up.

Although he'd been a skinny child, Dellen put on weight during his tweens and early teens. He was extremely sensitive about it and later blamed his father for feeding him too much pasta. His nickname during those years was Dellen the Melon. A former friend says that at one point he tried to destroy all the family photos of his pudgy past. In a letter from prison to an admirer asking Millard about his fashion preferences and hairstyles, he cites a photo of him that had appeared in the press: "You mention a V-neck and subtle mullet, which makes me think it was from my chubby years. (Just great)."

After his headline-making solo flights, he managed to win some respect from his classmates, although by this time, he no longer seemed to crave it. He soon dropped out of the Toronto French School, claiming that only a few of his teachers interested him, and he tried his hand at a number of pursuits, all of which—apart from a stint at culinary school—were related to the entertainment industries.

Millard took a 3D games animation course at Humber College but left after he got nabbed for plagiarism. (It's not clear if his departure was his choice or the school's.) He then moved on to makeup artistry, special effects, and photography, using his girlfriend at the time as his model in various softcore porno shoots. The most memorable of these, a photo series entitled "Cockpit," appeared on the adult website Suicide Girls in 2005. Among other things, it features "Josie," naked inside a Millardair plane, explaining that her "first official act as captain was to make the DC-4 a clothing-strictly-prohibited aircraft." Eight years later, upon hearing that her ex-boyfriend was about to be charged with murder, Josie, which is not her real name, took to Twitter in a misguided attempt at humour. "Nothing like finding out your evil ex-boyfriend was arrested for potential murder," she tweeted. "The only time it's ever okay for your ex to be more popular than you on Twitter is if he's suspected of murder is what I always say." Apparently, she thought better of the tweets and soon removed them.

BY 2007, WAYNE HAD APPOINTED his son and, more surprisingly, his ex-wife, Madeleine Burns, as vice presidents at Millardair. Burns, who had gone back to school to study interior design, was trying not very successfully to make it as a designer. She was concerned about her personal finances and worried that Wayne and Dellen would fritter away the Millard fortune, estimated by family friends to be between $10 million and $20 million. After she moved out of the Maple Gate house, she had acquired full ownership of a farm property she previously co-owned with Wayne. That should have been the end of her involvement, but she continued to play a financial role in the business. Wayne may well have encouraged her, either out of loneliness or a hope that they would get back together or both. He had never been as careful with money as Carl, who came of age during the Depression and had a reputation for being cheap. What's more, Wayne allowed Dellen to spend large amounts of money, never making any demands on his son other than that he show up at the hangar office from time to time.

AL SHARIF, THE FOURTH man hired at the revamped Millardair, was the only person prepared to speak publicly about Wayne's Waterloo venture after Dellen's arrest. He attributes this to the fact that he is a Texan, not shy, and not worried about possible retaliation from any Dellen cronies. Sharif remembers being taken aback when he first met Wayne's son. "Anyone that walks around with an orange mohawk, the elevator doesn't go to the top floor," he thought. As a consultant in an international air maintenance and overhaul business based in Austin, Texas, Sharif knew John Barnes, Wayne's right-hand man in the new Millardair operation, from Barnes's days at Toronto-based Skyservice Airlines. Back then, Barnes was a customer of Evergreen Air Center of Washington State, where Sharif worked bringing in commercial transport category aircraft for its MRO operation. Barnes suggested to Wayne that Sharif would be a good fit to line up clients for Millardair. The two hit it off instantly.

The problems began in early 2012, even before Millardair was operative, when the cost of hangar construction went far beyond Wayne's original assessment. The budget overrun left inadequate funds to purchase tooling and equipment, build offices inside the hangar, and hire the trained technicians required to secure regulatory approval. Sharif made Wayne Millard a proposal: Sharif could line up outside investors who would take a minority stake but still leave control of the business with the Millard family. Wayne turned him down.

"He advised me that this whole exercise was to provide Dell a secure future and provide him with a sustainable environment that he could grow within as a person and to learn the business," Sharif recalls. Wayne was adamant that he could secure the necessary funding through local banks. To help him out, Barnes polished the business plan while Sharif provided financial forecasting that took into account all the variables faced by a start-up MRO. "Dell went out locally and hired an accountant to assist Wayne with the books and to help him with the banks. Wayne was eventually successful in bringing a large sum to the table from one of the local banks. It provided more than enough funding to do what we needed to do," says Sharif.

The stalled operation was back in action. Barnes focussed on hiring the necessary staff for certification as well as acquiring tooling and equipment within Canada, while Sharif looked for bargains in the United States. By attending the auctions of defunct aviation companies, they managed to save hundreds of thousands of dollars on equipment. New employees were trained on the specific aircraft types they expected to service. But as all this was going on—and Sharif emphasizes that it was hard work—the accountant Dellen had hired kept expressing his doubts about the viability of the business. Sharif attributes his skepticism to the fact that he had no aviation industry experience and was used to working for commodity-driven businesses. He didn't understand that Millardair was in a service industry, where success depended on establishing relationships with airlines and aviation leasing companies. While Sharif acknowledges that the aircraft maintenance business is a competitive field, he was convinced Millardair had what it needed to make a go of it.

Unfortunately, along with the accountant, Dellen was putting up obstacles. According to Sharif, he was the only member of the team not to complete his assignment, which was to finish construction of the offices and clean up the hangar. "It was still full of Dell's toys—cars, hot rods, Jeeps, Jet Skis, airplanes," says Sharif. "There were also piles of junk from their old facility at Pearson strewn about the hangar." The law required potential customers to audit the Millardair facility and team to ensure they met minimum requirements, but the messy hangar made visits impossible.

Dellen also made modifications to the building without consulting anyone, using a cutting torch, for example, to remove structural components. "At every turn, he cut corners to save money without any experience or knowledge of the regulations involved, both from a safety standpoint and a regulatory standpoint," says Sharif. He maintains that it was only thanks to Barnes that Millardair gained the regulatory approval needed for the start-up of operations in November 2012.

Although nothing was guaranteed, Sharif says the team was finally starting to see light at the end of the tunnel. He had secured a commitment from one of Millardair's competitors to handle their overflow work and share revenues. And Barnes had a smaller Canadian airline ready to visit the facility. He and Sharif were also working on securing business from a large leasing company that had more than forty-five aircraft available for 2013 and 2014. "Wayne was very comfortable with the direction we were headed," says Sharif. A meeting was called at the Maple Gate house to go over what remained to be done before the first aircraft arrived for servicing.

When Sharif arrived at the Millard home, Dellen and the accountant began questioning him about why there were no contracts in place for the remainder of 2012 and all the way out to mid-2013. "Again, I explained to them that, legally, we could not secure contracts until we were certified by the Canadian regulatory authority and, realistically, we would not get a contracted commitment until the hangar was completed and cleared of all the crap laying inside. It seemed at the time that I was speaking to the wall."

The next day Sharif visited the hangar to assess the state of readiness. "I was sorely disappointed with what I saw," he recalls. "We were not close to being ready to present our facility to anyone. All of the items that Dell was responsible for were either not even touched or were behind schedule." When Dellen finally showed up around noon, as Sharif says was his habit, the two had a tense conversation in the middle of the hangar. To defuse the situation, Dellen invited Sharif to dinner that night.

They met several hours later at a steakhouse near Pearson Airport. As Sharif tells it, their business discussions were relaxed and normal, with Dellen asking why the family should continue to invest in the facility. Sharif explained yet again why the future was bright and how Dellen needed to do his part. After Dellen expressed concern that the family coffers were running low and said he was reluctant to keep pouring good money after bad, Sharif warned that if he cut and ran now, he would be lucky to get twenty cents for every dollar invested. He emphasized that the real value of the business lay in the coveted Transport Canada operational certification it had just received, the high-quality team it had assembled, and the potential customers being lined up.

"We parted pleasantly and nothing further was said between us until his father's death," says Sharif. "Two days after I returned home from Toronto, I called Wayne, and he and I spent a lengthy time on the phone going over Dell's and my conversation, going over everything that I was working on from a business stand-point. And again, I reiterated the fact that they needed to finish the hangar and the work would come. I would say that he gave me a vote of confidence and that he was very comfortable with the opportunities ahead."

Less than two weeks later, Wayne was dead. Everyone on the Millardair team was told he died of a brain aneurysm. Dellen took over as CEO. With the exception of Dellen's personal mech-anic, Shane Schlatman, all the employees were laid off. Within days, the transportation department certification that had been so hard to obtain was cancelled. Sharif thought maybe the pressure had got to Wayne. There had been rumblings that he might have started drinking again. It wasn't until the Tim Bosma murder made headlines that Sharif learned the truth: Wayne Millard had died of a gunshot to the left eye and the police had just reopened the file on his death, which had originally been ruled a suicide. "My immediate reaction was that Wayne's death was not a suicide," says Sharif. "He had more reasons to live than to die."

EIGHT

THE NEW CEO

Wayne Millard's body was discovered at his home on the evening of Thursday, November 29, 2012. The following Monday, Dellen texted Mark Smich, "Tomorrow I start firing people."

"Tru. Well im still online. Mite run one last game," his friend replied. "Whats the deal for tomoro? U busy i guess."

"Yea organizing a funeral & the layoff of 15 employees & renegotiating deals with banks is a few days work. A lot's happening fast. I'm getting sick too. yea at millardair, I'm sending everyone accept Shane home. noone knows yet."

Shane would become an employee of Millard Properties, another family company. His first assignment for the new CEO was to change the locks at the hangar. "tomorrow morning John [Barnes] & his associates lose access to the hangar," Dellen texted. "SPECIAL PROJECT: Either after hours tonight or early tomorrow morning Discreetly change the lock on the hangar entrance. I'll want 3 keys. 1 for me, 1 for you, 1 spare to be kept in the key cabinet."

As soon as that was done, Shane got back to work on Dellen's cars with no further distractions. "Suzuki done. Seat back in Caddy and working. Olds is lock able again. Working on Vette now," he reported in a text on the one-week anniversary of Wayne's death. "I am very happy working for you."

ON TUESDAY, MAY 7, 2013, the day after Tim Bosma's murder, Arthur Jennings stopped by his daughter's house to see his grand-kids before going to work. He was having coffee when he noticed his son-in-law Shane Schlatman's strange reaction to a text. It was from Dellen Millard, telling Shane not to come to work, which was very unusual. "He was expected to be at work no matter what," Jennings later tells the court. "I was led to believe Dellen trusted Shane so much he wanted him there all the time. He could live there if he wanted. The look on Shane's face was pretty shocked, surprised."

Jennings had also been working at Millardair, on an unpaid internship arranged by Shane. It was the final requirement to get his certificate in supply-chain management, which he had gone back to school to study in late middle age. The school was supposed to have arranged a placement for Jennings, but it failed to come through, leaving him to get his own gig. The Millardair internship, which had begun in February, was essentially a scam where Jennings put in the hours required by the school while everybody ignored the fact that at Millardair there was no supply chain to manage.

After Jennings left his daughter and son-in-law's house, he found the same text from Millard on his phone, which he had not yet checked that morning: "Airport politics no one goes to the hangar today, not even just to grab something." It had been sent at 5:55 A.M.

That was fine with Jennings. Even before he received Millard's text, he had decided to take the day off and enjoy the beautiful spring weather with his wife. He wanted to avoid all the menial tasks that awaited him at Millardair, including mopping the entire fifty thousand square feet of hangar floor. Neither Jennings nor Schlatman ever had any idea when the boss would show up or what he might want them to do. And when Millard did arrive, he was often in the company of Mark Smich and Mark's girlfriend, Marlena Meneses, who would both be assigned odd jobs ranging from painting to cleaning the washrooms.

On the day before Jennings and Schlatman were told to stay away, it had been business (or more accurately lack of business) as usual at Millardair, with most of the hours devoted to building and outfitting a special trailer for Millard. While Millard wasn't there that day, he did text Schlatman to let him know that he should stick around in the evening because Andrew Michalski was coming from Toronto to pick up his car. It had been at the hangar for five or six weeks, as Michalski's licence had been suspended. Schlatman had done an oil change and reattached a bumper. Michalski's friend Robert Bochenek—who, like Michalski, was living at Millard's house—drove him there. While at the hangar, Bochenek and Michalski admired a Camaro belonging to Schlatman and made a short video of him revving the engine. By about 8 P.M., all three men were on their way home in their separate vehicles.

As his father-in-law had observed, Schlatman was shocked when Millard texted everyone not to come in to work on Tuesday.

He messaged back in disbelief, "Including me?"

"Yes," wrote Millard. "Take the day off."

"Ok. Cya tomorrow then."

"See you Wednesday."

"Wednesday it is," wrote Schlatman, anxiously adding, "Did I do something?"

"Haha not at all."

"Ok I just don't wanna do anything to cause you any headaches."

"You are the relief to many of my headaches."

"Well thanks for that. I do try."

SHANE SCHLATMAN, A TALL, hefty guy with a sandy goatee, tells the court that in May 2013 he had known Dellen Millard for seven years. The two had met when Schlatman was working as a mechanic on the outskirts of Toronto and Millard would bring in his Jeep Wrangler TJ for servicing. Millard wanted to learn more about cars and approached Schlatman's boss about renting a bay at his garage. When he was turned down, Millard proposed that Schlatman, who was a talented mechanic, come and work for him at Pearson Airport on Saturdays. That was in 2010, by which time there was no longer any active aviation business at the Pearson hangar. According to Schlatman, he maintained the various Millardair and Millard family vehicles and built a kit car for Dellen. Eventually he was hired on full-time, earning $31 an hour, ten dollars more than he'd gotten at his old job. Though Wayne Millard was in charge, Schlatman reported to Dellen alone. "I always was directed by Dell," he says. "He would tell me what work to do, and I was not to listen to anyone else."

In 2011, as Millardair prepared to reactivate its aviation business, the company moved into two small rented hangars at Waterloo Airport as it waited for its new headquarters to be completed. Schlatman helped out by fabricating steel doors for the hangar, which opened in March 2012, and building and installing racking. But the bulk of his time was still spent on cars and personal projects for Dellen.

Dellen remained as uninterested as ever in the business Wayne was setting up for him and instead focused his ambitions on his farm. Along with planning to build his dream home at the rural property, Millard led Schlatman to believe that he too might have a family home there one day and work nearby in a special garage. In April 2013, Madeleine Burns applied on her son's behalf for the zoning permission required to construct a four-thousand-square-foot drive shed to house Millard's cars, trucks, and motorcycles. Millard and Schlatman had discussed a ninety-nine-year lease that would allow Schlatman to build a house on a slice of land carved out of the property.

The homes at the farm were to be constructed by Javier Villada, a contractor who had previously worked for Wayne and Dellen at Riverside Drive, Maple Gate Court, and Pearson and Waterloo airports. Whenever there was a big job, Villada would hire his four brothers—Alvaro, Francisco, Cesar, and Roberto—as well as his brothers-in-law, to work on an hourly basis. They had recently built the washrooms and office facilities at the new Waterloo hangar. Villada was also involved with Dellen in a company called Villada Homes, which, despite its name, was owned and run by Millard, with Villada occupying nothing more than a foreman role. The only homes the two partners had ever worked on were Millard's properties and his ex-fiancée's house in Oakville.

But Villada, a burly man of fifty, still dreamed of building a gated community country estate at the Millard farm.

He even allowed his pay to be cut to $22 per hour from $27, a pittance in real estate–crazy, renovation-mad Toronto. Villada, who by all accounts is a good contractor, should have easily been able to find work elsewhere, but he stuck it out with Dellen. Over the years, his relationship with the Millards had evolved into something almost feudal in nature. He not only did work for the family, but also lived in one of the Riverside Drive apartments and made himself available around the clock, seven days a week. After he borrowed $9,000 from Dellen to return home to Colombia for a family visit, the two argued about how much had been worked off and paid back. As if that were not enough, Villada had an arrangement to lease Millard's gas- guzzling red Dodge Ram from him for $450 per month. Yet even for this substantial fee, he would get last-minute requests from Millard to use the pickup.

One of these came on Saturday, May 4, 2013. "I believe Dellen called me to ask me to switch cars," Villada tells the court. The exchange was made at five or six in the evening in front of the Sears store at Sherway Gardens mall in the west end of Toronto. Millard took the red truck and gave Villada his Yukon to keep for at least a week. But then, later that night, Millard changed his mind. He and his girlfriend, Christina Noudga, showed up at Riverside Drive with a white van owned by Millardair. They left the van with Villada and took back the Yukon.

While he was at Riverside that night, Millard asked to see an apartment Villada was custom renovating for him, which included extra-high kitchen counters for his comfort. The next day, Sunday, Millard texted Villada requesting that he check inside the white van for an item Millard had forgotten. On Monday, Millard gave Villada $900 in back pay while he was working at widening the driveway at Maple Gate. Then on Tuesday, Villada received the same text sent to Schlatman and Jennings, warning him to stay away from the hangar where he had not been in weeks.

WHEN JENNINGS RETURNED TO work on Wednesday, May 8, he brought coffee and doughnuts for himself and Shane. They chatted briefly and put their lunch boxes away. As he crossed the hangar floor, Jennings was stunned to see the truck he had seen on TV the evening before. It was sitting in the middle of the hangar on a green tarp. As a truck aficionado, Jennings immediately recognized the chrome and steel running boards from the news report about Tim Bosma's disappearance. "My exact words to myself were, 'Oh my God, could that be the truck?'" he tells the court. "Except for the back bench seat, everything else was out of it," including the licence plates. There were some spray-paint cans on the tarp.

Because the truck made him "uncomfortable," Jennings stayed away from it. He didn't discuss it with Schlatman, who seemed unperturbed. Schlatman was preparing the vehicle to be painted red at a body shop north of Toronto. Millard had told the shop's owner, Tony Diciano, that it was a rush job. He wanted it done by Friday, but despite the fact that Millard and his family were long-time customers, Diciano said he would need the weekend. At Millard's request, Schlatman was stripping away the truck's emblems, lights, and any other bits and pieces that would get in the way of painting.

Sometime around midday, Spencer Hussey stopped by the hangar. He was a baby-faced young aviation enthusiast who, before Wayne's death, had been employed at the short-lived Millardair MRO. After he was laid off, he picked up some part-time work fixing cars and doing other odd jobs at the hangar and the farm. Working for $12.50 an hour was Hussey's way of keeping in Dellen's good graces. He didn't even complain when Millard made him drive all the way to Toronto to pick up his pay-cheques. Like Javier Villada, Hussey was counting on Millard's help to make his dreams come true. He had a plan to turn the hangar into an FBO, or fixed base of operations—a hotel for planes, as the hangar crew described it. While this was not as specialized or interesting a business as the MRO, or airplane garage, in which Wayne Millard had invested millions, it was better than nothing.

Throughout April 2013, Hussey had been arranging meetings with potential FBO clients and business partners, ranging from Bearskin Airlines to Esso. He kept Dellen Millard up to date with a stream of enthusiastic text messages and requests for meetings. At 7:53 on the morning after Tim Bosma disappeared, Millard replied to one of Hussey's texts: "Haven't forgotten about you, just haven't had a brake [sic] yet." A few hours later, he messaged again, asking Hussey to meet him at the airport the next day at noon.

Unlike Jennings, Hussey had not heard the news about Tim Bosma's disappearance, so he didn't think twice about the truck at the hangar. When he asked casually where it came from, Schlatman told him Dell had bought it in Kitchener. At his meeting with Millard, Hussey didn't raise the topic.

He remembers thinking Millard looked tired, with bags under his eyes, while his hair, which "he usually styled in some way, was just kind of thrown over." Hussey and Millard arranged another meeting for two days later, on Friday, May 10, with two other potential partners.

Later that afternoon, Schlatman tried, at Millard's request, to remove the windshield from Millard's red Dodge Ram truck, the one they had taken to Mexico two years earlier. To assist with this task, which he had never carried out before, the mechanic had ordered a special windshield removal kit, which was promptly delivered by nearby NAPA Auto Parts. Schlatman was a good customer, buying thousands of dollars' worth of parts every month. This, though, was his first purchase of a windshield kit. It was also the only one the NAPA sales rep had ever sold in his five years on the job.

The kit turned out to be a dud. Schlatman couldn't figure out how to work it and eventually gave up, leaving the windshield on the red truck intact. He tells the court that Millard never explained why he wanted the windshield removed and that he never asked. When Schlatman inquired as to how the black truck had gotten to the hangar when it had no front seats, Millard said he'd driven it while sitting on a pail. According to Schlatman, that was as far as the conversation went. It was a similar kind of explanation to the one Jennings received when, earlier in his internship, he had wondered aloud about the presence in the hangar of vehicles with their interiors stripped out and was told that Millard was highly allergic to mould. "It's strange to understand," Jennings tells the court. "I didn't ask questions. I didn't want to."

IGNORING WEIRD GOINGS-ON WAS a prerequisite for working at Millardair. When Dellen bought a $60,000 excavator, took it for a joyride, and blew out the engine, leaving it stuck in a swamp, Schlatman's reaction, he tells the court, was, "That's Dell." He and Hussey headed out to the farm to help remove the machine from the mud. They tried towing it out using a Bobcat, failed, switched to a snowmobile and, not surprisingly, failed again. When he finally realized this approach wasn't going to work, Schlatman attempted the unsuccessful "engine swap" witnessed by Chaz Main. In the end, Millard's mechanic had to call in backup in the form of another excavator, which was used to pull the damaged engine out and replace it with a new one. Only then could the excavator finally be driven out of the swamp, where it had been stuck for months.

Nor was Dellen the only Millard handing out strange work assignments. When Wayne was alive, staff might arrive at Millardair only to be told their job that day was transporting barrels filled with oil and kerosene to the barn on Dellen's farm for storage. On another occasion, employees were instructed to remove straw from the barn and spread it on the fields. Spencer Hussey thought they were doing it because Dell wanted to convert the barn into a house, while Javier Villada was told it was because the straw was a fire hazard. There was never an explanation that satisfied everyone.

Yet all this paled in comparison to the project that occupied Schlatman for several weeks during the spring and summer of 2012. Dellen had asked him to build a homemade incinerator. At Millard's request, he welded together three fifty-gallon green steel drums on a steel base. The device, which is shown to the court during Schlatman's testimony, looks like a high school student's entry in a science competition to build your own rocket ship.

"Whose idea was it to build this thing?" asks prosecutor Craig Fraser.

"That was Dell's," says Schlatman. He explains that Millard planned to use it to burn garbage.

"Did you ever use it for garbage?" Fraser asks.

"I didn't, no."

"Did Mr. Millard use it for garbage?"

"I do believe he tried, but it didn't work very well."

"Do you know what kinds of garbage would be burned?"

"From Riverside and Maple Gate. There was a lot of garbage produced from those properties. He wanted some way to dispose of it cheaper and quicker."

It was a preposterous story. Millard's residential properties all had regular city garbage, recycling, and compost collection. The idea that it made sense to drive more than one hundred kilometres to dispose of normal household waste in a homemade incinerator was beyond belief. Yet according to his testimony, Schlatman never so much as raised an eyebrow at the plan, even when he almost caused a serious accident. "Having to wash the barrels out real well. Had small fireball out of one barrel," Schlatman texted Millard on May 25, 2012. "Luckily had barrel facing out overhead door so No prob other than dirty underwear! Lol."

"Haha, shame I missed it," Millard wrote back. "So no incinerator today?"

"No lookin like monday it will be done."

On Monday, Schlatman and Millard exchanged more texts. "That's the idea," wrote Millard regarding a photo they had been looking at. "needs double the number of vents, and a guard to prevent egress of large embers and light."

Then Millard messaged his friend Mark Smich about getting together that evening: "We go do incinerator, cool?"

"Yo I'm down bro. I would even say come sooner then that. Then we can chill and talk about other shit as well."

Schlatman had fixed up a trailer for Millard to tow the incinerator from the hangar to the farm for its test. Whatever happened next was not documented at the trial, but the text messages available indicate that it was not a success. Millard asked Schlatman to make still more modifications. Schlatman promised that he would get to it as soon as possible but said he was being delayed by Wayne, who had asked him to measure the hanger.

When that task was complete, he texted Dellen about the incinerator. "Did you want existing air holes covered or leave them and add more?"

"If the new guards cover the old holes, leave em. if not, fill em," Dellen instructed.

"Ok guards will cover."

"Great, don't forget handles for easy moving," said Millard.

Two days later, Schlatman asked, "Incinerator up to snuff now?" Presumably it wasn't, because by June 18, after a month of experimentation, Millard finally gave up on homemade devices and instructed his mechanic to research professionally manufactured livestock incinerators.

"Cost on small 250 lb [capacity] incinerator is $11,390," Schlatman texted Millard the next day. "Next model is 500 lb and sells for $13,440. Tax and Shipping extra."

"Interesting, double capacity for 18% higher cost," said Millard. "And they run off propane?"

Schlatman confirmed that he was looking at the propane model.

"Put an order in for the larger one," Millard instructed. "Use the red Visa."

Millard's story about why he needed an incinerator had shifted by this point, but Schlatman was satisfied with the new explanation: his boss was thinking of getting into the pet cremation business. Millard told him that his uncle, a veterinarian, wanted to cut the high cost of destroying animal carcasses in Toronto. He thought he could "help his uncle out and possibly pick up business from other vets in the area," Schlatman tells the court. Millard, he says, was always looking for new ways to make money. It wasn't up to him to question what kind of profit margins there were in pet incineration, or why Millard would find it a more desirable career than aviation.

In his usual manner, Schlatman just did what he was told. He ordered the Eliminator from its Canadian distributor, Tristar Dairy, Hog and Poultry, based in Grunthal, Manitoba. When it arrived at the hangar, he unboxed it and took photos on his phone. On July 9, 2012, he wrote to Bill Penner, the sales representative he had worked with: "Hi Bill, received the unit on Thursday. Wow, very impressive." He had some problems getting the machine up and running, but after much back and forth with Tristar and the Georgia manufacturers, Schlatman finally succeeded. A six-hour test burn was conducted at the hangar, and Millard was instructed on how to operate the device. At his boss's request, Schlatman also constructed a special trailer so the Eliminator would be mobile and outfitted it with a generator and a propane tank. When everything was ready, the incinerator was moved from the hangar to its new home in the barn at Millard's farm. Just as he had photographed its arrival, Schlatman took pictures of its departure. On August 13, he sent another email to Penner: "BTW - SN 500 is working great now. Sounds awesome when the afterburner kicks in!!"

The Eliminator was paid for by Millardair, a purchase entered into the company books by Lisa Williams, a contract bookkeeper who originally met the Millards through Dellen's uncle, Robert Burns. Burns's veterinary clinic was next door to a computer and IT business owned by Williams and her husband. Williams tells the court that the incinerator receipt did not stand out to her, and she never made any inquiries about it. Somehow, however, her husband, Charles Dubien, who had installed the security system at the hangar, found out about the Eliminator and mentioned it to Dr. Burns, Dellen's supposed business partner. Burns tells the court he was shocked by Dubien's information. He had never once discussed going into the pet incineration business, with his nephew. He was completely satisfied with the carcass disposal company he had used for the past twenty-six years.

From Burns's body language and tone, it is evident that he despises Millard. While Millard tries to make eye contact with his uncle as he walks into court, Burns refuses to look at him. "He's my sister's son," he tells Tony Leitch. "Biologically, he's my nephew." Burns says he looked after Millard regularly from the time he was three, when Dellen's parents split up, until he was about fifteen, but he describes their recent relationship as "distant." His testimony, which is confined as closely as possible to details about the Eliminator, is interrupted twice for legal arguments. Burns spends less than half an hour on the stand

and police escort him out of the courthouse, keeping photographers at bay.

ART JENNINGS AND HIS son-in-law had come to an unspoken agreement to all but ignore the strange activities at Millardair. But on Thursday, May 9, Jennings broke that pact. While Schlatman was otherwise occupied, Jennings took out his phone and snapped several pictures of the black Dodge Ram, including close-up photos of the VIN through the windshield. He then called Crime Stoppers, gave the operator the number's last six digits, and asked her to check if it was the Bosma truck. "That's all I can tell you right now," he told her. "I will call you back if you check those VIN numbers."

"I was pacing, going outside, having fifteen cigarettes. I was hoping beyond hope it was not the truck and Dell was not involved. . . . She said, 'Yes, it is the truck. Where is it? Please tell us where it is.'" Because Crime Stoppers guarantees anonymity, it does not trace calls and is unable to do so. It relies on sources like Jennings who don't want to go to the police but have information about a crime.

Jennings told the Crime Stoppers operator that he couldn't tell her where the truck was and that he would call back later that day. "I went into shock. I went inside my pickup truck and vomited because I was that upset. I was upset for everybody." Most of all, he says, he feared for his family.

Although he phoned his wife, Jennings still didn't talk to his son-in-law. "I knew Shane and Dellen were so close that I didn't want to cause a rift between them," he says. At 4:30 P.M., he phoned Crime Stoppers back and they patched him through to the police. Again, Jennings refused to give them the truck's location, this time saying he would get back to them the next day after talking to his family. He sent Shane a text asking him to stop by his house after work. His daughter was there as well as his wife. Shane arrived and blew up. He said he was going to quit Millardair the next day and then he left.

Whether at the family meeting or shortly after it, a storyline emerged, one that Schlatman says endured right up to the trial: that Millard might have inadvertently tangled himself up with real criminals. "I thought maybe he had got himself into getting a stolen truck," Schlatman tells the court. "The Dell Millard I know, he's a nice guy. I would have never connected him with this."

Jennings's version is similar. "My concern was, 'What has Dell got himself into?' I didn't know how far up this went. I didn't want to bring harm upon myself or my family. It was better just to stay off to the side and let's see what happens."

Although Schlatman denies it repeatedly on the witness stand, his text messages suggest that he spoke with Millard after talking to his father-in-law. Just before ten that same Thursday evening, Millard, referring to the Bosmas, texted Schlatman, "I can't stop thinking about what that family's going through."

There is no record that Millard was replying to an earlier text from his mechanic, so Craig Fraser asks Schlatman what prompted that message if, as Schlatman claims, he had not talked to Millard about the Bosma truck. The witness can't provide any kind of credible explanation for the texts between him and

Millard that night. To hear him tell it, that first text from Millard arrived out of the blue, followed two hours later by another one about the truck: "I want to take it back, but I'm a little concerned about how that's going to play out," Millard wrote.

"Ya that's a tough call man," Schlatman replied. "Have you considered goin to cops? Tell em you bought this truck but you think its warm."

"Hypothetically: if this is the same one, I'm in a lot of jeapordy: what truck?"

Fraser asks Schlatman what the last text from Millard means.

"I assumed he was playing dumb not knowing what truck I was talking about," says Schlatman.

Another explanation is that Millard was feeding Schlatman his lines using the hangar code. He was telling Schlatman not to talk about the truck, that it was gone and had never been at the hangar. If anyone asked, all Schlatman had to say was "What truck?" It was okay to lie about it because Dellen was in jeopardy from the criminals setting him up, the same ones, no doubt, that his lawyer would later suggest were framing Millard. For Schlatman, this was justification enough for not telling anyone that Tim Bosma's truck had been sitting in Dellen Millard's hangar for at least two days.

ON FRIDAY MORNING, JENNINGS brought his son-in-law coffee and doughnuts, as if it were just a regular day. And in a sense it started out that way. The black truck was gone, the green tarp was gone, and the giant trailer that had been outside the hangar was also gone. "When I asked [Shane] where the truck was, I was told to mind my own business, stay out of it," Jennings says. He did, however, see tracks on the floor leading to one of the main doors for planes. They stood out, because earlier that week Jennings had been ordered to mop the entire hangar floor, an assignment he clearly resented.

Although he had told the police he would call Friday morning, Jennings didn't follow up. Instead, he and his son-in-law got to work on another trailer project for Millard, which Shane was adamant had to be done. Hussey stopped by for his meeting, at which Millard told him that all potential FBO partners would have to contribute $5,000 to the business. That was a significant amount for Hussey, who tells the court he was surprised by the demand. He left the hangar by 2 P.M., just before the police arrived.

Jennings also missed the police visit, as he was on a supply run to Home Depot. When he returned, he found his son-in-law and Millard talking. "Dell was looking at me. Shane would look at me, turn his head. They were having a heated discussion," he says. Millard came over and told Jennings to get all his stuff and go home.

"That's when I . . . found out that the police had been there," Jennings testifies. "He wasn't angry, just calm, same old Dell. It really had me confused."

Jennings collected his tools, his golf cart, which he worked on when there was nothing else to do at the hangar, and a meat smoker. He gave his Millardair key fob back to Schlatman. "I felt like a mouse in a trap," he says. "I didn't know if someone was going to come in and whack me. I had no idea. I didn't know what was going on. I packed up all my stuff, drove it home."

After the police left the hangar, Millard told Schlatman he had done nothing wrong. As was his custom, Schlatman didn't pose any uncomfortable questions. In the courtroom, Craig Fraser asks him why not.

"He had said he wanted to move the red Dodge pickup truck," Schlatman answers, as if that makes sense.

"Was this immediately after the police left?" asks Fraser.

"Immediate-ish," says Schlatman.

Fraser establishes that there had been no previous discussion about moving Millard's red truck, the same one from which Schlatman was asked to remove the windshield.

Schlatman says Millard told him "he wanted to have a vehicle outside the hangar in case the hangar was locked down. I was under the impression that for some reason the police might be back and not allow him into the hangar."

Schlatman quickly arranged for a friend who lived nearby to store the red truck. Millard drove it over and Schlatman followed in his black Dodge Caravan as the Waterloo Police surveillance unit watched their every move. The two men returned to the hangar in Schlatman's van.

"Any discussion about the events of that day?" asks Fraser.

"He was leaving to go to the bank and to see a lawyer."

Millard left in the Yukon, followed again by the surveillance team who would tail him up until his arrest.

"And that was the last discussion you had with Mr. Millard?"

"Yes."

Schlatman tells the court he has not spoken to either Dellen Millard or Art Jennings since that day. Some time after he left the hangar, Jennings went to the police. "I wanted to be proactive, not reactive," he testifies. "I didn't want myself or son-in-law involved. And I knew we weren't. I knew it was better to tell my story before they made me look like I was part of the crime, and I wasn't. He wasn't."

WHEN THOMAS DUNGEY CROSS-EXAMINES Shane Schlatman, he suddenly and somewhat unexpectedly assumes the role of everybody's favourite trial lawyer. The cross-examination takes place almost halfway through the trial in early April, at the point where most of the forensic evidence has been presented and a parade of highly anticipated witnesses, including the friends and girlfriends of Mark Smich and Dellen Millard, is about to begin. The Schlatman cross is an epic shaming that leaves the packed courtroom simultaneously riveted and uncomfortable. "Intense" is the word audience members whisper among themselves as they file out for the morning break. As common as this type of legal drama is on TV and in the movies, it's exceptional in real life. And when it does happen, it's a reminder that when it comes to public humiliation, the courtroom still trumps the internet.

Until now, Dungey has not spent nearly as much time at the podium as Millard's lawyers, Ravin Pillay and Nadir Sachak. (Dungey's co-counsel, Jennifer Trehearne, almost exclusively handled legal arguments in front of the judge.) But his brevity and liveliness have been much appreciated, as have the questions no one else asked. Why, for example, he wanted to know from Javier Villada, did Millard call his company "Villada Homes"? Villada replied that he had never really thought about it. Dungey was also sympathetic to witnesses the public liked and who were attacked by Millard's team—Igor Tumanenko, the Israeli army officer who spotted the "ambition" tattoo, for example—and tough on witnesses who did not make a good impression on anyone but Millard's lawyers.

In the latter category was Lisa Whidden, a real estate agent who sold a house for Millard and went on to become his lover. At the time of the Bosma murder, Whidden was helping him sell a condo in Toronto's Distillery District, a neighbourhood known for its night life, high-rise views, and youngish inhabitants. There were problems because, while Millard had paid a deposit to the builder, he didn't have ownership of the unit. He had neither paid off the balance nor obtained a mortgage, and was having difficulty raising the necessary funds. According to texts he sent to Whidden, he was in a real cash crunch.

Whidden, a strawberry blonde in a plaid dress who is seven years Millard's senior, smiled at him as she walked back and forth to the witness stand. Though she was never the number one girlfriend, she was still loyal. When Tim Bosma was missing, she refused to talk to the police about texts Millard had sent her on May 10, 2013. Among other things, the messages said "i'm too hot, stay away" and "I think someone i work with has set me up." The police had to handcuff a belligerent Whidden to prevent her from leaving with her phone, which was seized as evidence. She testified that the handcuffs made her bleed, seemingly expecting sympathy. When she told the court, for a second time, that she didn't see the relevance of certain questions, the judge had to remind her, "Ma'am, it's up to the jury and myself to decide what's relevant."

After Millard was arrested, another agent took over the sale of the condo from Whidden, who forwarded her contacts and helped out with an open house. In return, she received a commission. At first she said that it was $10,000 from Millard's mother, but then she clarifies that it may have been a $7,000 cheque signed by Burns but from a real estate brokerage firm.

Dungey acted dumbfounded. "You just get a cheque in the mail, ten grand from his mother," he said. "You're dating a guy for a year, not selling anything, and you get $10,000?" It was a bit of a cheap shot, but it also addressed a recurring Dungey theme: that the Millard family seemed ready and willing to pay people off.

The topic crops up early on in Dungey's cross-examination of Shane Schlatman, when he notes that the mechanic continued to work at full salary for Millardair right up until April 2014, even though there was no commercial activity at the hangar for most of the year. Should anyone have failed to pick up on Millardair's tendency to skirt the tax laws, Dungey leans on the podium and looks at the jury in disbelief as Schlatman explains his duties: working on Dellen's hobby cars, doing the occasional oil change, and taking vacations in Baja, all on the company dime. None of this had anything to do with aviation or actually benefited Millardair, Dungey suggests to Schlatman, who protests that a couple of the vehicles did indeed belong to Millardair.

As a defence lawyer cross-examining the Crown's witnesses, Dungey can ask leading questions not permitted during the prosecution's direct examination. He also has more latitude in the issues he can raise as long as it aids his client's defence. The main goal of cross-examination in a trial like this is to use the prosecution's witnesses to strengthen the defence's theory of the case. For Dungey, the main narrative he is advancing is that Mark Smich, his hapless druggie of a client, was controlled and manipulated by the evil Millard. To this end, Schlatman is portrayed as an example of Millard's handiwork: deluded, obedient, and forever loyal to his criminal master.

Dungey questions Schlatman about the time he was asked to remove the GPS from a Bobcat that arrived at the hangar out of nowhere one morning. It's an example of the type of issue that the defence can raise but the prosecution can't, and it lends credence to news reports from May 2013 that a chop shop was being run out of Millardair's facilities.

"Do you not find that a little suspicious?" Dungey asks.

"Not really. He told me he purchased it."

"Are you sort of closing your eyes here . . . when you take the GPS off it?"

Schlatman maintains he's not. "He's the guy with the money," he says of Millard. "If he wants it, he can just go buy it."

Schlatman essentially gives the same answer when asked about the appearance of a wood chipper, a Harley-Davidson, and a concrete floor polisher at Millardair.

"So your philosophy is 'I just do what he tells me, no matter what it is'?" asks Dungey.

"Yes," says Schlatman.

Dungey turns to the week of May 6 and Schlatman's arrival at work on Wednesday. He asks him if he was surprised to see the black Dodge Ram truck with its interior stripped out.

"Yes."

"How long do you think you spent looking inside?"

"Twenty seconds."

"Didn't see any unusual smudging on the dashboard?"

"No."

Schlatman says Millard brushed him off when he tried to get information, so he didn't persist. Instead, he just asked what should be done with the truck. "He wanted to paint it and we were going to modify the truck for more power and fuel economy," says Schlatman. The plan was to take it and the trailer Schlatman was building to Baja later that month.

Dungey asks if Schlatman didn't find it suspicious that Millard wanted to paint a stripped truck red and replace its perfectly good windshield, which would in effect change the VIN.

Schlatman says there are VINs in other places.

"Yeah, but unless there's a real problem, that's where they look," says Dungey. "You're not even going to ask, 'Why am I taking it out?'"

Schlatman claims that not only did he not ask but also he wasn't even curious. Although the disappearance of Tim Bosma and his truck was a huge story, he says he knew nothing about it because it's not his habit to watch the news or listen to the radio. When he did find out, his reaction was, "Art had already gone to Crime Stoppers so the police are already aware."

Dungey raises his voice and tells Schlatman that this is the same game he's played with all the vehicles. "Why don't you do your duty and call the police?" he asks.

"Friday, I talked to Dell," says Schlatman. "He said [he] hadn't done anything wrong. He was my friend. I believed him."

"C'mon, Mr. Schlatman, you saw the VIN number. . . . You use common sense, something's going over."

"At that time, common sense wasn't a strong point with me," says Schlatman, who is agitated now and raising his voice. "My brain was in a blur."

"How about Mr. Bosma?" snaps Dungey. "Was that a blur?"

"I don't know what you want me to answer. I was waiting to talk to Dell."

"So Dell's more important than the Bosmas and the missing person?"

"Maybe I didn't do everything I should have."

"No, Mr. Schlatman," Dungey blasts him, "you didn't do anything."

He accuses the witness of acting as if Tim Bosma didn't exist.

"Well, I wouldn't say that," says Schlatman. "The Dell I know would not be involved in something like this." That is the rationalization he repeats over and over again.

Dungey tells Schlatman that his loyalty to Millard trumps all, which is why, three years later, he is still not speaking to his father-in-law, who Schlatman believes "ratted Dell out."

"Your loyalty is so great, the hell with Bosma," Dungey roars in righteous anger. "It's just like the other vehicles. You turn a blind eye. You're not going to question anything."

"No, sir, I did not."

"Whatever Dell wants, Dell gets," shouts Dungey.

Schlatman answers with a muted yes.

Dungey asks him why he initially denied to the police that he helped move the red truck on the Friday afternoon. He says the only reason Schlatman eventually admitted it is that the officer who questioned him told him he could be charged with withholding. He was in a corner.

"I think I was more trying to protect myself," Schlatman says.

A few minutes later Dungey delivers the final blast—"You don't see anything, you don't hear anything"—and Schlatman is excused from the witness box. Hank and Mary Bosma both look at him as he walks past on his way out of the room, but he doesn't return their gaze. Outside the courthouse, he covers his face with a grey hoodie and gets into his van.

Social media erupts with praise for Dungey: finally, someone is holding a person accountable for the part he played in a tragic crime. Every story needs a hero avenger, and if the law won't allow the Crown attorneys to ask the questions needed to elicit the truth, then so much the better if Dungey can. The emergence of Smich's lawyer as the crowd pleaser at the Tim Bosma trial is just one of the peculiarities of the adversarial system, and an illustration of what can happen during a cutthroat defence.

NINE

SUSPICIONS

As much as Shane Schlatman was convinced his friend and patron couldn't be involved in something as nefarious as the disappearance of Tim Bosma, another group of people had the opposite reaction when they heard the news of Dellen Millard's arrest. One of these was a long-time employee of Millardair known for telling others that Millard was going to end up in jail. There were two stories he especially liked to recount, and they both took place in 2005.

The first involved Wayne Millard's plans to refurbish a Millardair DC-4 at Brantford Municipal Airport. On June 7, 2005, as Dellen was working on the plane, a seventy-four-year-old contractor fell from some scaffolding, hit his head, and died. As a result, Wayne was charged and sentenced to a $15,000 fine for "failing, as a supervisor, to ensure that the equipment, materials and protective devices" prescribed by law were provided. The prosecution disposition form, dated 2007, states that a "long time worker and friend of the owner of the company was working on an old airplane on a raised work platform. Platform did not have safety railings and the worker fell off, hit head on pavement and died. Company had ceased operations and had no assets. Supervisor was willing to step forward on behalf of company. Supervisor was current owner of what was left of company."

According to the Ontario Ministry of Labour accident report, the fall was witnessed by Dellen Millard and another Millardair contractor, who were also working on the plane. Years later, after Dellen was arrested, a family member of the late contractor contacted police to make sure that they were aware of the accident. The police looked into it and do not believe it to be suspicious.

Curiously, though, just three months after the Brantford accident, Dellen was tied to another falling death. His girlfriend at the time leapt off a balcony in New York City in what was deemed by police to be a suicide. According to the official report made available by the New York Police Department, twenty-year-old Rebecca (not her real name) jumped after talking to her boyfriend on the phone. That boyfriend was Dellen Millard. Over the years, he told a number of friends and acquaintances that he had been having sex with Josie, the woman who appeared in the Millardair porn shoot, while talking to Rebecca. In a condolence message posted online, Millard wrote, "Rebecca, on the surface you were wild and strong; beneath that, sometimes fragile and troubled; but under all of it, infinitely beautiful, sweet and giving. I wish you were still alive, but that now seems not to be; so I wish you are happy, or at least no longer sad. Ever since we very first met, that is what I have always wished for you. Oh dear Rebecca; difficult as times have been, I feel the good outweighed the bad; I feel blessed to have had our lives touch.—love, Del."

Madeleine Burns also posted many strange and religiously-infused comments about Rebecca's death. "Oh [Rebecca],

Losing you now is unendurable, immeasurable. We knew each other for only a short period of time, but your beautiful and tender spirit touched my heart," Burns wrote. "Rebecca, you are now at peace, surrounded with angelic joy, free from the depths of human suffering. I believe that those who love you will be reunited with you once again. Rebecca, it is just a matter of time. BLESS YOU, Madeleine"

A few days later, as she arranged for a mass to be held at a church near her home, Burns wrote, "Darling Girl, today my prayer to OUR FATHER IN HEAVEN is that I may, through this veil of tears, find acceptance and one day be able to rejoice that you have returned home.

'. . . THY WILL BE DONE . . .'"

Over the next three years, she continued to post comments in a similar vein—saying, among other things, that Rebecca's death had been "the most difficult and confusing time of [my] life." Curiously, unlike other friends of Rebecca who shared their memories, Burns and her son were never acknowledged or thanked on the website by Rebecca's parents.

Although he had moved to New York to be with Rebecca, just before her death Millard returned to Toronto, where he soon became involved with a new woman, wooing her with helicopter rides, trips to see art installations, and talk of a future together. A year or two later, that relationship also ended badly, with both Millard and the woman accusing each other of assault. Police pressed charges against the woman, but not against Dellen Millard.

For his next serious girlfriend, the young woman to whom he would eventually become engaged, Millard went with someone his mother recommended. Jennifer Spafford was the ballerina daughter of one of Burns's childhood friends, and by all accounts she and Millard were a striking couple who impressed others with their good looks and outwardly happy relationship. Millard took her travelling to Europe and Asia, treating her to expensive spas and a lifestyle well beyond the reach of a ballet teacher. In 2010, they bought a house in Oakville for $600,000 in cash, which was registered in Spafford's name and renovated by Javier Villada. Up until Millard's arrest, she drove a car registered in her ex-fiancé's name and lived in one of his condos. When Madeleine Burns was asked what her son's fiancée was like, she replied that she was "a nice girl but expensive." Apparently, even Millard was shocked at the cost of the designer wedding dress friends say Spafford selected to go with the Tiffany engagement ring he gave her.

Despite their break-up, Spafford and Millard remained friendly. On the night Wayne Millard was found dead, in November 2012, she was at the Maple Gate house with Dellen and his mother. And she and Millard texted back and forth the week Tim Bosma was murdered, arranging breakfast and yoga dates, and flirting. Along with Lisa Whidden and Christina Noudga, who was Millard's official girlfriend at the time, that made Spafford love interest number three.

Noudga was introduced into Millard's circle by a former boyfriend who knew Andrew Michalski. She was also from Etobicoke, though she was slightly younger and attended a different school from most of the Millard entourage. Her parents were immigrants from Ukraine who had come to Canada around 1995, when Christina was three. The family lived modestly in a small bungalow. Dellen Millard offered Christina a taste of a more lavish lifestyle. "She really worshipped Dellen," said a former acquaintance who didn't want to be named. "I remember talking on the phone with her for, like, forty-five minutes, and she said how Dellen was a genius, the hardest working guy she's ever met, going on about how great he was."

Noudga's Facebook profile photo at the time of Millard's arrest showed her wearing a red dress and embracing Millard, who is kissing her on the forehead. He is front and centre, while her face is hidden by her long dark hair. To show off her rich, good-looking, older boyfriend, Christina is willing to conceal her own face. Yet despite her devotion, she never received the full Jenn Spafford princess treatment. No house, no car, no engagement ring. Even as she took on an ever more central role in Millard's life, she continued to live at home with her parents and work at part-time jobs to pay tuition.

Until the trial, the news media often featured the same two photographs of Noudga. One, taken after Millard returned from the Baja race in 2011, shows a pretty young woman in a leather jacket holding Pedo the puppy and smiling sweetly down upon him; in the second, Noudga grins broadly and looks supermodel-esque. She's dressed in a red jumpsuit, ready to go skydiving with Millard and a group of his identically clad friends and relatives, many of whom were visiting from France. Noudga's YouTube account, under the name ChristinaEnn, shows an uglier side of her, however. In a video titled "Equadorian," posted in 2007, she and her friend Karoline secretly film an Ecuadorean couple going for a walk in a snowy wooded area. "The Ecuadoreans are taking a trip," says one of the girls in a whispery voiceover. "The Ecuadorean girl is very ugly. The guy is way too attractive to be with her." As the couple starts walking up an icy hill, taking care to avoid falling, the narrator keeps up her commentary. She seems irritated that the Ecuadoreans haven't slipped. "What the fuck is your problem? I live in fucking Canada," she says. "Why the fuck haven't they fallen?" Then she and her friend laugh about how the couple have spotted them and realize they're being talked about and ridiculed. Christina and Karoline are mean girls.

They were also both friends of Laura Babcock, who vanished in the summer of 2012, almost a year before the murder of Tim Bosma. The disappearance did not receive media attention at the time, but things changed after Millard's arrest. As soon as Babcock's ex-boyfriend Shawn Lerner heard Millard's name mentioned in connection with the Bosma case, he contacted Babcock's parents, who then got in touch with the police. Babcock's phone bill showed that the last eight calls she had made before she disappeared were to Dellen Millard.

In the view of the police, it wasn't that surprising that Babcock would go missing of her own volition. Although she was a recent graduate of the University of Toronto in English and drama and came from a stable middle-class family, Babcock had experienced a lot of upheaval in the last few months before her disappearance. She was no longer the bubbly flautist who had joined the high school marching band, or the young woman who had charmed customers at the toy store where she worked part-time. She had had a mental health crisis, had combined recreational drugs with her prescription meds, and had been asked to leave her parents' home. This caused the police to think of her as a possible runaway or a voluntary disappearance. According to Lerner, when he had originally brought Babcock's phone bill and other information to their attention, the Toronto cops brushed him off and accused him of playing CSI.

He says the police even suggested to him that because he wasn't a family member, he didn't have the right to file a missing person report. The obvious inference was that they thought he was some kind of stalker, a perception supported by the fact that it was Lerner, the ex-boyfriend, and not Babcock's parents, Clayton and Linda, who originally reported her missing, on July 14, 2012. Lerner has always been exceedingly diplomatic about the Babcock family's handling of their daughter's disappearance. He explains that because she was no longer living at home, her friends were naturally the first to note her prolonged absence. He emphasizes that the Babcocks notified the Toronto Police that their daughter was missing a few days after he did and were interviewed by detectives from 22 Division in Etobicoke, the same Toronto suburb where the Millards lived. When Babcock's phone bill arrived in the mail, he says her parents shared it with both him and the police and asked the police to contact Dellen Millard.

But the police appear not to have acted on the phone information, and the Babcocks didn't push further other than to repeat their request. They seem to have believed that ruffling police feathers could hinder rather than help the investigation. And despite the fact that Babcock had never disappeared for an extended period before, they had an almost irrational faith that nothing bad had happened to her. Perhaps, they thought, she had just left on some kind of adventure from which she would eventually return.

Lerner was more suspicious. Over the course of his dealings with the Toronto Police, he became convinced that once they heard about Babcock's drug habit, they were less diligent. When he contacted Sergeant Stephen Woodhouse, the officer in charge of the investigation, to check if he had spoken to Dellen Millard, Woodhouse did not return his emails. Because Woodhouse's voice mail was often full, Lerner was almost never able to leave a phone message, and on the rare occasion that he could, he says no one got back to him. (Later, in a May 2013 story in the *National Post*, Woodhouse stated that the original police investigators were not aware of the relationship between Babcock and Millard, and contended that her phone records were not brought to their attention at the time.)

Out of frustration, Lerner decided to contact Millard himself soon after Babcock's disappearance. He got no response until he sent Millard a text saying he had Babcock's phone bill and was wondering about her last eight calls with him. Millard responded immediately, suggesting they get together at once, as early as that afternoon. Lerner couldn't make it until the next day, and the two men agreed to meet for coffee at a bookstore Starbucks west of Toronto. Millard was sipping a drink and leafing through magazines when Lerner arrived a few minutes late. Millard initially denied having spoken with Babcock, changing his story only when Lerner produced Babcock's phone bill from his bag. Oh, yes, Millard then recalled, she had been looking for drugs.

Lerner pressed to find out more, but Millard cut the conversation short, saying he had to hurry to another engagement. After the meeting, Lerner says, he tried again to get Sergeant Woodhouse to talk to Millard and to trace the iPad that Lerner had loaned Babcock to help her look for work and a place to live. He had given it to her the last time they met, on June 26, 2012, at the food court in the Eaton Centre shopping mall in downtown Toronto.

By that point, the glowing, brown-haired girl-next-door, whom Lerner had dated for more than a year before they broke up in December 2011, had transformed into a skinny blonde who sometimes went by the name Elle Ryan. Not long after her split from Lerner, she had moved in with a new boyfriend. The relationship ended badly a few months later when she went to the police and had David Austerweil arrested for assault, theft under $5,000, and the sexual assault of a friend. The charges, which were dropped after Babcock vanished, stemmed from an incident that took place in February 2012. The *Toronto Star* reported that Austerweil, Babcock, and a friend of Babcock's were taking a variety of drugs when the women started stripping and kissing each other for an online sex cam. According to Austerweil, Babcock was registered at the site, where anyone can sign up to perform live sex acts and receive payment.

Since graduating from university, Babcock had been at a loss about what to do with her life. The mental health problems she had fought against for years had begun to take over, and she went from doctor to doctor looking for a diagnosis and treatment. A few weeks before the sex cam incident and the arrest of Austerweil, Babcock had been caught shoplifting a lipstick from a Winners store in downtown Toronto. When security guards stopped her, she repeatedly banged the back of her head against the building's exterior wall, causing the injury that Austerweil says police later blamed on him. His broken finger, he said, was the result of him hitting a wall in frustration after Babcock punched him repeatedly.

Her relationship with Austerweil over, Babcock moved from one friend's home to another, sleeping on their couches and wearing out her welcome with her increasingly erratic behaviour.

She felt she couldn't go home because her parents had asked her to leave after she threatened her mother with a wooden spoon. In an effort to keep her safe, Lerner paid for Babcock to stay at the Days Inn, now a Howard Johnson, in the west end of the city. While it wasn't the greatest accommodation or location, the hotel accepted dogs, and that was important for Babcock, whose small white Maltese, Lacey, accompanied her almost everywhere. A few days before she disappeared, Babcock dropped Lacey off at her parents' house along with a shoebox full of cash.

LAURA BABCOCK LIKED TO meet men through online dating sites. If they met with her approval, she would sometimes invite them out again with friends, including Christina Noudga and Karoline. Most of the time, the man would end up picking up the tab for all the young women. Then, as part of their game, they would figure out which of the women the man should date. Babcock liked to play matchmaker—and sometimes match un-maker. This type of fooling around was fun at first for many of her friends, but it often lost its appeal and resulted in rifts. Not long before Babcock disappeared, her friendships with Christina and Karoline had reached a breaking point. Babcock had moved in on Noudga's territory, sleeping with Millard and gossiping to her friends about it.

Babcock told her uncle Thomas Ryan, who would get married two weeks before she went missing, that she wanted to bring a date to his wedding, a wealthy guy who was a pilot and photog-rapher. But Ryan had heard that Babcock was running with a bad crowd and was worried about her showing up with a brand-new boyfriend.

Before she made her last phone calls to Dellen Millard, on July 2 and 3, 2012, Babcock phoned Nicole MacLeod—an old high school friend with whom she had recently got back in touch—looking for somewhere to stay. "I was in no position to be able to offer my home at the time," Nicole later wrote on Websleuths about the July 1 call. "And that's something that eats away at me pretty hard sometimes. I know if I have kids someday, I will be that mom that lets kids stay when they need a place to go."

AFTER BABCOCK DISAPPEARED, Nicole MacLeod joined the Help Us Find Laura group on Facebook, set up by Shawn Lerner. In his first post, on July 18, 2012, he wrote, "This is Laura's friend Shawn. I logged on to her account to create this group. I am sorry if I got your hopes up when you saw she was online but I just wanted to create this group through her account so I can invite all her friends. As you may have heard Laura ('Elle Ryan' to some of her friends) has been missing for the past 3 weeks."

Lerner urged anyone with any information to contact him, the police, or Crime Stoppers. And on the off chance that Babcock herself might see his post, Lerner wrote, "Laura, in case you are reading this know that we love you and are worried sick. If you don't want to be found, you don't have to tell us where you are. Just get in touch with someone to confirm you are safe."

Lerner made a poster and asked for help distributing it, adding that Babcock's father, Clayton, would cover any printing and travel costs. MacLeod volunteered to help with the poster and leaflet campaign, as did other friends. On August 4, Lerner announced: "$5000 Reward for anyone who has information that enables us to locate Laura. Cash and no questions asked. Please help us spread the word."

Through July and August, worried friends checked in to the Facebook group, asking if there was any news and making suggestions. Dellen Millard never joined the group, but Christina Noudga and Andrew Michalski did. Noudga did not participate in any of the discussions. Michalski tweeted from his Twitter account asking if anyone had seen "Ryan."

In the fall, another of Babcock's friends posted her information on The Dirty (www.thedirty.com), a gossip site featuring both celebrity news and trash talk about the non-famous. Babcock had been a fan of The Dirty and read it loyally, so her friend thought it might be a good way to get a message to her. "She has not been heard from by her parents or friends since June 30 and everyone is worried sick," the friend wrote. "Since she was last seen, there has been no activity on any of her social networking accounts, credit card, email or cellphone."

The Dirty posting led to a clue that Babcock might be in Las Vegas, working at a strip club called the Rhino or close by. Shawn Lerner and Babcock's mother contacted the club and Las Vegas Metropolitan Police but got nowhere. By the new year, the Facebook postings had slowed to a trickle. On one of the last posts before the news of Dellen Millard's arrest broke, Nicole MacLeod commented, "I think about Laura a lot. . . . I really wish I had been able to help her somehow before she went missing. . . . The lack of coverage still disturbs me to this day."

MISSING

TIM BOSMA

PLATE NUMBER
726-7ZW

The Hamilton Police Service is seeking the assistance of the public in locating a missing 32-year-old Hamilton man.Timothy Bosma was reported missing to the Hamilton Police Service on May 6th, 2013 in the Ancaster area.

The Hamilton Police Service and his family are concerned for his well being and are asking for the help of the public in locating him. Timothy was last seen in his 2007 black Dodge Ram 3500 pick-up truck with license plate number 726-7ZW. Timothy was last seen wearing dark blue jeans, work boots, and a long sleeve shirt.

Hamilton Police continue to investigate and are asking anyone with information on the whereabouts of Timothy Bosma to contact the on duty CID investigator from Division 3 CID at 905-546-4930 or

CRIME STOPPERS AT 1-800-222-8477

The mystery of Tim Bosma's disappearance made headlines across Canada.

Dellen Millard photographed on the day of his arrest, May 10, 2013, four days after the murder of Tim Bosma.

Mark Smich under police surveillance, the week before his arrest on May 22, 2013.

Mark Smich with Marlena Meneses at the wedding of Smich's sister, May 19, 2013, less than two weeks after Bosma's murder.

Toronto Police Service
News release

46 College Street • Toronto, ON • M5G 2J3   www.torontopolice.on.ca

**Missing woman,
Laura Babcock, 23,
Update to investigation**

Above: Missing woman Laura Babcock, 23

After the arrest of Dellen Millard, Toronto Police released a notice for missing person Laura Babcock, who disappeared in July 2012. Both Millard and Smich face first-degree murder charges in the death of Babcock, who dated Millard.

The Eliminator, bought by Millard in 2012,
was used to incinerate the body of Tim Bosma.

Forensic anthropologist Dr. Tracy Rogers climbs inside to retrieve as much of Bosma's
remains as possible, both for the prosecution and his family.

Bosma's Dodge Ram 3500 was examined at an OPP facility in Tillsonburg, Ontario.
It was found in a trailer in the driveway of Dellen Millard's mother,
Madeleine Burns, in Kleinburg, Ontario.

The Millardair hangar at Waterloo International Airport
became a storage facility for Dellen Millard's alleged thefts.
Millard and Smich transported the Eliminator and Bosma's body here.

Dellen Millard's defence team, Nadir Sachak and Ravin Pillay,
were a contrast in courtroom styles.

Mark Smich's legal team, Thomas Dungey and Jennifer Trehearne,
used a cutthroat defence, blaming Millard as the shooter.

Christina Noudga (centre) with lawyer Paul Mergler and her mother.
Noudga's attire and her courtroom behaviour caused a stir.

Detective Greg Rodzoniak (left) and Staff Sergeant Matt Kavanagh
head into court on February 9, 2016 in Hamilton.

The prosecution team addresses the media after the guilty verdict.
Assistant Crown attorneys Craig Fraser (left), lead prosecutor Tony Leitch (centre)
and Brett Moodie (right) were methodical and relentless in their pursuit
of a first-degree murder conviction.

A tearful but composed Sharlene Bosma, with Hank Bosma (right) and family behind
her, addresses media and supporters after the verdict. "For Tim's murderers, their life
sentence begins now. And ours began over three years ago when they murdered Tim."

That all changed when Dellen Millard, the last person Laura phoned, was charged with murder. All of a sudden, her disappearance was in the headlines and her pictures were all over the news and social media. During the final week of May 2013, with new information sufficient to obtain a search warrant, police and forensic vans descended again on Dellen Millard's farm. This time they were looking not for evidence related to the Tim Bosma case but for clues that would help Toronto Police with their reinvigorated investigations into the disappearance of Babcock and the sudden death of Wayne Millard, which had originally been deemed a suicide. Working alongside Waterloo Regional Police and Ontario Provincial Police, homicide detectives from Toronto supervised the search of a piece of land close to the barn, later described as "an area of interest." Among other things, police used a ground-penetrating radar device. The search lasted three days and was occasionally hampered by fog and rain.

At a news conference held the following week at Toronto Police Headquarters, Detective Mike Carbone revealed to reporters that the search had yielded no new evidence. A homicide cop who had only recently been put in charge of the Laura Babcock and Wayne Millard cases, Carbone faced a barrage of questions from reporters about the earlier handling of these investigations. By the end of the twelve-minute news conference, he looked like a man whose bosses had sent on suicide mission. His situation wasn't helped by the fact that he was wearing a dark wool jacket on a June day. His forehead glistened ever brighter as he insisted to skeptical reporters that the Wayne Millard and Laura Babcock investigations had been, in his chosen words, "thorough" and "traditional."

Carbone remained on message, dodging the many questions about why no one had ever followed up on Babcock's phone bill. He suggested too that there may have been a sighting of Babcock after July 4. And without anyone in the Toronto Police having given prior warning to Babcock's parents, he said she was "known to be involved in the sex trade business as an internet escort" and had a non-traditional dating relationship with Millard.

"We were stunned," Clayton Babcock said after the news conference. "She also had a university degree. She had her issues, but she is a very nice young woman."

In the normally cop-friendly *Toronto Sun*, columnist Joe Warmington wrote that even some police officers on the case were taken aback by Carbone's statement. "'It was dirty because we don't even really know how accurate or extensive that is,'" Warmington quoted an unnamed detective as saying. The detective called it nothing but an exercise by Toronto Police to "cover their butt on what they didn't do."

On the Help Us Find Laura page on Facebook, Shawn Lerner posted that Babcock's life had been turned upside down in a matter of months. "I don't know exactly when or how the drugs and this apparent involvement in the escort business started. The first I learned of either was in talking to some of her friends after her disappearance. I'm not trying to justify her actions, I just want to provide some context for what she was going through at the time. I think the police were content to close the book on this case as soon as they heard the words 'drugs' and 'escort.' I hope the public doesn't feel the same way since we need everyone's help to find her and bring her home safe."

TEN

THE BROS

Dellen Millard acquired his burner cell phone in March 2013. Even though the Toronto Police had inexplicably failed to follow up with him about Laura Babcock's last calls to his regular cell, Millard knew he might not get that lucky again. He realized that his own phone could connect him to people he didn't want to be connected to. What he failed to understand was that the pings from his cell phone also told an important story. Early in the trial, the prosecution introduced a PowerPoint exhibit tracking the movement of Millard's and Smich's cell phones, as well as the new burner phone registered in the name of Lucas Bate.

The presentation began with a display of calls made from the Bate phone on the evening of Friday, May 3. Two were to men selling Dodge Ram trucks: Dennis Araujo, at 8:33 P.M., followed by Omar Palmili, at 8:36. Less than half an hour later, at 9:01, a call was made on Millard's phone. All three of these calls bounced off cell towers near Millard's Maple Gate home. The same pattern occurred on Saturday, May 4, as the burner phone was used to contact truck sellers while Millard made and received calls to friends on his personal phone. Once again, the cell tower information suggested the two phones were together at Millard's home.

Andrew Michalski, Millard's worshipful Baja companion, who was living at Maple Gate at the time, tells the court that he recalls his friend looking for a truck that weekend. Millard showed him a Kijiji ad for a black Dodge Ram 3500 pickup on his computer. "He asked me if he should steal it from the asshole or the nice guy," Michalski says. "I told him to fuck off."

"Why was that the response you gave?" asks prosecutor Craig Fraser.

"I didn't think he needed to steal a truck."

"'Asshole' or 'nice guy.' Did you know who he was referring to?"

"No."

That May 4 afternoon, the burner phone had been used to call Omar Palmili, Igor Tumanenko, and Tim Bosma, and test drives were set up for the next day with Palmili and Tumanenko. Most likely, Tumanenko, the Russian who had served in the Israeli army, was the seller Millard referred to as "the asshole." The nice guy could have been either Palmili or Bosma, but in the courtroom a lot of people automatically assume Millard was referring to Tim Bosma. It's an uncomfortable moment in Michalski's testimony, which is overall very damning for both accused.

Michalski makes a far better impression in real life than he does on Facebook. He is big and tall, with chin-length hair pulled back in a partial ponytail. On his first day of testimony, he wears a light-blue sports jacket, white shirt, and black pants. For the three days he is on the witness stand, he is accompanied in the courtroom by his mother, brother, and aunt. He is respectful of court procedures, and he and his brother allow the media to photograph them as they arrive at and leave the courthouse. He is a confident and credible witness.

Michalski says that on the Sunday before Tim Bosma disappeared, he left the Maple Gate house at about 1 P.M. to go rollerblading along the Lake Ontario waterfront with his cousin. He remembers having seen Millard alone at the house that morning, before Millard's cell phone data put him near Mark Smich's mother's Oakville home in the early afternoon. By 3 P.M., both Millard's and Smich's phones, along with the Bate phone, were in North Toronto, near Igor Tumanenko's apartment building. The Bate phone was used to call Tumanenko to tell him the potential truck buyers were waiting downstairs. During that same one-hour period, the Smich phone received texts from Marlena Meneses, his girlfriend, and the Millard phone received a text from an unknown number. All of these communications pinged towers near Tumanenko's home. At 4:36, when the Sunday test drive was over, the Bate phone was used again to call that other possible nice guy, Omar Palmili. He was lucky enough to sleep through it.

Michalski remembers speaking to Millard and Smich in the kitchen at Maple Gate at about five o'clock that afternoon. They told him they had been on a test drive and Smich said he was sick.

"That was their excuse for not stealing the truck," Michalski says.

"Can you recall anything else they said?" asks Fraser.

"They mentioned they were going to see another truck later on in the week," says Michalski. He tells Fraser that Millard's demeanour was normal, while Smich looked visibly sick.

Fraser asks why Michalski didn't say anything about the truck stealing plan.

"I think I was more minding my own business than anything," Michalski says.

The next day, Monday, May 6, Michalski left early to work a seven-to-four shift at the Campbell Soup Company in Etobicoke. He didn't see his housemate Millard, who met his mother for lunch at a Bier Markt restaurant, where he picked up a certified cheque for $420,000 to help him out of his condo-closing difficulties. At some point during the day, Millard also gave Javier Villada, who was working at widening the Maple Gate driveway, some $900 in back pay.

By about 8 P.M., texts between Millard and Shane Schlatman were bouncing off a tower near Smich's home. Millard was picking up his friend for another test drive. From 8:45 to 9:00 P.M., both the Smich and Millard phones were pinging towers in Ancaster as they sent and received texts. At 9:05, the Bate phone also pinged an Ancaster tower, when it called Tim Bosma. It was the last communication the burner phone ever made. The Smich phone texted Meneses from Ancaster at 9:20 P.M. and then either shut down or was turned off for the next twelve hours. The Millard phone stayed on, receiving a series of texts that evening from Lisa Whidden, Millard's realtor girlfriend. During the early morning of May 7, they text chatted casually about pets as the body of Tim Bosma was being incinerated within metres of Millard.

The message telling Schlatman and Jennings not to come to the hangar was sent at 5:55 A.M., minutes before GA Masonry's video camera recorded the Eliminator being towed into the hangar. A few hours later, when he was back at home, Millard sent his text reassuring Schlatman that he hadn't done anything wrong and should just take the day off. Meanwhile, Smich, who had returned to his mother's house in Oakville, charged up his phone and received all the text messages he had missed overnight, including several from Meneses, who had been worried about whether her boyfriend, who she knew was out stealing a truck, was okay.

Andrew Michalski's first sighting of Millard on Tuesday, May 7, was late in the afternoon, when Michalski got home from work. "He was on the computer. I asked him if they got the truck, and he said yes."

"If you can reflect back, was there any manner, demeanour, associated with it?" asks Craig Fraser.

"I don't remember the demeanour."

Why had Michalski asked him if they got the truck? Fraser wants to know.

"I was just curious."

"Do you recall, after Tuesday, May 7, when it was that you next saw Dell?"

"I don't believe I saw him that week," says Michalski, who first learned something was wrong when Mark Smich contacted him the following Friday night, after Millard's arrest.

MATTHEW HAGERMAN, WHO AS a high school student had introduced the older Dellen Millard to his circle of friends, tells the court that in the year before Tim Bosma was murdered, the group surrounding Millard—including himself and Andrew Michalski—had begun to disconnect. "Everybody got busy with their own lives," he says. "We were all backing away. We all had our own things happening." But the more Hagerman talks, the more it becomes apparent that his definition of disconnecting won't be shared by everyone. By his own admission, he and Millard texted each other several times a week. And when Millard's driver's licence was suspended in October 2012, for reasons that are not revealed in court, Hagerman acted as his personal paid driver.

While Hagerman was no longer living in Millard's basement, as he once did, he was still closely tied to the friend he said he had known for as long as he could remember. His grandmother Dina had cared for Millard's grandmother when she was dying of cancer. Until Wayne Millard died, Dina had looked after his and Dellen's many pets at Maple Gate, done laundry for Wayne, and prepared some of his meals. Despite these connections, Hagerman was spared the social media notoriety experienced by Shane Schlatman and Andrew Michalski. Unlike them, he never had his name bandied about on Facebook and Twitter as a possible accomplice in the Bosma murder. In fact, until he was called to testify at the trial, he had successfully avoided the unflattering spotlight this tragedy has cast.

A slight, bearded man with a hipsterish look, Hagerman appears visibly anxious in the courthouse halls before his testimony begins. When he leaves court, he hides his face behind a scarf, a toque, and sunglasses and dives into the back of a waiting car. He is accompanied throughout by his father and another middle-aged man. Hagerman walks tentatively to the witness box and back, sometimes casting a quick glance at Dellen Millard. On the stand, he fights to hold back tears as a side of his life that has remained hidden is exposed.

Craig Fraser displays what is known as an extraction report on the courtroom screens. It shows text messages between

Hagerman and Millard from October 2012 taken from Millard's phone. The first message is sent at 5:20 P.M. on October 2, 2012, from Millard. "Need a lookout on walkie talkie tonight. 10pm-3am. $50 or credit towards future grabs," he writes. "Interested?"

"I have a movie date at 10:20," Hagerman answers. "Movie runs until 12:30 so i'd be able and willing to help around 1. Where is this going down?"

"That might actually work out. Waterloo."

"Lol okay. What are you going to be thieving?"

"Lawnmowers. 2 ride ones."

Although Millard arranged to pick up Hagerman at a nearby park, the heist fell through. The lawnmowers had been moved before the gang of thieves could get to them. Millard texted Hagerman that they would have to steal them the following spring.

Two and a half weeks later, on October 19, another "mission"—as Millard and his crew called them—was planned. "Just scoped a construction project with a lot of trees being prepped to be planted," Millard texted. "You want some 20′ maples?"

"Lmao what. How is this going to work?"

"Gotta scope night security. $100 to each lookout upon mission success."

"What's the mission? Must be dangerous if you're paying :o"

"Not dangerous for lookouts. Along the same lines as the last one but bigger. 3 am-5am. I'm going to catch some sleep."

"Okay. Goodnight sweet prince," wrote Hagerman. It was the type of line he liked to use.

"Kowalski will get you if you're down," Millard wrote. Kowalski was a nickname for Andrew Michalski, who would be along on the mission, as would Mark Smich and Steven Kenny, another member of the Millard circle. They would be stealing a Bobcat. Although the mission was planned for 3 to 5 A.M., it ran late, like almost everything Millard organized. It wasn't until 4:15 that Hagerman was picked up at his parents' house, where he lived.

Hagerman was deposited on a rural road north of Toronto with a walkie-talkie, Kenny was stationed on another road, and Michalski drove around in the more immediate vicinity, keeping an eye out for anyone who might spot the thieves. Millard and Smich were pulling a trailer. They grabbed the Bobcat, stashed it in the trailer, then drove to the Millardair hangar at Waterloo Airport, where everyone convened at 7:30 A.M. Shane Schlatman removed the GPS from the Bobcat.

An emotional Hagerman tells the court that this was the only time he ever served as a lookout on one of Millard's missions. Millard looks on and smirks.

ON MAY 9, 2013, HAGERMAN had just returned from a vacation and was back to working his regular evening shift bartending at an Etobicoke pub. His father stopped by to give him his newly repaired phone. As soon as he checked it, Hagerman saw he had missed a series of calls from Christina Noudga, whom he knew casually as Dellen Millard's girlfriend. The number and frequency of the calls made him assume right away that something must be wrong, but when he tried to phone back there was just dead air. His phone had not been properly repaired and the speaker was broken. He couldn't hear anything.

After a few more failed attempts at calling, Hagerman started communicating by text. Although Millard never identified himself as the user of the phone, Hagerman was aware right away that the person on the other end was Millard, not Noudga, and that he wanted to ask him a favour. "He was feeling some heat. He wanted me to hang on to something for a few days," Hagerman tells the court, adding that Millard reassured him it was nothing serious.

In a text message, Hagerman asked what the "toys" Millard wanted him to keep were, so that he could prepare himself.

"A toolbox," came the reply at 1:52 A.M.

"Haha full of guns," Hagerman texted back.

Millard responded just with three dots (". . ."), sidestepping further questions.

To calm his nerves, Hagerman texted two close friends about getting together to discuss the "rather shady" situation. As he recalls, he met up with one of them and then returned home to await Millard's arrival. At 4:10 A.M., he received a text from his friend that read simply "2." It meant he was to meet Millard in the driveway in two minutes, Hagerman tells the court.

Craig Fraser walks across the courtroom to pick up a yellow-and-black Stanley toolbox in a transparent plastic evidence bag. He takes it to the witness stand and places it in front of Hagerman.

"Does that look familiar?" he asks with distaste.

Hagerman says it does; it's the toolbox Millard gave him.

"Did it have a lock?"

"It had a small padlock."

Fraser asks what vehicle Millard was driving when he pulled up that Friday morning.

"The Yukon," says Hagerman. "The windows were very tinted, but I was sure there was someone else in the car. I couldn't say who."

What did Millard say? asks Fraser. How was he acting?

He was dishevelled, says Hagerman. "I asked him if everything was okay, and he told me it was better if he didn't tell me." According to Millard, Hagerman would need to hang on to the toolbox for "a couple of weeks, tops."

Did Hagerman ask what was inside?

Hagerman says he didn't, because he was familiar with the toolbox. He had seen it at Millard's Maple Gate home many times.

"What did you associate that box with?" asks Fraser.

"Drugs that were brought out at parties."

"In the discussion up until the point he hands it over, did he ever say, 'There are drugs in here'?"

"No."

"Did you ask him?"

"I didn't, no. I figured it was what I had always seen inside of it."

Hagerman stored the toolbox in his parents' basement fruit cellar. "It would have been slightly concealed but not trying to be hidden," he says. "It was out in the open on a shelf."

"Did you attempt to see what was in the toolbox?"

"Never once."

Fraser wonders why earlier, when Hagerman was messaging Millard, he had made a joke about there being guns in the toolbox, a text Hagerman later deleted, along with many others.

Hagerman says it was an unfortunate attempt at humour, that he had no idea there could really be a gun in the toolbox. "Dellen was not someone who had an interest in guns," he insists. "I never saw one at the Maple Gate house ever."

"Can you tell us what the reason was for the police to come see you on four different occasions?"

They were suspicious of his involvement with Millard, says Hagerman, admitting he wasn't truthful when investigators talked with him on May 14, 15, and 22. That changed after Hagerman confessed to his father what was going on. Together they got a lawyer, and Hagerman finally told police the truth on May 30. His father lent him the money for the lawyer, which Hagerman paid back over the next six months.

"CALL ME ASAP," Andrew Michalski texted Matt Hagerman at 10:53 P.M. on Friday, May 10, about three and a half hours after Dellen Millard was arrested.

When he replied at 2:30 the next morning, Hagerman asked, in his typically jokey way, "What's the situation crustation [sic]?"

"We have a situation," Michalski responded at 11:15 A.M. "I need to meet you at your park today."

The two men agreed to meet in the late afternoon, with Michalski telling Hagerman, "It's really important we talk. It's about the thing someone gave you."

Hagerman assumed it was about the toolbox and asked if Millard was in trouble.

On the witness stand, Hagerman describes Michalski as being in shock. "That is when I found out he was living at Dellen's house at Maple Gate and that the cops had shown up . . . and raided the house in the morning," he says. "And that is when I first heard about Dellen's arrest."

"Was there discussion about what you had and what he had?" asks Fraser.

Hagerman says Michalski had been given a blue backpack and that Michalski knew Millard had given Hagerman something. "We were both in a panic," he says. "I was upset. This thing got thrown in my lap just a couple of days ago. And I just wanted to get rid of it."

ALTHOUGH MICHALSKI HAD SEEN Facebook posts about the disappearance of Tim Bosma and knew Millard had been going to steal a truck, he had not put two and two together when Mark Smich called him just before 9:30 on Friday night. It was the first of five phone calls they made to each other over the next few hours. Smich told him that "they've got Dell, and I should get all the drugs out of the house," Michalski says.

As soon as he got off the phone, Michalski grabbed his blue backpack, filled it with all the drugs he could find at Maple Gate, stashed it in the trunk of his car, and moved the car from the driveway to a spot across the street. He also texted Hagerman, because Smich had told him to bring "what Matt Hagerman had" and the drugs to him. He says he had no idea what item in Hagerman's possession Smich was referring to.

The next day, Michalski went to work, an early Saturday shift at Campbell's. In the lunchroom on the TV, he saw that Millard had been arrested for forcible confinement in the Tim Bosma case and started to panic. "I realized what I had in my car and it needed to go to Mark and that was it," he states in court.

At two o'clock, he left work early and headed for Hagerman's house. He suggested to his friend that they should use the Hagerman family car, since Matt's parents were away at their cottage. When asked about Hagerman's demeanour, Michalski says, "I don't remember. I think both of us were uncomfortable."

Smich wanted them to bring the toolbox and backpack directly to his girlfriend's sister's apartment, where he was temporarily hiding out. "But when I saw the news, I didn't want to see him, make contact with him," says Michalski. He arranged a drop-off behind a Shoppers Drug Mart store near Smich.

As he made the twenty-minute drive down the QEW to Oakville, with Hagerman at the wheel, Michalski kept in touch with Smich by text. Hagerman turned on the radio to confirm that Millard's arrest was all over the news, as Michalski had said. When he heard a report about the Bosma case, Hagerman pulled the car over and demanded they get rid of the backpack and toolbox right then and there. They didn't, but in the ensuing panic and confusion, they ended up at the wrong drop spot, a Shoppers Home Health Care Outlet instead of the store Smich had in mind. At the back of a small strip mall, they went down a concrete staircase to an electrical room and left the backpack and toolbox for Smich at the foot of the stairs.

Smich wanted to send his buddy Brendan Daly to do the pickup, but he wasn't answering texts or calls. He had to rely on another friend, Arthur, to do it. Arthur's last name isn't revealed in court, but Smich's co-accused on his 2012 mischief charge for graffiti was Artour Sabouloua, age twenty-one, of Oakville. According to Daly, Smich referred to Artour as his bitch.

In spite of the fact that Daly saunters up to the witness box with his hands in the pockets of baggy jeans that are about to fall off his backside, he makes a credible witness. He is the friend pictured in the surveillance photos of Mark Smich and has important knowledge of what exactly happened in May 2013. After Daly's parents realized he had become inadvertently involved in the Tim Bosma murder, they hired a lawyer on his behalf. Daly's counsel advised him to tell the truth, which he appears to do. It is a popular misconception that lawyering up means shutting up and saying nothing. In cases like Daly's—where someone has knowledge of a serious crime but was not a party to it and is unlikely to face charges—a good lawyer will generally advise his or her client to come clean and ensure that justice is done.

Daly, who is a few years younger than Smich, lived around the corner, less than a minute from his friend's house. They had met three or four years earlier, when Daly spotted Smich sitting on his porch and they struck up a conversation. It was their habit to smoke up together almost every morning. In 2013, neither of them was working and Marlena Meneses was often around.

Daly didn't notice anything out of the ordinary about his friend's behaviour until the Thursday night of the week Tim Bosma was killed. He was waiting outside Smich's mother's house to collect some marijuana. "I remember Dell's truck zooming by, Mark hopping out, running into the house, sending Marlena out a couple of minutes later, and then she basically told us to scram." He found it strange that Mark, whom he thought of as his best friend, didn't say anything to him. As Daly recalls, Smich told him about Millard's arrest very soon after it happened, when he became nervous and jumpy and moved into Marlena's sister's place.

Smich told Daly there was a gun in the toolbox and that one of the reasons he had moved was that he didn't feel safe being in the same place as the firearm, which he had stored in the bottom of either the washer or dryer in his mother's garage. "He was just trying to lay low there, avoid being seen by anybody," says Daly. "I think that he said people were looking for him."

The next day or over the weekend, Smich told Daly that people were coming to get him. For some reason that is never explained in court, he was especially scared of the victim's friends. "These guys don't fuck around, they're going to come back. They're going to find me," he said. "I fucked up, man. I fucked up. These niggas are coming to get me."

Smich deleted his Facebook account, got rid of his phone, and generally acted paranoid. Daly had never seen him in such a state. He would use Marlena's phone or borrow Daly's, going out on the balcony to make calls or send texts. When he gave the phone back, all the recent activity would be deleted. When Daly asked Smich if he was involved in the Bosma case, Smich snapped at him, a reaction that Daly describes in court as more "defensive" than angry. The mood changed very quickly. Daly was nervous and let the subject drop.

Several days after Millard's arrest—perhaps when he had begun to think he might have escaped police notice after all—Smich told Daly that the gun in the toolbox was his. The conversation took place while Smich was showing his friends a YouTube video about ammunition. "Some zombie bullets thing [that] went with the gun he wanted," Daly says. But Mark didn't purchase that gun, he adds. Dell bought the gun that used the so-called Zombie bullets, designed to expand upon impact.

Daly says he advised Smich to "put on a work vest and hard hat and go bury [the gun] somewhere. Just pretend to be a city worker." But Smich told him he needed money for a lawyer and so intended to sell the gun as well as the weed in Michalski's blue backpack. He asked Daly to arrange a meeting with a friend of his, nicknamed Bleach, who might want to buy the gun. Daly texted Bleach. "I said, 'Do you have money?' He said, 'Why?' I told him Mark had something he wanted to get rid of. That was the extent of the text messages."

Smich was also feeling pressure from his mother and his older sister, Andrea. According to Daly, the media had shown up at their house, where preparations were taking place for his middle sister Melissa's wedding on May 19. While Smich's mother waited outside in the car, Andrea arrived at Elizabeth Meneses's apartment. She was "yelling at him, telling him to get rid of everything. And then she started yelling at me," Daly says. She told him it was a stupid idea to try to sell the gun. It is never explained how she came to find out about the gun.

As far as Daly remembers, the meeting with Bleach took place in the park beside the apartment building where Smich was staying. Mark wanted $1,000 for the gun, but Bleach had only $100 so the gun was never produced for him to see. A small marijuana transaction may have taken place. Daly says he thinks that he and Bleach hung out afterward and that Mark went his separate way. Daly doesn't know what happened to the toolbox or the gun. The first time he has seen Mark Smich since his arrest is in court.

SHOCK AND OUTRAGE BEST describe the reaction to the testimony of Matt Hagerman, Andrew Michalski, and Brendan Daly, coming as it did on the heels of Shane Schlatman's cross-examination. For many spectators, it was inexplicable that among all the people who had known something about Tim Bosma's case, not one did the right thing. On social media, Millard's friends became known as Millard's minions and Millard's morons. Once again, it fell to Mark Smich's lawyer to express the collective anger, this time targeting Matt Hagerman. Dungey was the right lawyer at the right time, so long as you were prepared to overlook the evidence which showed that his client, his client's ex-girlfriend, and his client's sister all had knowledge of the crime and did nothing about it.

Right from the start of his cross-examination, Thomas Dungey makes it clear that there is more to Hagerman than the tearful young man the jury has seen for the past two days. He holds up a bound copy of Hagerman's four police statements with bright-pink Post-it Notes sticking out all over. According to Dungey, they mark the many lies Hagerman has told. He says Hagerman's strategy was to tell the police as little as he could get away with, revealing new information only after it was uncovered by investigators. "You can sit there now and snivel, Mr. Hagerman," Dungey says. "The reality isn't that you lied once or twice. You lied at least forty times." As an example, Dungey cites how Hagerman misdirected the police when they asked if Millard had gotten in contact with him. "You were indicating that you got texts from Christina's phone. You never mentioned it was Millard," he says.

"You were his best friend?" continues Dungey, changing tack.

"I was friends with him over years," says Hagerman. "I knew him from a young age."

"Why does he come to you in the middle of the night, four in the morning, to hide a toolbox?"

"Either because I was a close friend or my house is the closest distance."

Dungey says Millard could have hidden the toolbox at the farm, the hangar, any of his other properties. "You couldn't have possibly thought it was drugs," he insists, refusing to accept that Hagerman didn't suspect it contained something else when Millard, dishevelled and agitated, dropped it off at four o'clock in the morning after a flurry of urgent texts.

Hagerman says it never occurred to him.

"Well, why are you so scared when you're going to drop it off in Oakville if you think it's drugs?"

"Because a friend of mine had been charged with a theft," says Hagerman, referring to one of the two original charges laid against Millard, which were theft over five thousand dollars and forcible confinement.

"Well, if you never thought he would have been involved, less reason to ditch it," says Dungey.

Again, Dungey insists that Hagerman knew, and again the witness denies it.

"Never crossed your innocent little mind?" says Dungey with contempt.

"I swear to you."

"You, the innocent little criminal, you suspected more than just a truck being stolen."

"I thought what I had in my possession wasn't of interest to the police."

"You had no consideration for the Bosma family or Mr. Bosma."

"I didn't want to be involved with the situation," says Hagerman. "I called Crime Stoppers."

"Well, that can't be proved," says Dungey. (Because Crime Stoppers operates on the principle of anonymity, Hagerman's claim would be difficult, if not impossible, to confirm.) "You can easily say that, can't you?"

"I told them that the other suspect they were looking for might be Mark Smich," Hagerman says. "I told them about the farm and the properties."

Dungey demands to know why Hagerman didn't call the police, and then asks him, "What are you snivelling about?" *Snivel* is definitely the word for which this cross-examination will be remembered.

"I'm nervous right now."

"You're snivelling for yourself. You're not snivelling for the Bosma family."

"I think, Mr. Dungey, we can lower the tenor with respect to this witness," says Justice Goodman.

Dungey goes back to hammering away about how Hagerman lied repeatedly, up until his fourth interview with police. Then he says, "You even lied to your father."

"Yes, I lied to a lot of people I cared about."

"When did it dawn on you you should come up with some semblance of the truth?"

Hagerman says it was when his father pointed out to him that the toolbox was locked and there could have been anything inside it.

"You were afraid it would all of a sudden come out that you were a criminal," says Dungey, pointing out that even in his fourth and final interview, where he supposedly told the police everything, Hagerman still didn't mention the Bobcat mission. "Stealing a Bobcat, Mr. Bosma's truck, you didn't see any parallel there?"

"It never crossed my mind. We were there about the toolbox," says Hagerman. "Knowing what I know now, I could have changed how things transpired."

"It took three years to come to this conclusion?" asks Dungey.

"I've been thinking about this every day for three years," he answers with a big sniffle. "I eventually told the truth."

CROSS-EXAMINATION OF WITNESSES is an opportunity for a defence team to build its theories of the crime and make the case for its client's innocence. And if necessary, the lawyers will also try to destroy the witnesses' credibility. While Dungey is determined to portray Dellen Millard as a master manipulator who dragged his friend Smich into a murder, Nadir Sachak wants to dispel the image of his client as controlling, someone who forced others into a life of crime. Yes, the rich guy liked stealing for kicks, he argues, but it was the crazy, violence-prone Smich who transformed theft into murder. When Sachak questions Hagerman and then Michalski, he makes it clear that they participated in Millard's thieving missions voluntarily.

"There is no duress, right?" Sachak asks Hagerman.

"Correct."

"There's no control?"

"Correct."

"There's no domination over you?"

"Correct."

To Michalski, Sachak points out that he was ready and willing to go along on the Bobcat mission even before he knew what it was about. He wanted to participate so much that he was prepared to ditch his girlfriend, who was staying over for the night.

"It was voluntary?" says Sachak.

"Yes," answers Michalski.

"Consensual?"

"Yes."

Sachak drives the point home. "Willing?"

Michalski agrees, but pushes back. He tells Sachak he didn't actually want to do it. Though he is not at all analytical, Michalski explains that, for him, there's a difference between willing and wanting to do something—that he was willing to participate in missions even if he didn't particularly want to.

"I don't want to get into semantics," Sachak replies. "There was no coercion, control, domination. You and your friends wanted to steal for a sense of adventure?"

Again, Michalski agrees, but as contradictory as his answers seem, in the courtroom they add to his credibility as a witness. Michalski isn't minimizing his misbehaviour and criminal acts to make himself look better. He is simply acknowledging that a part of him always knew better and didn't want to do the things he did, even if he went along with them willingly.

Michalski's and Hagerman's testimony about the thefts is not good news for their once good friend Dellen Millard. Both of them are testifying against their own interests, albeit in the face of undeniable text message evidence. With Hagerman, the best that Sachak can really do is to contrast the thieving missions with the events of the night Tim Bosma was murdered in an attempt to show they are completely different operations. He describes the past missions as methodical and carefully thought out. "There are precautions taken to ensure you guys don't get caught and if need be to abandon the mission," he says. The implication is that the theft of Tim Bosma's truck doesn't fit the pattern, therefore it could not have been planned by Dellen Millard. It's not much to work with, but it's all Sachak's got.

He has more to go on with Michalski, who, Sachak reveals, was arrested by police for the first-degree murder of Tim Bosma on May 13. In the police statement he gave at the time, Michalski said Smich sounded forceful and angry when he called him on the night of May 10 after Millard's arrest. "There are numerous calls and texts between you and Smich," Sachak tells Michalski. "They deal with one topic and one topic only. Smich wants those drugs in Dell's house. He wants you to meet with Hagerman. He wants the thing that Hagerman has . . . Smich made it abundantly clear he wants the toolbox . . . Smich is directing your movements. He's quarterbacking your movements."

Michalski agrees that he did what Smich wanted on Friday night—but not on Saturday. He answers repeatedly that he refused to deliver the toolbox and backpack personally to Smich. He was scared of where that might lead, which was why he arranged a drop spot. He sticks to his story throughout repeated questioning by Sachak, and then by Dungey, who attempts to get Michalski to admit he was doing Millard's bidding and trying to frame Smich by dropping the gun on him.

Dungey knows that Michalski is a far stronger witness than Schlatman or Hagerman. He's not telling preposterous stories like the former and, unlike the latter, he is owning up to his bad behaviour. The jury might not like it if Dungey directly attacks Michalski, so he starts off gently.

"You come from a good family," Dungey says. "What caused the thievery?"

Michalski answers that he felt safe around Millard.

"Why is that?"

"I can't explain it."

"Thinking you were indestructible?" says Dungey. He suggests there was a special kind of bonding between Michalski and Millard, and Michalski agrees.

"If you hadn't met Mr. Millard, you wouldn't have got to stealing things?"

"Probably not," says Michalski. "He had money, he could protect me. I felt confident he would do that for me."

"Did he tell you that?"

No, says Michalski. It was a feeling he got.

As he did with Hagerman, Dungey has a bound copy of the transcript from Michalski's first interview with police. It's ninety pages long, and Dungey says that for the first sixty pages, Michalski is resisting the officer.

Michalski denies that he was lying. "I was basically talking to get comfortable with the situation," he explains.

"I appreciate that. I have empathy. But these are police officers asking specific questions, and you're just not telling them the truth," says Dungey. "You've been put into this position because of Mr. Millard, that's correct?"

"Yes."

"You know he's involved?"

"Yes, sir."

"You leave out the pertinent fact of Mr. Millard and the stealing of the truck?"

"Yes, sir."

Dungey suggests again that it's because of what he repeatedly calls the "bonding" between Michalski and Millard, that it must be very strong if Michalski is protecting Millard when he himself might face first-degree murder charges for a crime he did not commit. "You hold back, and at times you lie to police, until you get to the point you realize you're in big trouble, because you want to protect your good friend Millard."

"And myself," says Michalski. "I'm also trying to escape from underneath it, just to not be involved."

Somewhat disingenuously, Dungey tells him that he wasn't involved, that he wouldn't have gotten in trouble.

"But I am here," says Michalski. "I am involved."

When Dungey suggests, as he did so effectively with Schlatman and Hagerman, that Michalski was just trying to protect Millard, it doesn't work. Michalski has already undermined that idea when Dungey asked him earlier about Millard's motives for stealing. "Why does this guy with all this money, all the possessions he has, why does he have to go steal off somebody a truck? In your mind, why do you think he does this?" Dungey asked.

"For the thrill of it," Michalski said.

"For the thrill of it," Dungey repeated for emphasis. "Because he's getting a thrill out of this thieving?"

"That's correct," said Michalski.

When Michalski has said this, it's hard for Dungey to argue now that he really wanted to protect Dellen Millard.

Dungey and Ravin Pillay, Millard's lead defence counsel, both have a tricky time cross-examining Brendan Daly, because his testimony supports some elements of their individual defence theories and undermines others. One minute Daly says something that works in either Millard's or Smich's favour, the next minute he makes the same defendant look bad. For example, Daly tells Pillay that Smich has a mean streak and difficulty controlling his anger, that his talk about violence sometimes made Daly uncomfortable. But when Pillay cites lyrics found on Smich's iPad—"My 380 [gun] is no stranger / When i'm angered you're in danger"—Daly says firmly, "No, I don't remember that." And while Daly readily agrees with Pillay that Smich talked about owning a gun and said it was his gun in the toolbox, he also insists that Smich told him Millard also had a gun.

Likewise, Daly agrees with Dungey that Smich feared Millard was going to try to frame him. He confirms that Smich needed money to hire a lawyer, which is why he tried to sell the gun. But when Dungey suggests to Daly that he wasn't pressured into helping with the sale, Daly firmly contradicts him, answering, "Yeah, I was." Daly also won't go along with Dungey's narrative that Smich was expecting only a drug drop-off, not the toolbox, and that he never owned a gun.

"Mr. Smich never told you that his gun was the one in the toolbox," Dungey says.

"Yes, he did," says Daly.

ELEVEN

INVESTIGATIONS ARE ONGOING

In late May of 2013, a small local newspaper on Manitoulin Island, in Lake Huron, got a big scoop when it learned that Ontario Provincial Police officers had been to Little Current, the island's largest settlement, to investigate a sailing trip Dellen Millard had made in the summer of 2011. Investigators arrived after Chris Blodgett, whose family owned and operated Discovery Yacht Charters in Little Current, recognized a familiar red mohawk on the evening news and realized Millard had been a customer. "His name never left my memory, especially considering the strange circumstances of his charter," Blodgett told *The Manitoulin Expositor.* Millard had rented a sailboat for a ten-day cruise of the North Channel. Thanks to his aviation background, navigation skills, and previous charter experiences, he easily met the requirements to sail a Discovery vessel. Blodgett remembered him as intelligent and well spoken, despite the hairstyle. Nor was it Millard's fault when the yacht suffered a mechanical failure while at anchor and Blodgett was called out to fix it.

Once he climbed on board, however, things got strange. Blodgett noticed spots of blood around the boat and asked what was going on. Although media outlets would later report that there was blood all over the yacht, making it sound like a grisly murder scene, in reality it was more like several drops in a few different locations. Millard explained that his companion was having her period and the toilet had blocked, which made sense to Blodgett and could also have accounted for why she didn't come out to say hello. But as the news about Millard emerged, Blodgett started to wonder why he hadn't seen the supposedly menstruating woman. He remembered too that Millard had originally left port with one young woman only to return her to shore and set off again with a second woman. He realized he hadn't seen either Millard or the second woman actually leave the boat when it was returned to Little Current.

The police performed forensic tests on the boat Millard had rented and grilled Blodgett about the details of everything that had taken place, including where exactly on Lake Huron the yacht's mechanical failure had occurred. Once officers were spotted at the Little Current docks, it didn't take long for news to spread through town of a missing woman and a blood-drenched yacht. *The Manitoulin Expositor* wrote the story up and, from there, it was a short hop to the internet. Within no time big city media had made the trek north and reporters from Toronto were insisting on speaking to Blodgett. Along with the syndicated article that had created the impression there were large amounts of blood all over the boat, a TV reporter tastelessly joked that Blodgett should offer special rates to "crime tourists" and inaccurately suggested on the evening news that Discovery Yacht Charters would be cutting rates to improve its image.

Things went from bad to worse for the tour operator when the police released a statement labelling Blodgett's concerns "unfounded," which deeply upset him. "After spending hours in interviews with investigators, fielding repeated calls from the police, having them come to my home and getting hounded by the media for days on end, I don't understand why they would choose to leave me looking discredited," he told the *Expositor*. "Don't get me wrong, the police took my report seriously and all the officers involved in this case were extremely respectful, polite and professional to me through the entire process. I just don't understand why the word 'unfounded' would be chosen when they clearly received information that my report to them was accurate, deserving of investigation and not exaggerated based on what we had seen aboard that boat back in September 2011.

"Honestly, what should I have done?" he asked.

The *Expositor* put that very question to the OPP and was told that *unfounded* is police jargon for when an investigation is wrapped up with no further concern about criminal activities. In this case, both the young women who had been on the yacht with Millard had been identified and found to be safe and secure, so the police were closing the file. "The information brought forward by Mr. Blodgett was valid, and he should be commended for that," Staff Sergeant Kevin Webb, commander of the OPP's Manitoulin detachment, told the *Expositor*. "He took initiative, recognizing some information that may have been useful for the police. We are all very pleased he did."

The yacht story was among the last Millard-related pieces to be published before news of the Tim Bosma and Laura Babcock investigations drifted out of the headlines. It coincided with a series of press reports about stolen vehicles at the Millardair

hangar, including one about Marty MacDougall, a film produ-
cer, whose Harley-Davidson motorcycle had been stolen in its
trailer from his back driveway in downtown Toronto the previous fall. While on vacation in Ireland, MacDougall received a
text from Hamilton Police telling him his motorbike had been
located, albeit in pieces, at a hangar at Waterloo Airport. The
Harley had been up for sale on Kijiji when it was stolen, and
MacDougall suspected someone might have done a reverse
lookup of his phone number to figure out where he lived and
where they could find the bike. According to witnesses, two men
in a black truck had backed in and taken it away. In addition
to the $35,000 Harley, police found multiple stolen vehicles and
parts at the Millardair hangar. They were in the process of being
repainted and their serial numbers were ground away. The operation had all the characteristics of a chop shop operation.

As the defence lawyers and prosecutors began their work
to prepare for the trial of Millard and Smich, Detective Matt
Kavanagh spoke to *The Globe and Mail* about the murder of
Tim Bosma one last time. He said there may not have been a
third suspect after all. "As an investigator, you always talk about
tunnel vision, and I think it'd be tunnel vision for me to say that
I definitely believe there's a third person or to say there wasn't,"
Kavanagh said. "It's possible that there's only two involved, and
it's also possible that there may have been a third. And so we're
looking into that and we still have some doors to shut, some
avenues of investigation. In reality, it could have been Smich.
Smich could have got out of the Bosma truck and into the Yukon.
So that's why I say I'm not sure."

OVER THE SUMMER OF 2013, there continued to be the occasional revelation about the Bosma case, but for the most part it had entered that phase of pretrial limbo where nothing very significant comes out in the news. Millard and Smich made a couple of brief procedural court appearances in Hamilton. A letter written by Millard to a jailhouse groupie, in which he proclaimed his innocence, found its way onto Facebook. And an eBay account in Millard's name showed that in October 2012 he had purchased two concealment holsters from Barsony Holsters & Belts in Oregon, including a brown leather shoulder holster for a Walther PPK and an IWB, or inside the waistband, holster for a Smith & Wesson Bodyguard .380.

It wasn't until September 2013 that Millard returned to the headlines in a big way. Police searched his farm for a third and final time. It was the most dramatic of the searches, drawing in Toronto homicide detectives, uniformed officers from the local Waterloo force, forensic technicians in lab coats, and an OPP hazmat team with oxygen tanks strapped to their backs and gas masks covering their faces. The road was lined with fire trucks, buses, and vans carrying television news crews. Forensic tents were erected, huge piles of straw were pitched from the barn, and dozens of barrels were removed for testing. The operation, police said, was related to the disappearance of Laura Babcock. It was the second and far larger of the two farm searches looking for evidence in her case and it is not yet known what, if anything, it yielded. Online sleuths speculated wildly about the barrels (the ones that it was later revealed at trial were moved by Spencer Hussey and other Millardair employees) and about a stained board that a photographer snapped being carried out of the barn.

When the search finally wrapped up, the only new information provided to the public came in answer to a reporter's question about the mysterious barrels. "The content of the barrels is known and determined not to be relevant to the investigation," said Staff Inspector Greg McLane, head of the Toronto Police homicide unit. It was the last comment he would make on the investigation before responsibility for all communications related to the Tim Bosma, Laura Babcock, and Wayne Millard cases was handed over to the OPP's Major Case Management task force.

From the police's point of view, the lack of leaks—and therefore lack of news—pertaining to their investigations was a good thing, but it caused frustrations to run high for both the public and reporters. In 2013, the news event Canadians searched for more than any other was, according to Yahoo Canada, the murder of Tim Bosma. Google Canada ranked Tim Bosma fourth on the list of the year's top trending searches, behind Toronto's globally notorious mayor Rob Ford, the late *Glee* star Cory Monteith, and the late *Fast & Furious* actor Paul Walker, but ahead of the Boston Marathon bombing and the birth of future British monarch Prince George. At CBC News websites, traffic spiked whenever new developments appeared in the Bosma case, while at *The Hamilton Spectator*, the continuing coverage of the young father's tragic death was the most read news story of 2013.

In Toronto, questions arose about the police's handling of the disappearance of Laura Babcock and the death of Wayne Millard. Would Tim Bosma and Wayne Millard have still been alive if there had been proper follow-up on Babcock's last phone bill and the police had checked into Dellen Millard in the summer of 2012? With two major investigations underway in their jurisdiction and the Tim Bosma trial pending, the Toronto Police had an excuse for not answering difficult questions about their performance. A full-fledged inquiry, if eventually it was decided one was needed, couldn't be launched until the courts had completed the trials, and that could take years. Not to mention that Laura Babcock was still missing and the police had nothing new to tell the public about the case. As for Wayne Millard, he had been cremated almost a year earlier, so it was hard to imagine what evidence investigators could possibly discover.

AS IT TURNED OUT, the lack of news did not accurately reflect what was going on behind the scenes. The police almost always know more than they are telling. The Bosma, Babcock, and Millard murder investigations were no exception. Throughout the spring and summer and into the winter of 2013–14, investigations were active on multiple fronts, using computer and mobile-device forensics, DNA, and more.

Over the course of his work on the Bosma case, James Sloots, one of the forensic biologists who examined the Bosma truck in Tillsonburg alongside officers Banks, McLellan, and Jones, wrote twelve different reports relating to DNA evidence, including the DNA found in and on the truck, the Eliminator, and the three black nitrile gloves seized from Dellen Millard's pocket at the time of his arrest. The first report was prepared on May 14, 2013, when Sloots looked for, and failed to find, blood on Dellen Millard's shoes and on leaves taken from under the Eliminator. The last report was dated September 11, 2015, as pretrial motions got going.

As he begins his testimony at trial, Sloots, who wears round glasses and has a professorial air, tells the jury, "I'm going to put on my teacher hat and give you a DNA 101 course." He wants to familiarize them with the language he uses and what a DNA profile can and cannot reveal. He reminds his listeners that half their DNA comes from their mother, half from their father. Only 1 percent of an individual's DNA is unique; the other 99 percent is shared by the entire human race. DNA can be found in blood, semen, saliva, mucus, muscle, bone, teeth, skin, and hair follicles. Not all samples taken from a crime scene will generate a sufficient quantity of DNA to proceed with testing. Sometimes, a bloodstain, for example, will yield only enough DNA for a partial, as opposed to a full, profile, which is drawn from fifteen different tests taken at fifteen different locations along the DNA strand. In the case of the blood from the Bosma truck, Sloots was easily able to get a full DNA profile and look at all fifteen DNA locations. When multiple samples of blood DNA from the truck were compared to DNA taken from Tim Bosma's toothbrush, a match was made. Although the possibility of the blood in the truck randomly matching Bosma's is one in eighteen quadrillion (a quadrillion has fifteen zeros), in court the somewhat confusing practice is to say that the person whose DNA is being tested for a match—in this case, Tim Bosma—"cannot be excluded as the source of the blood."

Sloots also tested blood found on the Eliminator by Hamilton Police. They submitted three swabs to the Centre of Forensic Sciences, but it turned out that none was sufficient to test for DNA. In December 2013, Sloots and a technologist travelled to the OPP headquarters in Orillia, Ontario, where the Eliminator had been stored, to see if they could find other samples. They took swabs from stains on the metal lip in front of the burn chamber and a metal ledge below the load door.

"Would your expertise be the same or better than a police agency?" prosecutor Craig Fraser asks Sloots.

"We see a lot of blood under a lot of different conditions," says Sloots. "We have a lot of expertise in looking at blood in different conditions."

From one of the stains identified on the ledge, Sloots was able to get a full, fifteen-test result, the same level of match obtained from the bloodstains in the truck, with the same random match probability of one in eighteen quadrillion. From another stain on the ledge, he got results from thirteen of fifteen tests, for a one-in-3.7-trillion random match probability. "It's a little more common," he tells the court, with no irony intended.

When Sloots first examined the three black nitrile gloves seized from Millard's pocket at the time of his arrest, blood was found on two of them. The exterior of the first glove had particles of blood dust on it and a mixture of male and female DNA. Inside the glove, there were DNA profiles for two males and one female. The second glove had a visible bloodstain and the DNA of a male and a female. The third glove had a female DNA profile and no blood found.

After establishing the presence of DNA on the gloves, the police obtained warrants to get full DNA profiles for Smich and Millard, who were, of course, in custody. They also arranged to get what's known as a castoff DNA sample from Christina Noudga, Millard's girlfriend. Officer Jennifer Granatier, who was then with the Hamilton Police surveillance unit, was sent to tail their "target" on September 18, 2013. She was looking for any material Noudga might discard in public—a cigarette butt, drinking straw, or paper coffee cup, for example.

Granatier waited outside the Noudga family home until Christina emerged in the morning. She followed her on the bus and subway to the university campus where Noudga studied. After Noudga bought a drink at a Booster Juice, Granatier retrieved the discarded cup and straw from a recycling bin. Sloots then compared the Noudga DNA, which was enough to run all fifteen tests, to the female DNA profile on the nitrile gloves. The DNA on the first glove was determined to be that of Tim Bosma, Dellen Millard, and Christina Noudga. The second glove had Millard's and Noudga's DNA. The third glove had only Noudga's.

ROBERT GERARD, A FORENSIC chemist at the Centre of Forensic Sciences, handled the gunshot residue, (GSR), forensics. Along with examining the so-called tapelift samplers or dabbers, taken from Tim Bosma's truck in Tillsonburg, Gerard also processed the toolbox. "I sampled the inside of the tray and then I sampled the inside of the actual box," he tells the court. He examined his samples on a scanning electron microscope, which produces images using a beam of electrons.

Gunshot residue is composed of the particles produced when a firearm is discharged and a cloud of vapour escapes. The largest source of GSR is the gun's muzzle, but it can also be expelled from ejection ports and cylinder gaps. The particles can end up on the shooter's hand and clothing, and on anything else in the area. The identification of GSR requires the presence of lead, antimony, and barium fused into a single microscopic particle. Gerard found one GSR particle in the toolbox tray.

In court he is asked by Craig Fraser if that's a significant finding. "Yes," says Gerard. "It shows an association with a firearm." Either a particle from a firearm landed in the box, a firearm was placed inside it, or someone with GSR on their hands handled it. He explains that it's not possible to tell how the particle got there or how long it was in the tray. Such particles don't evaporate or decompose, he says. "They stay there until removed by washing or handling."

With the Bosma truck, Gerard worked with a total of twelve GSR tapelift samples compared to the more standard figure of four for a typical vehicle examination. Although Gerard did not do the sampling himself in this case, he describes for the court the process typically followed. He says that for a drive-by shooting, he would sample the window area. For a getaway car, he would test the driver's door, steering wheel, and stick shift. For a firearm discharged inside a vehicle, he would sample the roof liner and other flat surfaces. In all these cases, samples would be taken exclusively from the interior as the mud and dust on the outside of a vehicle make it too difficult to find samples on the exterior.

Gerard's resulting report, prepared on June 28, 2013, showed two GSR particles on the front dash, one on both the front and rear doors on the driver's side, none on the passenger side front door, and two on the passenger side rear door. There was one particle found on the rear passenger seat and one on the back of the rear passenger seat. Nothing was found on the driver's side seats. On the roof liner, twenty-six particles were found on the driver's side. On the passenger side, where the front and back sections of the liner were sampled separately, ten particles were found in the rear and thirty-five in the front.

"What is the significance of thirty-five?" Fraser asks.

"Thirty-five would to me indicate a firearm was discharged very close to that area or someone had a lot of GSR and rubbed it into the roof. The most likely scenario is a firearm discharged close to that spot."

"Can you provide any opinion as to where the shot came from?"

"No."

"Is this a limitation generally or one specific to this case?"

"You can't use GSR to determine firing angles or anything of that nature," says Gerard. "All I can say is it's very likely a firearm was discharged within the vehicle but I can't say from which spot or which angle."

"Are those unusual values for you to see in your work?"

"For inside a vehicle, yes. I've never seen that many within a vehicle. Generally, I might get a few on the stick shift or steering wheel."

"Would it change if there were more than one shot?"

"No, because I can't distinguish," says Gerard, explaining that it's not a linear process. Firing a gun twice wouldn't necessarily double the amount of GSR. "The number of particles generally doesn't tell you how many shots were fired. The number of particles produced on any one discharge is a random chaotic event."

IN PARALLEL WITH THE work being done by the scientists at the Centre of Forensic Sciences, specialists from the OPP's technological crimes unit and Hamilton Police conducted extensive searches on Millard's and Smich's various computers, tablets, and phones. The OPP team was led by Detective Sergeant Jim Falconer, who searched for evidence on the four computers and one USB hard drive seized from Millard's Maple Gate home. Another member of Falconer's team worked on an iPad and BlackBerry belonging to Mark Smich. Hamilton Police were responsible for Millard's phone, as well as Hagerman's, Michalski's, Noudga's, Meneses's, and Daly's, among others. To examine a computer, the first thing investigators do is make a true copy, or what they refer to as "an image." For phones, it is often not possible to do this, and they have to perform what is known as an extraction. Extracting data from phones and mobile devices involves more variables and is a far more complex process than taking an image from computers. In all cases, to ensure that the original is kept intact, police work only with the copy.

Once it has been confirmed that a computer copy has been made correctly, forensics officers assess the best type of software to use based on usage patterns. In the case of Millard's Maple Gate computers, a decision was made to use C4All, a program developed by the OPP to search for picture and movie files, and Internet Evidence Finder (IEF), a commercial program sold by Magnet Forensics. "It's very efficient at searching computer data for internet browsing and electronic communications," including browser history, messaging programs, and Facebook activity, Falconer tells the court. "It wraps it all up in a nice package."

Then it's time for human beings to review the data. In this case, there were five OPP employees working for roughly two and a half months under Falconer's supervision on the Bosma, Babcock, and Wayne Millard investigations. The final report presented at trial represents the fruits of their work in regard to the Bosma murder.

The report corroborates much of the testimony heard in court. For example, Falconer's team found that dating back to November 2012 there was extensive evidence of internet browsing for a Dodge Ram truck on Millard's computers. There were also photos of the yellow-and-black toolbox that held the gun; video of the Eliminator, taken in September 2012; invoices for Villada Homes; and information about Millardair and other Millard properties.

ONE OF JIM FALCONER'S key findings relates to the Walther PPK the prosecution believes was used to kill Tim Bosma and then transferred to Mark Smich in the toolbox. The backup files for text messages sent and received by "Dell's iPhone," which Falconer recovered from one of the Maple Gate computers, showed a series of conversations between Millard and Matthew Ward-Jackson, a drug and gun dealer who went by the name of "Iish," or "Iisho." Millard had met Ward-Jackson through Mark Smich, who had gone to Catholic elementary school with him in Mississauga in the 1990s. Ward-Jackson loved low-rider cars, Hispanic gangs, and tattoos, which he had all over his body, including on his face. Like Smich, he was an aspiring rapper, most recently using the identity Krucifix14. Many of his friends and hangers-on had no idea what his real name even was.

On February 5, 2012, when Ward-Jackson texted Millard asking for Smich's new phone number, his real name showed up on Millard's screen. A few days later, when Millard contacted him about buying a gun, he texted, "Jackson? that your last name?"

"Yea," Ward-Jackson acknowledged, before providing the details of the gun: "Walther pk 9mill tomorow 2200? Proper one."

Millard asked him if he could come down on the $2,200 price and if it included ammunition.

"Na walther is a really proper wanted one. And yes I can give y grains. I tlked the guy down from 25 cuz I thought ya wouldn't wanna spend that. I can get him to bring me it now would u like it foreal?"

"Let's do it," said Millard. "pick it up tonight?"

"Can u be at my house soon? Lakeshore one?"

"30-40 mins. send me the address, encase I mix up which building."

Ward-Jackson pushed for the habitually late Millard to be punctual. "5:30 at 2537 lakeshore. 22 cash plz I'm doing ya a big favor trust. I'm not making a penny. My guys comn from niagara so plz be on time. I don't wanna look stoopid."

"I'll be there," Millard promised.

At 5:50, Ward-Jackson asked Millard if he was close by, to which Millard answered he was. At 6:22, Ward-Jackson texted that the Niagara guy was late but would be at his house in ten minutes.

"K," answered Millard. "I have till 7."

"Yea ill be there in a second and ima hop in ya car and im off to niagara ima pay dude myself. So just have it counted I gotta run. And its legit u won't have problems if u need lessons tomorow I'm free and we can go over every piece ok?"

"it's counted," said Millard. "yea going over it tomorrow some-time after 2pm is good."

Ward-Jackson brought the gun down to Millard's car at 6:45. A few minutes later, after they had parted company, it dawned on

Millard that he had forgotten an important question about the gun and whether it could be traced to any past crimes. "btw is it clean or dirty," he texted Ward-Jackson.

"Clean," came the reply.

The next day, February 13, Millard messaged, "this afternoon still good for grabbing grain?" He was referring to bullets.

Ward-Jackson said it was.

Millard said he would eat and then stop by.

"Yeah come to royal york and dundas. Td bank," said Ward-Jackson, adding that this was his second home, or "base." The TD branch was the closest landmark.

Millard arrived at 6:30 and texted that he was parked on a side street.

"Yes sir, see my benz parked across the street. park beside it and ill send butler dude down."

Millard didn't see Ward-Jackson's Mercedes. "have your butler scoop me inside the td entrance, I need to use the ATM anyways," he said.

"Its directly across the street," said Ward-Jackson about his car.

"omg I'm on bloor, fml," texted Millard. He'd shown up at the wrong place.

When Millard pulled up outside Ward-Jackson's home five minutes later, Ward-Jackson sent his "butler" down. This was Joseph Michael Horth, known to Ward-Jackson's crowd as Spiken Mike. Horth was a small fifty-something man who had fallen on hard times, lost his teeth to crystal meth, and supposedly been rescued from a life of homelessness by Ward-Jackson. In return, Horth did Ward-Jackson's bidding. Sometimes, this was indeed butler-type work, like fetching Millard and cigarettes for the boss. At other times, it involved physically punishing activities, like hanging on to the wheels of souped-up trucks and going for a few slow revolutions around the parking lot or being strapped to their roofs for a bumpy ride. These feats, carried out for the entertainment of others, were videotaped and posted to YouTube to preserve the moment. There is even a video where Horth is assaulted and abused on camera. He is given a shot of alcohol before facing punishment for supposedly failing at his butler duties. Then he is kicked in the testicles by a man whose face is not shown. There is laughter from onlookers off-camera. Afterward, as Horth is doubled over in pain, hugging a dog for comfort, he is given another shot of booze to help him recover. All the while, he recites that he deserves to be punished.

On this particular evening, however, all Horth had to do was escort Millard from his car to Ward-Jackson's living room for his gun instruction. "I'm chilling," Millard texted the butler's boss, who had not yet arrived. "I await your presence."

From the lack of texts over the next few hours, it appears that Millard and Ward-Jackson spent the evening together. In the early hours of February 14, after leaving his gun dealer's base, Millard texted Ward-Jackson, "btw happy Valentine's day." He also snapped some pictures of his new Walther PPK, which Falconer would later uncover in a folder labelled "DellsHard/Pictures." The embedded GPS metadata shows that the photos were taken near his Maple Gate home.

Several months later, on September 22, 2012, again in the early morning hours, Millard sent another photo of what is presumably the same Walther PPK—which is famous for, among other things, being James Bond's gun of choice—to Christina Noudga. It was found in the backup file for her iPhone on a laptop computer seized from Millard's bedroom.

A third photo was discovered in yet another backup file on one of the Maple Gate computers, this one for a device labelled "Mark's Ipad [sic]." The "start date," or first syncing with the computer, of Mark's iPad is recorded as having occurred on July 5, 2012, shortly after the disappearance of Laura Babcock, who had been loaned Shawn Lerner's iPad. The last backup of that device to Millard's computer is on January 2013. Its serial number shows it is the same iPad that was seized from Mark Smich's mother's house on the day of his arrest. The original gun photo, which was taken with the iPad, had been deleted from the device by the time Smich was arrested, but the backup photo shows part of a gun that resembles a Walther PPK being held by two grubby fingers with dirty fingernails and a freckle on the index finger between the nail and the first joint. Barely visible in the bottom left corner is a partially covered face that appears disproportionately small due to the perspective. Falconer says the person's clothing—what looks like a grey hoodie—and facial hair on the upper lip led him to believe it is Mark Smich. Another photo on the iPad shows Smich has a freckle on his index finger.

The photos recovered demonstrate that both Millard and Smich had handled the Walther PPK that the police believe was used to kill Tim Bosma.

ON FEBRUARY 18, 2014, ONE of Millard's Valentine's Day gun photos was sent by email to Christianne Lys, a Toronto Police supervisor in Forensic Identification Services, who has specialized in fingerprints since 2003. The original photo showed part of a hand holding a gun including a very clear finger pad.

Lys received this image of a finger, but she was not given any information about the case it related to. Her task was to try to find the person's identity by analyzing the ridges on the finger in the photograph.

Lys has worked with digital images of fingers before and says that, depending on a number of factors, including the resolution of the photograph, it's possible to make an identification. A good-quality photograph of a finger, with sufficient clarity and detail to proceed with testing, is sometimes preferable to an actual lifted print. "It can be easier, as it doesn't have the same distortions," she tells the jury.

One of the first things Lys did with the image was to reverse it so that the finger had the same orientation as prints in the RCMP's automated fingerprint identification system. She then marked up the printed photo and submitted it to the database, which uses a matching algorithm to provide a list of twenty possible matching candidates. Lys examined these all by eye. With the best match, there were seventeen points of comparison. She says all seventeen matched the left index finger of Dellen Millard, which had been entered in the database on May 11, 2013. As is standard procedure, Lys's identification was peer reviewed by another qualified examiner, who agreed with her assessment.

CLOSE TO A YEAR after the murder of Tim Bosma, on the morning of April 10, 2014, completely unbeknownst to the press, Dellen Millard and Mark Smich were transported from their respective jails to make an appearance at the Toronto West Court. Millard was charged with the first-degree murders of his father and Laura

Babcock, and Smich was charged with the first-degree murder of Laura Babcock. Because there was not a journalist in sight at the strip mall courthouse—located just blocks away from the intersection of Jane and Finch, a neighbourhood synonymous with violence in the minds of many—nothing is known about how the accused reacted to the charges or if any of their family members were present. Their lawyers later informed reporters that their clients intended to plead not guilty to all the charges. Deepak Paradkar, who still represented Millard at the time, pledged to defend him zealously, adding that he didn't see a "common link" between the three murders for which his client stood accused. Thomas Dungey said nothing other than that his defence would be vigorous.

Unusually, the police did not hold a proper press conference where reporters could ask about the investigations and what led to the new charges. Instead, Staff Inspector Greg McLane of the Toronto Police homicide unit read from the official OPP statement at a media event that lasted just a few minutes. Also contained in the press release was another startling piece of information: police had arrested Millard's girlfriend, Christina Noudga, who would be charged as an accessory after the fact in the murder of Tim Bosma.

Curiously, the police made no mention of several related charges that had been laid two days earlier, on April 8, against Matthew Ward-Jackson. He was charged not only with selling Millard the Walther PPK in February 2012 but with trafficking him two other guns later that year, including the firearm allegedly used to kill Wayne Millard. At the time he was charged, Ward-Jackson was already in custody for a separate set of charges relating to possession of an AK-47. He had been arrested in January 2014 and denied bail.

On the same day the new charges were laid against Millard and Smich, Noudga was taken to Hamilton for questioning while search warrants were executed at her home, where she lived with her parents and younger brother and sister. Although the police had identified Noudga as a key figure in the case early on, she had always declined to talk to them and lawyered up soon after her boyfriend's arrest. Her lawyer, Paul Mergler, declined to comment on the charges against her.

THE DAY AFTER CHRISTINA NOUDGA's arrest, she appeared at Hamilton's John Sopinka Courthouse to hear the charges against her. She was variously described by reporters as nervous, scared, and pensive. She wore a brown leather jacket, turquoise T-shirt, and black pants. She bit her lip and fidgeted as she stood in the prisoner's box. The Crown stated that the charges against her stemmed from actions she took on Thursday, May 9, 2013, when she allegedly assisted her boyfriend, Dellen Millard, in covering up the murder of Tim Bosma.

Sitting five metres away from Noudga in the front row of the courtroom was Sharlene Bosma. She watched the brief proceedings stoically, but later, outside the courtroom, she broke down in tears. Although the police had informed her two days earlier of the impending arrest, she was still shocked by it, and seeing Noudga in person had taken its toll. After composing herself, she spoke with reporters for a minute or two. "I'm not sure that I can take any more surprises," she said, standing on the courthouse steps. It was a beautiful early spring day, much like the one on which her husband had gone missing. "I always say that everybody has so much that they can take, and I'm reaching the limit. And I just hope that this is it. That we're done now."

TWELVE

THE GIRLFRIENDS

Until she was arrested, Christina Noudga refused to talk to police about what happened in May 2013. She appeared not to be bothered that a man had been murdered, that her boyfriend was in jail, and that she had information critical to the case. It took the realization that she was finally being charged as an "accessory after the fact to murder" to convince her to make a statement.

"I had plans to go abroad, get on with my life," she tells the Crown's Tony Leitch.

"This is Dell's mess, not mine," she later explains to Thomas Dungey.

As Noudga sees it, she's been unjustly humiliated in public and by the courts. "I'm arrested for what?" she asks. "For something stupid that maybe [Dellen] and Mark did."

Only once in her five days of testimony does Noudga mention Tim Bosma's name. Never once, as she sits in the witness box facing the victim's mother, father, and widow, does she show any hint of empathy or remorse. She displays no awareness of how offensive it is to describe a man's cold-blooded murder as "something stupid" and a "mess," an annoyance that has interfered with her plans, something that has caused her to be charged— wrongly, as she sees it—as an accessory after the fact to murder.

At the time of her testimony, Noudga's own trial is scheduled to take place a few months later, in November 2016. As a result, she asks for protection under the Canada Evidence Act. Unlike in the United States, where witnesses can refuse to answer questions by pleading the Fifth Amendment, in Canada they must answer or face possible charges for contempt of court. Any evidence Noudga gives at the trial of Dellen Millard and Mark Smich, however, cannot be used against her at her own trial. Unless she perjures herself or gives contradictory testimony, she is protected by the Evidence Act from incriminating herself. At her own trial, of course, she cannot be compelled to testify.

When Noudga arrives at court for her first day on the witness stand, she does not disappoint the photographers and TV crews waiting to capture her entrance. She and her mother, who holds her daughter's arm, both wear long dark coats and mirrored sunglasses to hide from the cameras. In Noudga's case, she has draped a black-and-white print scarf around her head as if she were an Islamic woman forbidden from revealing her face in public. Her mother opts for a toque-style hat pulled down over her forehead and a winter scarf wrapped around her lower face. The unseasonably cold April weather helps make them look marginally less ridiculous.

Under her coat, for her first day of testimony, Noudga is wearing a cream-coloured blouse, a black pencil skirt slit up the back, and maroon suede stilettos. She is tall and slim with excellent posture and walks speedily to the witness box even in heels.

Although she doesn't appear nervous, when the court registrar asks if she wants to be sworn on the Bible or to solemnly affirm, she answers, "Yes."

Noudga has declined to meet with Tony Leitch for witness preparation. Her brief period of cooperation with police and prosecutors ended with the two interviews given shortly after her arrest. Leitch makes it clear that there's no deal between Noudga and the Crown with respect to the evidence she is about to give. Her lawyer, Paul Mergler, sits in the public gallery with her mother.

As is customary, Leitch's first questions touch on personal history: how Noudga came to meet Millard in 2010, when she was eighteen and he was still with his fiancée, and how by 2013 she had become his girlfriend, staying over at his house five to seven nights a week. Noudga's original connection to Millard was through Andrew Michalski, who knew her ex-boyfriend, though she and Michalski were never especially friendly and haven't seen each other since May 2013. She explains that in the year before the murder of Tim Bosma, Mark Smich replaced Michalski as Millard's best friend. "It kind of just crossed over," she says. As a result, Noudga was regularly in Smich's company as he and Millard smoked dope, played video games, and "focussed on Mark's rap career."

"Was there any person [Millard] spent more time with than Mark?" asks Leitch.

"I think me and Dellen spent more time together than Mark and Dellen," says Noudga. While she admits to being extremely jealous of other women, Noudga does not appear to have been perturbed by her boyfriend's peculiar relationship with Smich.

Nor did she mind spending the occasional evening hanging out with Matthew Ward-Jackson, the alleged gun dealer, if it made Millard happy. Anything, it seems, was better than worrying that Millard was in the company of other women.

Leitch asks about the term *mission*, and Noudga says it was how she and Millard referred to a variety of activities: everything from buying weed to grocery shopping to touring Millard's properties. She says the word had no criminal connotations apart from purchasing marijuana. When Leitch shows her a photo of the Walther PPK that Millard texted her in September 2012, Noudga denies having any memory of it. As for the Eliminator, she says her boyfriend told her that it had been purchased to burn scrap metals from his aviation business.

LEITCH ASKS NOUDGA ABOUT a text message sent to her on Saturday, May 4, 2013, two days before the murder. "I've got some mission prep to do, reaching Waterloo soon, you're welcome to tag along," Millard wrote.

There's a long silence while Noudga looks at the message, which is displayed on the courtroom screens, before answering that she doesn't recall what happened that day. "Nothing stands out to me," she says, adding that when she and her lawyer were preparing for her testimony, they went back only as far as May 6.

Noudga also has no memory of stopping with Millard at his Riverside Drive property in the west end of Toronto later that Saturday evening to pick up Millard's Yukon from Javier Villada and give him the white van. Nor does she know what Millard meant when he sent her a text message after his Sunday test drive with Igor Tumanenko.

"No go today," he wrote. "I will be around later if you want to chill."

"Did you ever talk to him about that test drive?" asks Leitch.

"No," says Noudga. She repeats that she can't recall anything that happened before May 6.

"Okay," says Leitch, "let's talk about Monday, May 6, 2013. Did you see [Millard] that day?"

"I don't think so, no."

"Do you want to see the texts that were sent between you?"

"I think they'd be helpful."

Leitch puts them up on the screens. There's a message to Noudga about Millard's lunch with his mother, Madeleine Burns, whom he refers to as Rabbit. He'd complained the week before that he was having "a bit of constipation with that ass rabbit" because she wasn't helping him out fast enough with his condo financing woes. But that Monday, Burns had come through by taking funds from a line of credit on her house. "Finally pulled that rabbit out of my ass, went downtown, paid for the condo, and showed it to my mum," he wrote to Noudga at 7:38 P.M. on the night of Tim Bosma's murder.

Two minutes later, he told her, "I'm on my way to a mission now. If it's a flop i'll be done in 2 hrs. If it goes . . . it'll be an all nighter."

At 10:47 P.M. Noudga asked Millard if he was finished.

"Gonna be an all nighter," he replied at 11:34 P.M.

Leitch asks Noudga what Millard meant here by a "mission."

"I have no idea what he was referring to."

"Did you ever ask him later?"

"Never got the chance to," she says. "He was going to be work-ing late in the evening, so by the time he was going to see me I would probably be asleep."

"No prior discussion about what he was doing that day?"

"I knew he was inquiring into purchasing a vehicle."

Noudga says Millard had mentioned buying a truck the month before. "I was like, 'Cool.' End of conversation."

"Do you recall any specifics?"

Noudga says she can't.

Leitch puts up more texts from Millard.

"Yo," he wrote at 6:40 the following morning from the hangar.

"Early morning," Noudga replied.

"Need a break, I've got a moment to relax," he texted just before 8 A.M.

Noudga asks her boyfriend if he's still working.

"Stage 1 complete, taking a respite," he says.

He's back home at Maple Gate and there's some talk of them getting together, but they can't coordinate a time.

"K then later," says Millard. "I'm gonna take a nap."

"Good choice :)" says Noudga.

Leitch asks her why she told Millard it was a good choice.

"Because I was still in bed and I didn't want to get out," she says. She had no desire to run over to Millard's to be with him during his break, she tells Leitch. And, no, she had no idea what he was taking a break from or what "Stage 1" meant. She assumed it related to whatever he had been working on through the night.

Noudga says Millard "was always very ambiguous" about what he did all day while she was at university and at the part-time job she had as a lifeguard.

"Did that bother you?" asks Leitch.

"Originally, but then after a time I just stopped asking questions," she says. The only thing she admits to persistently inquiring about is the affairs she suspected Millard of having with other women.

Just before 6:30 that Tuesday evening, Millard texted Noudga again. "Had a nice 5 hour nap & bath, refreshed and ready for the next stage of mission digestion," he wrote.

"Lol mission digestion," said Noudga.

"(:" came the reply.

Noudga explains that she found *mission digestion* a funny term. She even laughs in court about it. "Yeah, I thought it was just a weird way to name one of his missions."

"Right," says Leitch. He asks her about the smiley-face emoji.

"I think it's funny when you say 'emoji,'" says Noudga, laughing again as she tucks her hair behind her ears. It's unclear if she's forgotten why she's here in court or just doesn't care.

In the early hours of Wednesday morning, Millard texted Noudga to tell her he was about to take another nap. When she woke up and read the text, she responded by asking him how the mission went.

"1.5 hr nap & still going," he replied.

"Nap-texting too."

"Still going on mission."

"Quite the long mission."

"Very, want to come help?"

"What do you need help with?"

"Nvm," he said, meaning never mind. "I'm letting my craving for your company get the best of me. Still in Waterloo, I don't have time yet."

"Oh boo, you've gotten me all excited."

In court, Noudga claims to have no memory of what they were talking about or why she asked how the mission was going. "He's been referring to the mission in the past couple of days," she says. "I wasn't sure what it was, so I used his words back at him."

Leitch asks if she had any idea why the date fell through.

"He never told me why. I was expecting to see him throughout the entire week, but he kept blowing me off," Noudga says. "It was kind of annoying, you know?"

When she finally did get the chance to see her boyfriend, she jumped at it.

"Tiny mission tonight, could use your help," he wrote on Thursday afternoon.

"Sure. Pick me up at 8:30," she texted back.

"Are you home?" asked the habitually late Millard at 9:37 P.M.

"Yes," said Noudga. "But I don't enjoy waiting around for you."

"Do you actually love me?" wrote Millard.

"Why do you ask?"

"Roll a joint. I'll pick you up in 10 mins."

Noudga lived with her family in a much less affluent part of Etobicoke than the one her boyfriend lived in. When Millard showed up at their bungalow in his red Dodge pickup, he was towing the trailer that contained Tim Bosma's truck.

Before Noudga got into Millard's truck, he gave her the digital video recorder he had brought from the hangar, the one with the brief clip of Millard, Smich, and Pedo from early on Tuesday morning. She took it to her bedroom while he waited outside. When she returned, they headed north to his mother's house in

Kleinburg, smoking weed along the way. She thought Millard seemed tired and sad.

"What did you think you were going to help him with?" asks Leitch.

"I didn't have the faintest idea."

"So you get in the car. What's the discussion?"

"I'm not sure what the discussion was. He gave me what I thought at the time was a stereo." Noudga didn't ask for any explanation because, she says, Millard was always "ambiguous."

"Did you ask him what he was doing for a week?"

"I didn't specifically ask him what, but I asked how it went," she says. "If I asked specific questions, he'd answer ambiguously, so I just stopped asking questions."

As her testimony progresses, it becomes clear that this is the Noudga narrative, her explanation for her participation in the events of May 9 and 10. She never asked questions, so she couldn't have known what had happened that week. After Millard's arrest, she simply moved the DVR farther back into her closet. Police photos taken when officers searched her bedroom show clothes and underwear all over the floor, used coffee cups, an unmade bed. In the closet, with junk piled on top of it, is the DVR, which the police will take away as evidence.

"Did you not think it might be relevant?" asks Leitch.

"I didn't think of it at all."

"Your boyfriend is arrested. At some point it must have dawned on you that this could possibly be evidence."

"This specifically? Never dawned on me."

Noudga's answers are frequently accompanied by eye-rolling, laughing, and sighing to show how stupid it is to imply she should be curious about the DVR in her closet or the contents of the trailer she and Millard pulled to Kleinburg.

"Should I have asked every time he showed up at my doorstep pulling a trailer?" she says. "It was like a normal evening."

Leitch asks Noudga to refresh her memory by reviewing the statement she gave to police after her arrest.

"Um, okay," she says, making it clear that she thinks this is another bad idea.

"What did you think was in the trailer?" he asks again after she has a moment to read.

"A Mother's Day present for his mother," says Noudga. "This was later an idea I came up with, like, when I was talking with his mother about what was in the trailer. The word *Tesla* was thrown around, because she wanted an electric car."

When Noudga and Millard reached Madeleine Burns's house, Millard backed the trailer right up against the garage door, smashing a light on the exterior wall. Noudga says she thought that positioning the trailer in such a way was just another one of the weird things he regularly did.

"Did you see Madeleine Burns?" asks Leitch.

"She came out and was like, 'What is this? Why are you putting it here?' And he was like, 'Don't worry.'"

When Burns asked her son why he was being so evasive, he didn't answer, says Noudga.

"At this point, we were both extremely stoned," Noudga recalls, laughing. "Then we both said bye to her and left for Waterloo."

"How long is that drive?"

"Forty-five minutes to an hour." She makes a scornful face, adding that she and Millard didn't talk much along the way. "It was more of a sexual expedition," she says. "Well, he was driving, and I was performing sexual favours for him, so there was no discussion to be made."

Noudga is smiling. She appears pleased with herself. Earlier, when asked how she got her nickname Rubikinks, she said the "Rubi" part came from her ability to solve a Rubik's Cube. Leitch said he didn't need to know about the "kinks" part. (The jury had already heard from other witnesses that Kinks was the name assigned to Noudga in Millard's phone contacts.)

Leitch asks Noudga how long the sexual act in the truck continued. He is trying to show that it can't account for a complete lack of conversation on the drive.

Noudga claims to have serviced Millard for half an hour once they hit the highway, leaving just fifteen or twenty minutes to talk. Their subsequent conversation revolved around the fellatio, she says, tossing her hair.

When they arrived at the hangar, they exchanged the red truck for the Yukon. She tells Leitch she believes she was there for just ten minutes.

Although Noudga said in her post-arrest statement that she and Millard had moved boxes at the hangar and that she wore gloves, she has since changed her mind. She says she is convinced that the box-moving happened on a different evening and that she wore gloves only to move the incinerator at the farm.

"We leave and were about to get on the highway when Dell interjects and says, 'Oh, one more quick stop.'" He wanted to go to the farm and move the incinerator from the barn.

"What did Dellen say when you were in the barn?" asks Leitch.

"He said, 'Oh, the floorboards are creaking under its weight. I don't want it to break.'" She and Millard gloved up, hitched the four-thousand-pound Eliminator to the Yukon, and towed it to a treed laneway, where Chaz Main would find and photograph it later that day.

"Is it that he wanted to have it a little bit concealed?"

He didn't want "a random contraption standing in the middle of the field," says Noudga. She maintains that the purpose of concealing the machine was to hide it from prospective thieves, and not in anticipation of a police search. She estimates the whole operation lasted no more than fifteen minutes. She took off her gloves and either gave them to Millard or put them on the floor of the Yukon.

Noudga's first day of testimony wraps up with her account of heading back to Toronto with Millard to drop off the toolbox.

THE PUBLIC REACTION TO Noudga's performance on the witness stand was unequivocal: she was reviled and mocked in both mainstream and social media. The *Toronto Sun* featured her picture on its front page with a tabloid-style headline about her sexcapades. In *The Hamilton Spectator*, Noudga was excoriated by court columnist Susan Clairmont, who wrote that "of all the unsavoury witnesses the jury has heard from at the Tim Bosma murder trial, she is the least likable of the lot." On Twitter, a photo circulated of Thomas Dungey's head grafted onto the leather-clad body of a machine-gun-toting Terminator renamed the Dungenator. "I'll be back for the truth, Christina," the caption read. Inside the courtroom and out, expectations were running high that Dungey's cross-examination would both call Noudga to account and yield some answers.

For one brief moment as her second day of testimony begins, Noudga appears slightly chastened by the negative reaction she has provoked. But she quickly reverts to Mean Girl mode when Leitch points out to her that her timeline of events doesn't add up and shows her slides displaying the cell tower pings. Noudga looks at him as if he were incompetent. "Oookaaay," she says condescendingly.

The phone records show that Noudga was at the farm later and for a longer period than she has claimed. They also show that on the earlier "sexual expedition" to the Waterloo hangar, four calls were made from Noudga's phone.

"Um . . . hmm," says Noudga as she examines the screen, at a loss to explain. She says that she didn't make any calls. "On the drive back from [the farm], I know I gave him my phone," she adds.

"Did you lend him your phone more than once that night?"

"I may have."

Leitch tells her that nine calls in total were made to Matt Hagerman on her phone. "You were in a position to hear those nine phone calls," he says, "and you have no recollection of what was said?"

"Not the exact words and phrasing. . . . I know I lent him my phone to get in contact."

"I'm asking you what Mr. Millard said to Mr. Hagerman in those nine phone calls."

"I don't recall," says Noudga, now looking vaguely worried.

While she originally said they left the farm at 12:30 A.M., she shifts the time to 3 A.M.

Leitch asks what time she thinks they arrived at the farm from the hangar.

"Like one or two."

"So you were there two hours?"

"No."

"So how long were you there for?"

"Maybe an hour at most."

The implication is clear: if Millard and Noudga spent about an hour at the farm, then they were also at the hangar for longer than she has acknowledged. That, in turn, casts doubt on her claim that she was mistaken in her police statement about moving boxes at the hangar. The missing hour or two has to have been spent somewhere, because the phone data shows conclusively when Noudga and Millard travelled from the farm to Hagerman's.

Noudga says she was exhausted and falling asleep when they pulled up at his house. She may have waved at Hagerman, who she remembers laughing with Millard. Then she and her boyfriend returned to Maple Gate at about 4:30 A.M., had sex, and went to sleep. When Millard woke up an hour or two later for an early morning meeting at the hangar, they had more sex. Then he left.

At noon on Friday, May 10, Noudga texted him, "Hope your days [sic] going well," followed by a photo of herself with Millard's dog Pedo in bed. She received no reply. At 3:50 P.M., she messaged again: "Text me when you can, I want to see you tonight." At 8:04, she wrote, "Hellooooo?" And at 9:10, she texted, "Call me." By this time, of course, Millard had been arrested. There was no call. Noudga didn't know it, but he was busy being questioned by the Hamilton Police.

Worried about Millard's lack of response, Noudga called Andrew Michalski, who told her Millard wasn't at home but that Pedo was. She then phoned Smich.

"I said, 'Hi, Mark, is Dell with you?' He said, 'No, but don't worry about it, Christina. Shit went down. Just don't worry about it.'" She was irritated with Smich for not answering her simple question and for getting her "panicked."

Not long after, Madeleine Burns phoned and told Noudga to come to Kleinburg immediately. She sounded hysterical. Noudga persuaded her mother to drive her there and wait outside while she went in to speak with Burns. Noudga's mother, who had trained as a doctor in the former Soviet Union, was concerned someone might need medical attention, but after Noudga talked to Burns, she reassured her mother and told her to go home.

Burns informed Noudga that Millard had been arrested for forcible confinement and the theft of a truck. She said Dellen's lawyer expected the media would soon be arriving at her house and she wanted Christina to accompany her to a hotel. Noudga says Burns kept asking, "Do you think the truck is in the trailer?" and "What if the truck is in the trailer?" Noudga claimed not to know what was in the trailer.

At the hotel, which is never identified, they checked in and drank some wine before deciding they should go to Maple Gate and pick up chequebooks, power-of-attorney forms, and some $5,000 to $6,000 in cash that Millard kept for emergencies. Once back at the hotel, they had more wine. "We started brainstorming as to what may have happened," says Noudga. "There's this giant trailer which he didn't really give much information about."

"At some point, do you look at any media?" asks Leitch.

"No, it was too disturbing."

"How do you know?"

"Well, it was really stressful. I never expected Dell to get arrested. I don't want to see what's going on. I don't want to know any of this," says Noudga. "You watch the media, and everything gets twisted around in your mind."

"At this stage, you're saying you and Ms. Burns are not looking at media?"

"Together, we came to that conclusion," says Noudga. "My biggest concern was, Holy shit, we touched the trailer, and if the truck is in the trailer, we're going to get drawn into the mess."

Leitch asks who she means by "we."

"Myself and Madeleine. Dell was not a concern, because he was arrested."

Burns was worried because she had tried to open the trailer to see what was inside.

"We kind of sit there, and we're like, Should we go back? Should we do something?"

They decided that they should indeed go back to Burns's house and wipe down the parts of the trailer they had touched. Noudga estimates that by this time it would have been the early hours of Saturday, May 11. When they got to the house, Burns gave Noudga a cloth and some dishwashing gloves and went to feed her cats and fetch a few things.

Noudga wiped down the trailer hitch and chain and the locks on the trailer's two side doors, anything she remembered touching the evening before. Burns opened the garage door, which gave them access to the back of the trailer, and pointed out to Noudga the areas she had touched when she had tried earlier to get in through its rear doors only to find them locked. When the cleanup was done, they returned to the hotel. It was still dark out.

Back in their room, there was "more brainstorming, a lot of crying, hugging, consoling . . . [while] drinking copious amounts of wine," says Noudga. "I think we ran out of wine by the time it got light out, but we were still in a lot of distress."

Later that day, they learned from Deepak Paradkar that Millard was being held at the Hamilton-Wentworth Detention Centre. The lawyer also advised Noudga against going to the courthouse where Millard would be charged that day. She says she was not aware at the time, or for months afterward, that Millard was not allowed to have contact with her.

IN CONTRAST TO CHRISTINA NOUDGA, Marlena Meneses, who testified before her, does not deny knowing about the events of May 2013 or the plans to steal a truck. She was at the Maple Gate house with Andrew Michalski while Millard and her boyfriend, Mark Smich, were discussing stealing a truck and looking at online ads. She later told Smich she thought the planned theft was a stupid idea, but he was determined to go ahead with it and didn't respond to her concerns.

On the night of the Ancaster test drive, May 6, Marlena went to visit her older sister Elizabeth. Her phone records show that she texted both Millard and Smich while they were near the Bosma home. Meneses remembers that the last time she spoke to her boyfriend that evening was just after 9 P.M., when Smich told her he was busy driving. She later became worried when she didn't hear from him. "I knew they were going to go steal a truck," she says. "I didn't know if he got hurt or what was going on." She texted Andrew Michalski, who told her not to worry and who then tried to contact Millard.

"Yo," he wrote just before 8 A.M. on Tuesday, May 7.

Millard replied immediately. "Sup?"

"Marlena was worried about Mark just wanted to figure out where he was."

"He's with her."

"Proper?? she called me at 6 in the morning asking where he was, if I knew where you were. Everything be irie?" he says, using Jamaican slang.

"Just swell. Marlena's a child and worries too easily."

"I told her that you guys were fine and that it's not the first time this has happened and won't be the last."

After leaving the hangar that morning, Millard and Smich headed to Oakville, where they picked Meneses up at 8 A.M. Security video seized from her sister's apartment building shows her taking an elevator to the lobby and leaving the building. Outside, Smich gets out of Millard's Yukon, walks over to his girlfriend, and greets her before helping her into the car.

The jury has seen this video during the testimony of Michael Plaxton, the forensic video analyst with the Hamilton Police, and it has also seen the surveillance photos of Meneses walking arm in arm with Smich following Millard's arrest, as well as the many selfies she and her boyfriend took on his iPad. Now the jurors are finally getting to see and hear from Meneses in person. With her hennaed red hair, big eyes, heart-shaped face, and tiny body, she resembles a Japanese anime doll. She is wearing tight black pants and a black T-shirt covered by an open blue-and-white print blouse. Her very high black suede heels seem to be hurting her feet, causing her to limp ever so slightly as she makes her way to the witness stand. She sits down and smiles at the constable, who gives her water. Mark Smich watches her intently and Dellen Millard gives his now familiar half-smirk.

Meneses and Smich went everywhere together, and they were often in Millard's company. While Christina Noudga had university and a part-time job to occupy her, Meneses and Smich were unemployed and free to tag along with Millard. They made an unusual trio.

Craig Fraser asks Meneses to describe the nature of the Smich–Millard relationship.

"They were really close, like brothers. I would say Mark cared for Dellen more than he cared for other people," she says. "He was in love with him."

"That's a strong term, Ms. Meneses," says Fraser. He asks her to elaborate.

"You could just tell that was Mark's feelings toward Dellen."

Meneses was nineteen when Tim Bosma was murdered. She had dropped out of high school after she met Smich, who was six years her senior. They met at a Tim Hortons in Oakville in early 2012. "I looked over at him. He gave me some look. His eyes were all big and it was like he was in love with me," she says. "My friend told me to go over and talk to him, and I did."

They were "dealing" for the first few weeks—which is "like when you're with someone but you're not fully dating, just getting to know each other"—and then she moved out of her mother's home into Smich's mother's house, where she lived for the next year. She and Smich were often together night and day. Aside from his drug dealing, their sole source of income was doing odd jobs at the hangar. In return, Millard bought them food and clothes and paid for their phones.

Meneses says she wasn't entirely happy with the arrangement, that it was disgusting cleaning the washrooms the hangar construction team used. "A girl my age should get paid more than food and money on a phone. There were things I wanted to do, go to school, college."

It's a statement that doesn't quite ring true. As sweet as Meneses appears at times, she also seems aimless and unmotivated. She has racked up an impressive number of bad decisions for someone so young. And despite her protestations that she didn't want Mark to steal, she regularly looked the other way when her boyfriend went out on thieving missions and dealt drugs.

Meneses also only got a real job after Smich told her she had to start bringing in an income, at which point she went to work in the cold cuts section of a Metro grocery store. Millard had helped her put together a resumé, which stated that her career objective was "to be an awesome employee at your establishment." She listed her defining characteristics as being cute, motivated, energetic, consistent, and attentive. Her work experience included cashier at Tim Hortons, car detailer at Millardair, and bartender at "Smichy's". Her references were Dellen Millard and Mark Smich.

While Meneses readily acknowledges that she would go to Millard for advice and that he did her favours from time to time, she also says she never much cared for him and found him somewhat creepy. "I would say we were more acquaintances than actual friends," she tells the court.

Once Millard and Smich had picked up Meneses on the morning after Bosma was murdered, Millard drove them to Smich's mother's house a few minutes away.

Fraser asks Meneses to describe the atmosphere in the car.

"Very happy. They're just really happy, saying they wanted to celebrate," she says. "They just said that their mission went well."

There are gasps in the courtroom. Mary Bosma fights back tears, and her husband looks straight ahead. Smich and Millard are both sitting just a few feet away from them. Marlena Meneses doesn't know where to look or what to do.

WHEN MENESES SAYS SHE learned from television news on the evening of Friday, May 10, that Millard had been arrested, she may be conflating memories. The arrest wasn't announced until the next day, but the story of the missing man was at the top of the news Friday, including reports about one of the suspects' "ambition" tattoo. Smich was there with her. "I freaked out," Meneses says. "Like, 'Why is your friend on the news, and why is he arrested for that?' [Mark] was kind of like, 'Oh, shit,' and grabbed my phone and started calling people."

Meneses bites her lip and says she didn't know who Smich called or why. All she knew was "that there were drugs in Dellen's house and he wanted to get them out." When she got home from work the next day, Smich told her a gun had been dropped off in a toolbox.

"Did you ask where Mr. Bosma was?"

"He told me Mr. Bosma was gone, gone."

"Did he say how Mr. Bosma was 'gone, gone'?"

"He just said Dell murdered him."

Mary Bosma is crying.

"Did he tell you how Dellen Millard murdered him?"

"That he shot him."

"Did he tell you where he was shot and when?"

"He told me it was when they did the test drive."

"Did he tell you why?"

"No."

"Did he tell you what he did?"

"He told me he did nothing, that Dell did it all."

"Did you know of the incinerator at the time, Ms. Meneses?"

Meneses replies that she'd seen the Eliminator at the hangar. She says Millard told her it was for animals at his farm. "I said, 'But you don't have any animals,' and he kind of just left it at that."

When she heard on the news how the incinerator had been used, she asked Smich about it.

Fraser asks what she did when she learned Tim Bosma was dead and incinerated.

"Nothing," she says. "I should have. I regret it. I could have stopped so much stuff. I should have."

Meneses says that when she suggested to her boyfriend that he talk to the police, he told her he just wanted to go to his sister's wedding the following Sunday, May 19. They didn't discuss it again.

"Did you ever ask Mr. Smich why Mr. Bosma was shot, killed, and burned?"

"No, I never asked."

"Why didn't you?"

"I don't want to know," she says, as if reliving the experience. "I was with the guy. I don't want to know anything."

"Did Mark get rid of that gun?"

"Yes."

"How did he get rid of it?"

"He told me he wrapped it in duct tape and buried it. He said somewhere in the forest," says Meneses, but he wouldn't tell her which forest or where it was.

"YOU LIVED BY A code," says Nadir Sachak to Marlena Meneses in his cross-examination. "That code was to be forever faithful, loyal, and dutiful to your lover. Protect your lover. . . . Your biggest thing is when someone is not faithful to a husband or lover."

Meneses agrees with Millard's lawyer that this was what she felt and, despite everything, still believes.

"In order to be with Mr. Smich, you had to accept that the person you loved could not have harmed a human being, would never shoot another human being, would not burn another human being," says Sachak.

"Yes," she says, sniffling into a tissue. Over her three days on the witness stand, she often has to dab away her tears.

"Your universe as you knew it would collapse. You gave up everything in your life to be with Mr. Smich, to be faithful to him, to be loyal to him?"

"Yes."

Sachak shows pictures of Meneses and Smich at his sister's wedding. She is wearing a strapless black dress with a hot pink shawl and matching pink shoes. Smich, for once, is dressed in clothes that fit. Although Meneses has just finished describing how upset the death of Tim Bosma made her, in the photos she and Smich are both smiling broadly.

Sachak asks her if that's how she grieves.

She looks ashamed. In her version of events, she has cast herself in the best possible light, yet the pictures tell another story, one in which Marlena Meneses focuses only on an imagined future. In that world, she's planning on having a baby and marrying Mark Smich, the drug dealer, not going back to school. She texts her sister Elizabeth from the reception, where she's happily getting drunk and eating dinner. "Our wedding is next," she writes.

Having dealt a blow to Meneses's credibility, Sachak will attempt to destroy the most important part of her testimony: her statement that in the car Millard and Smich were celebrating Bosma's murder. He asks Meneses why she never mentioned that the two were celebrating until April 16, 2016, when she was interviewed by prosecutors in preparation for her April 21 court appearance. "That's the first time in three years that you've ever made any reference to them celebrating," he says. "Right?"

Yes, says Meneses, but she insists she always told the police that Smich and Millard were happy, "not that they were celebrating, but they were very happy." She will not budge, and she is not open to the possibility that she might be mistaken. Until this trial, it seems she could not admit to herself, let alone the world, that Mark Smich was celebrating the murder and incineration of another human being. Even as she cooperated with the police, Meneses continued to profess her love for Smich and live by her code. For two years, she was faithful to him while he was in jail. And then she found a new boyfriend and her loyalties shifted. The code no longer applied to Mark Smich.

THIRTEEN

LETTERS

Sandwiched between the testimonies of Marlena Meneses and Christina Noudga—the final witness for the Crown—there was one other witness to take the stand briefly at the Tim Bosma murder trial: Sergeant Kerry Duench of the Hamilton Police. Duench helped execute the search warrant at Noudga's house after her arrest. She is there to testify that in the top drawer of Noudga's bedside table, she found a series of letters that appeared to be written from jail by Dellen Millard. During Noudga's testimony, those fifty letters are introduced as evidence. In a signed admission statement prepared by Millard's lawyers, the accused has agreed that he wrote the letters.

The letters are extremely valuable, because they show Millard's attempts to fabricate alibis, tamper with witnesses, and suborn perjury. They also provide a glimpse inside his mind.

Key details about the letters' transmission are not presented in evidence; the jury hears only that they were delivered to Noudga by Madeleine Burns at meetings that took place once or twice a month, often at a Canyon Creek steakhouse near Noudga's home.

Over lunch or dinner, Noudga would collect her mail and give Burns letters to take to Millard. While Millard's letters defied a court order barring him from communicating with his girlfriend, Noudga, until her arrest, was free to write to him. As the facilitator of this exchange, Burns violated a court order. She was never called to testify, however, nor has she been charged in relation to this case.

Throughout the trial, many observers tweeted at journalists asking why Burns, who came to be known online by her nickname, Rabbit, was not facing charges and did not come to court to support her son. The reporters were not allowed to answer even though they knew that Burns was under subpoena and excluded from the courtroom, first as a possible Crown witness and later as a potential defence witness. If they did so, they would have risked being found in contempt of court for publishing critical information that the jury had not heard. Jurors did not know that Burns might testify. Nor did they know that her subpoena had been served by Detective Matt Kavanagh on January 4, 2016, at the Toronto West Court on the first day of Millard's preliminary hearing to decide if he should stand trial for the murder of his father, Wayne. Two months later in March, when Justice Diane Oleskiw ruled that Millard would be committed for trial, no news media reported her decision.

According to Noudga, Burns started delivering Millard's letters in late May or June 2013, though at first she would just show them to Christina and not allow her to keep them. As far as Noudga remembers, they mostly described Millard's life in jail, interspersed with declarations of his love for her. The letters stopped, for reasons unknown, in January 2014. Some sections of the letters in evidence have been redacted and are not shown to the jury or made public. The earliest letter found in Noudga's bedside table was dated July 25, 2013, and titled "A Letter To an Arabian Princess." The spelling mistakes are Millard's.

I have a new prized possession. It's a little scrap of paper with a muddy paw print on it. It's fabulous! Thank you— you really do know me better than anyone else. It's the perfect gift in this place. When I was first brought in they treated me as though I were Hannibal Lecter. Paraded down the halls in chains and surrounded on all sides by a team of guards. I suppose the attention should have been flattering. For the first two weeks I was kept naked in a bare video recorded cell, and given only bread and jam to eat. In conversation the presiding psychiatric, [name redacted], actually admitted he was trying to see if he could make me suicidal as part of his pet project to figure me out. He called me an "enigma." He never did get a chance to finish his experiment. I managed to slip out of his clutches and into prison orange clothing. The good doctor does not realize the service he actually did me. He applied such great pressure in his quest to crack my spirit—what he accomplished was hardenning me, like loose carbon turned to diamond. Once I almost broke down. I had taken a Styrofoam cup and broken it into little granuels. I was pushing them about on the floor into different geometric designs. Almost immediately there was a bang at the door. "What are you playing with?" I replied that it was Styrofoam, that I wasn't aloud to read, or draw, and so that was all I had available. The guard confiscated the Styrofoam granuels, and I was back to absolute deprevation. I sat, hugging my knees, and began to cry. I wiped away the first tears with a forearm and the words tattooed there immediately jumped out. Here was text the doctor could not confiscate. "I am heaven sent, don't you dare forget." I had forgotten, and thanks to that tattoo, at the moment I needed reminding, I got it. I stopped crying and smiled. If the doctor had not been so cruel, I do not think I would be fairing so well now. I've been in "the hole" for two months. This is where other prisoners are sent for misconducts, such as fights: They come, they stay for a couple of weeks as punishment, and they go back to their respective ranges. They think this is punishment? Ha! I have clothing, pencil, paper and books. As my great grand mother would have said "tis luxury." The challenge is no longer enduring the day to day realities of prison life, it is bearring the loneliness. Being separated from you is terrible. All the pleasures of modern society; cars, movies, restaurants, itunes, I can do without. My favorite activities; sailing and flying, I could do without. What I long for most is to wake up next to you. I miss you so much— gonna cry.

Your letter has uplifted my spirits like an infusion of helium! I love you like I've never loved any other woman. I'm coming for you.

After lead prosecutor Tony Leitch reads this aloud in court he asks Noudga what she had written to Millard. (Her letters to him have never been found.)

"Um . . . hmm," she says. "Probably, you know, generic: 'I love you, I long for you . . . don't worry, you'll get through this.'"

Leitch reads the second part of Millard's July 25 letter, in which he segues abruptly from his fantastical account of life in jail and declarations of love for Noudga into not so subtle instructions for her.

> Some day sooner or later X may be forced to give a statement, or be sepinaed to take the stand. People often make small lies, and are caught lying by the details. X NEEDS to know, what the police already know, so that X doesn't say anything contrary. X must have this information! Police know Mark gave Dell a locked toolbox. They know Mark told Dell it contained drugs; and that Mark wanted Dell to hide it. They do not know if Dell was told the combination. (Dell will say he did not know the combination.) Police know that Dell used Christina's cell phone to text Matt and ask him to hold the toolbox. Police do not know if Christina was in the Yukon, only that Dell had access to her phone at the time. Matt stated he could not see into the Yukon. (Dell will say the toolbox remained locked the entire time. Christina may have seen it in the car, but it was closed, never openned. Dell will say he borrowed Christina's phone to send some texts. The only reason he gave was that Mark had made a terrible mistake and Dell was trying to contain it. Dell will say he left Christina and Pedo at Maple Gate, taking her phone with him, saying he had to meet someone briefly, and would be back soon. Dell will say he returned to Maple Gate without the toolbox, and returned Christina's phone to her, with

the text history cleared.) Police know that after Dell's arrest Matt returned the toolbox of drugs to Mark. After Mark's arrest police found the toolbox EMPTY in Mark's basement.

"Any idea who X is?" asks Leitch.

Noudga says implausibly that she doesn't. She does, however, concede that the letter was odd. "I didn't see any reason for him to hide the fact that I was in the car," she says. "I probably responded with a vague 'Okay, that's interesting,' and then moved on with talking about my day. I never agreed or disagreed."

"Did you realize what he was asking of you in this letter?"

"I didn't realize it at the time, but looking at it now, he's obviously asking me to tamper with evidence and testimony."

"Did you go to the police?"

"No."

"Why did you choose not to go to the police?"

"I didn't want to be involved," she says. "Not so much [due to] the love I had for him. It was more so I had plans to go abroad, get on with my life."

The fact that Millard was charged with first-degree murder was apparently inconsequential to Noudga. "I didn't want to make a statement," she tells the court. According to her account, it never occurred to her that the police might be interested in the letters. "I just left them there and they collected dust," she says.

"Were you prepared to lie for him?" asks Leitch.

"No."

Along with Millard's letters, police also seized various notes, diary-like musings, and draft letters from Noudga's room. Leitch shows her some of her writings.

"This is your own handwriting?"

"Uh, yeah."

"Do you see what you wrote?" Leitch asks. Then he puts his earlier question to Noudga again. "Were you prepared to lie for him?"

"I wrote that with thoughts of maybe helping him out," she says of her notes, which are not shown in court. "I thought about it, but I wasn't prepared to do it."

"Put it in writing but thought better of it? That's your position?"

"Yes."

Leitch shows a second letter to the court, this one from August 2013. It follows the same pattern as the first. Millard alludes to Smich getting him in trouble, saying he should have paid more attention to a piece of advice he heard on *Breaking Bad*: "Never trust a drug addict." He professes his undying love for Noudga. "I adore the effect your spirit has on me," he writes. "It's like sunshine to a meadow." And then he tells her that to get around the damning cell phone evidence, he may claim to have lent out his phone.

Millard gives the impression of having way more confidence than someone in his situation should have. "The entire case is circumstantial and full of holes," he declares. He asks his girlfriend to check Smich's Facebook page for pictures of Mark working at the hangar and, if she finds the photos, to send them to him.

Noudga tells the court she couldn't have done that even if she'd wanted to, as she deleted her Facebook account shortly after her boyfriend's arrest, and it would have raised suspicions if she'd used someone else's account. Throughout her testimony, she insists she didn't oblige Millard in any of his requests, other than to send along some sexy pictures of herself. His letters seem to support her claims, as he becomes increasingly anxious about her willingness to help him.

UNTIL HE LANDED IN JAIL charged with first-degree murder, Millard exerted a lot of control over Noudga, whose goal was to have him love her as much as she loved him. Although she denies it in court, her text messages about all-nighters and mission digestion can be interpreted to mean she was not only aware of Millard's murder plan but also approved of it. Judging from their texts and letters, it appeared that Noudga regarded Millard as a kind of superman unbound by society's rules, the perfect mate for the brilliant, sexy woman she imagined herself to be. To Millard, Noudga—with her lack of empathy or moral core—was a suitable candidate for number one girlfriend. But he was not prepared to be exclusive: on the side, he also continued to see the realtor Lisa Whidden, and Jenn Spafford, the glamorous ex-fiancée who was still enjoying the use of his car and one of his condos. Once he was behind bars, however, Millard realized that he was going to have to offer Noudga more if he wanted to keep her loyal. In September, he wrote promising her children and a life together.

> Pedo is my child in name and spirit, but the most basic life goal is to have children of my own flesh. My one true fear is to die before being a father.
>
> I usually keep my hopes and plans to myself. Did you know my plan for us and the sailboat? I know I told you I was buying one soon. It was supposed to be this summer.

What I didn't tell you was that as early, next spring, as weather would have allowed, I planned on Michalski bringing it, with me, to Toronto. By then you'd be done with your school year. I wanted us to set sail, just you, me and Pedo, and we'd head for the Atlantic. From Halifax we could go where ever the wind blew us. The winds would probably favor Norway, with a stop in Iceland. Then south to Scotland and England. I figured we'd explore each by harbouring and renting a car. After that the summer would be ending and you'd have to decide if you wanted to fly back for school in Canada or keep on going. I don't think it would be hard to convince you to keep on going. . . .

. . . I planned to sail the world with you. I hoped to time our ship's return to Canada with you pregnant. So we could each benefit from the advice of, and share in the joy with, our mothers.

It chews me up on the inside knowing what I'm missing; worrying what I may never have. If I beat the charges, this dream could still be realized. . . .

. . . I knew before I was arrested that I wanted you to be the mother of my children. I was waiting for you to finish school. I was waiting for my business to stabilize. I was waiting for us to explore the entire globe. Maybe I was waiting for me to be just a little more mature; to be better emotionally settled. But I've known for some time that I had finally found the girl I have spent my entire life waiting for. And now I'm in jail. Fuck!

What if I don't beat the charges? What if I'm given a life sentence? I'm sure you would book overnight trailer visits.

But for how long? I'm certain that if I win the trial we'll have children. But would you have children with a man in prison for life? It may not be a fair question, but these aren't fair times. It's on my mind and will be every day.

P.S. Even as a prisoner I could make a better husband and father than most free men.

As Tony Leitch reads this letter aloud in the courtroom, it causes extreme discomfort. The Bosma family is visibly shaken. Members of the normally stoic jury look horrified. And when the gallery of spectators files out for the afternoon break, they are pretty much speechless.

In keeping with his habit of following declarations of love and devotion with requests for favours, Millard's next letter to Noudga tries to enlist her help as a "secret agent," a career, she tells Leitch, she had long fantasized about.

I've always been able to achieve extraordinary goals. Winning back my liberty . . . Wow, maybe it's beyond me, on my own. Maybe all the things I've achieved have been. I've always gotten help in one form or another. To get out of this bind I need help. I won't ask you to give testimony that could be disproved. What I've written to you is a "rough draft." I wanted your feedback. I WONT have you made a witness if you don't want to be. I can't promise the prosecussion won't subpoena you and force you to testify though. We need to get our stories straight. I need to know what you're willing to do? And of course nothing will go without being checked against phone and internet records.

You said you wanted to be a secret agent. Be mine? Life has a funny way of giving us exactly what we wish for.

Here's your chance to be a covert operative. I wished for two years off work. I wished for a challenge worth devoting myself to. Seems I got it. You know what I wish for now? My liberty. Yours and Pedo's company. Freedom and exploration. To get these things I need to win at trial. To win at trial, I need help. Help could be testimony. Help could be other things too . . . like secretly delivering a message . . . just staying quiet has been an immense help already. If Mark and Andrew had done the same this would be a lot easier. Poor Andrew, shit his pants and spilled his guts. And treacherous Mark; got himself charged by trying to put it on me. These are the most lethal pieces currently played against me.

By October 1, when he wrote the following letter, Millard regarded himself as a jailhouse lawyer, proposing concrete action plans for Noudga. While some of his legal points are correct, others are not. His allegations about the Hamilton Police are unfounded. And he continues to be obsessed with Michalski and his evidence.

None of the science included in the disclosure is hugely relevant. I'm assuming they have Grissom from CSI Las Vegas working the case, and will discover and prove everything that science can. If they miss something, then bonus. If they fake something, then it's a chance to catch them faking. The science shows a body was disposed of. It does not, in this case, show how someone died.

If someone dies accidently, and then the body is disposed of, that's not murder. If someone dies accidently during a robbery, that's murder. Because the robbery is intentional, even an accidental death can become a murder conviction. Most of the evidence points to me going to buy a pickup. This results in an acquittal, and I'm a free man. But there's a problem, and it's the testimony of Andrew Michalski. Cops tricked him into thinking a) that he was charged with murder, which he was not, and b) that they already had the evidence, he was just confirming a tiny meaningless piece for them. Andrew told police that on May 5th I showed him a picture of a black dodge pickup truck, printed from the internet, and told him there were two trucks to choose from, and that I asked "who's should I STEAL, the nice guy's or the asshole's?" It took five hours of interrogation and Andrew contradicted himself many times, but that's what he gave them.

Fucking panzy, scared into giving up a true friend. He doesn't understand the law. He doesn't know what the words mean. He's the only piece of evidence that puts me in the category of intentional robbery. His testimony, not forensic science, is going to get me convicted. He is the most important, single piece of the case against me. . . .

. . . His interrogation seems guided. As if the detective were hinting at what Andrew should say: When Andrew said "no Dell didn't tell me anything about anything" the detective gets angry. When Andrew says "there was a picture of a truck" the detective is all warm and cudly. We are going to argue that Andrew was given the message that he wasn't going home until he said what police wanted to hear. That he was untruthful, so that police would let him leave. The interrogation really does look that way too. . . .

Andrew's a bit gullible when it comes to authority. He is probably mad at me, blaming me for his frightenning interrogation, so that he doesn't have to admit to himself how completely he has thrown me under the bus. All he had to do was say nothing, but instead he tried to talk his way out.

Andrew needs to say I showed him a picture of a truck and asked "who's I should BUY." That he changed it to steal because, before the interrogation began, cops told him they wanted to hear about the planning of a truck robbery, and he wasn't going home until he told them what they wanted to hear. . . .

. . . Someone needs to shake him up. I protected him by telling him nothing. He should never have moved things after I was arrested. That was Mark who brought heat to him, not me. . . .

. . . It was Mark who fucked up a truck robbery, not me. And just because I helped clean up Mark's mess, does not mean I should also pay for it. Especially not because of a technicality in the law. Especially not because Andrew didn't know how to keep his mouth shut. I need him to undo the damage he has done me!

I love him and I know he loves me. He has a loyal heart. If he knew that his words were going to get me a life sentence, he would want to change them. Show him how he can, and he will change them.

Millard regularly warns Noudga to get rid of the evidence. "If ever there were letters to destroy, these are they. Reread them," he writes. "Destroy them now." Millard is also paranoid about those close to him being watched. "My mum's house is under very elusive surveillance," he tells Noudga. He suggests that Noudga's and Michalski's phones are obvious targets for bugging. He asks, "So are you my secret agent? Careful what you wish for." He gives her the name of a lawyer, Christopher Tarach, to pass on to Andrew once she makes contact. "Chris already knows my case. He will probably take Andrew for free," Millard says. "If need be Moose [another friend] could donate 1000.00 (warn him not to use his bugged phone)."

Millard tells Noudga that her most important role will be on the witness stand at his trial.

> Protecting your credibility and preparing to give testimony is how you can help me most. Do not allow that to be sacrificed by trying to solve less important issues.
>
> The second most important role, is getting Andrew on board to help. He's got to say he never heard anything about any thefts or plans to steal anything, especially nothing about stealing a truck. He heard I wanted to buy a truck. Lots of people heard buy, he was just being pressured, coached even, by police. . . .
>
> . . . Bringing Andrew back to my side, brings me back from losing, and puts me at a tie. Your testimony, though, will be what wins it. . . . If Andrew wants to be helpful, maybe he can contact Matt. Andrew's good hearted, but a tad bit slow. If he does want to help, impress upon him how important it is to keep any contact with you a

secret. If he goes to talk to Matt, he must not say where he got his information. He needs a cover story completely thought out in advance.

Help me ObiwonRubikinks, you're my only hope.

The letter includes a large sketch by Millard of Noudga dressed in a Star Wars–style helmet and goggles. He is a gifted sketch artist.

As Leitch reads the letters one by one into the record at court, he stops regularly with questions for Noudga.

"Did you ever think holding on to [the letters] could protect you in some way?" he asks.

Noudga looks blank.

He rephrases the question. "Did you have any concerns about anything Mr. Millard might do?"

She says she didn't. A few minutes earlier, she had insisted she kept the letters only because "I always wanted him to love me back the way I loved him." Now, she says, looking back, she sees "it was very stupid, very idiotic, of me."

IN OCTOBER 2013, MILLARD STARTED teaching himself Ukrainian in jail and writing passages of his letters to Noudga in her parents' native tongue. In a letter that was also a language-learning exercise, Millard wrote several phrases in Ukrainian, including "Dellen loves Christina," "Never a lender nor a borrower be," and "First learn the alphabet."

"Prior to incarceration," asks Leitch, "had he shown any interest in the Ukrainian language?"

"It wasn't on the top of his language list," says Noudga, who, despite her infatuation with Millard, seems to have sensed on some level that learning Ukrainian might be a ploy to ingratiate himself with her. Although he was also learning Spanish and was interested in a lot of languages, Millard had never before tried to talk to her in Ukrainian. Yet after a few months in jail, he was signing his letters to her with the Ukrainian phrase meaning "your man" or "your husband."

Millard was also obsessed with surveillance. In a letter sent in October, he tells Noudga that a recent visitor to his mother's house, who stopped by when Madeleine Burns wasn't home, was pulled over by police fifteen minutes later on Highway 27 "by an unmarked cruizer (the kind that look like cop cars, but the word police is obscured). It seems like a routine traffic stop, until he's ordered out of his car, and the car is searched. Nothing was found. Then to top it off, he was asked what he was doing at my mum's."

Millard says these cops are "real undercover," who can't be detected. He was sure they knew that his mother and Christina were meeting. "I hope you read these letters in an enclosed place where none of the public can see you," he says. "I hope you take this warning very seriously."

Despite the perceived danger, Millard still wanted Noudga to contact Michalski with what he called "Mission Impossible, James Bond, super spy perfection." He was okay if she played the romance card. "I don't mind you being publicly flirtatious if it's in my favor," he writes. "Just so long as all of him stays on the outside of you."

A few days later, Millard told Christina he needed her phone records for May 5, 6, 7, and 8. He wanted incoming and outgoing calls and texts, with times and locations. "Send me a copy AND keep a copy for yourself," he says. "So that I can write you about them, and we can cross reference."

Leitch asks Noudga if she obliged.

"No," she says. "I thought it was, like, a waste of time."

"Was that your response?"

"I don't know if I used those exact words. . . . I was probably like, 'I don't think you need the phone records, because I know what I was doing the entire week.'"

As frustrated as Millard may have been with Noudga's lack of response to his requests, he kept on cozying up to her. "I was going to wait to hear from you before writing this letter, but I don't want that much time to go to waste," he writes on October 27. "So until I do hear from you, I am going to continue writing as if your response is a resounding Yes! That you will be my secret agent; effectively my savior.

"Only the craftiest of coyotes will be able to avoid charges like witness tampering or perjury," he continues. "Of paramount importance is that you keep our contact secret."

Noudga maintains that she didn't know at first that a court order forbade Millard from communicating with her. She says a few of her friends and both her parents were aware she was in contact with him.

By mid-November 2013, six months after his arrest, Millard was still discussing phone location data, although he admits to Noudga, "Because there is still so much disclosure to come, it is not certain what defense I will use." He wanted her to testify that he had a habit of lending his phone to Smich and to help him find any possible supporting evidence. "This can be done in the positive, ie: someone called my phone [and] instead of me answering, Mark would answer and say that I wasn't there. Or, this could be done in the negative, ie: someone saw me, but I did not have my phone on me." He asks Noudga if Snoff and Kodiak, the code names he has assigned to Hagerman and Michalski, "will help create the precedent. Careful what you tell them. Be sure they will help before giving them any information."

"Did you reach out to them about this phone issue?" asks Leitch.

"No," says Noudga.

"In your time with Mr. Millard, did you ever see him loan his phone to Mr. Smich?"

"I've seen him not have it, but I've never seen him lend his phone."

Somewhat ironically, Noudga appears—according to her testimony on this point—to have been almost as unhelpful to her jailed boyfriend as she was to the police and prosecutors. She maintains that in the same way she ignored his requests for her phone records, she didn't engage with him about what defence strategies he might use at trial.

Millard also worried about his mother's role as intermediary. In one of his letters, he describes an incident where Burns called him from a pay phone and put Noudga on the line.

> It was wonderful to think you could hear me on the phone. I could almost feel your presence. Even now days later, it puts the hint of a smile on my face.
>
> But, it was also reckless of my mum to do that. Your credibility as a witness is the ace up my sleeve. If either you or her are under surviellence, what are you gonna say when the prosecution pulls out a snapshot of you in the

phone booth, with phone records, and jail records, to say
I was on the other end of the line?

...A phone call you can't talk back on is not worth
the risk. There were a hundred officers assigned to this
case. It doesn't take that many to listen to the jail phone,
and fetch coffee. These aren't traffic cops. They're like the
KGB. You, and my mum, are the only people who haven't
given any statement at all. Your names are probably on a
board in some detective's office with big question marks
beside them. I don't think my mum appreciates that police
focus could be on her, and you. I need you to appreciate
it. I need you to play the role of the illusive spy. Illusive,
cunning and catious; if you can be these things, I can get
out of here and be yours again.

According to Noudga's account of this phone call, she did
not say a word, just listened as Millard sang the Oasis song
"Wonderwall" to her. The lyrics, especially the chorus about
being the one to save him, likely struck him as relevant.

Leitch is skeptical. "He has the opportunity to speak to you in
person and all he does is sing 'Wonderwall'?"

"Correct."

"How does he know you're there?"

"His mother mentions it to him."

"Did you ever do this again?"

They never had any further voice contact, she says.

As 2013 drew to a close, Millard's letters suggest he was becoming increasingly worried that his hold on Noudga was weakening.
He asked one of his visitors in jail to reach out to her. And in an

interview with the *Toronto Star*, weeks in the making, he laments not being able to speak to Noudga due to the no-contact order. "We were in love," he declares for the world to read.

Before the *Toronto Star* article appeared, on December 30, Millard had informed Noudga that he was speaking to a reporter, who had also expressed interest in talking to her. "I shrugged my shoulders, and said I did not mind. But when he contacts you, I think, you should not talk to him," Millard writes. "Don't say anything to him, not about me, not about you, not about the weather. I don't know yet if what he is going to write, is going to help me, or hurt me."

For her part, Noudga let Millard know that she'd "withheld" a lawyer, to which he responds, "Oh how I miss your diction! Its 'retained,' my love." The two of them regularly corrected each other's language mistakes. He called her his "english professor," probably because she gave him grief over his atrocious spelling, while he took aim at her vocabulary mix-ups and malapropisms. (In court, for example, she confused *recant* with *recount* several times.)

Millard also encouraged Noudga to keep active on his behalf. "Surely your super spy self can get in touch with Kodiak. How about going to Yuri's and getting him to call in a plumbing emergency. Or, going to the same New Year's party," he writes in early December.

"We can't know what to say until disclosure is fully in. That's still months down the road," he says. "More disclosure could change everything and require a different approach with what will be best for you to say. What Kodiak needs to say is already clear, that won't change."

"So this is a reference to you testifying," says Leitch.

"Uh, yes."

"How do you respond?"

"I don't mention it, really. I had other plans for New Year's and Christmas anyways, and that's what I talked about." She says Yuri was a friend of hers, Millard's, and Michalski's.

When Leitch reads the translation of a date written in Ukrainian in the next letter, Noudga corrects him, as she has done on a few previous occasions. "You need a new translator," she says.

"You could be right," Leitch says. "Maybe we should have hired you, Ms. Noudga." Then he asks if she was still in love in December.

"Unfortunately so," she says, but adds that her feelings were contradictory. When she expressed this to Millard, he responded, "What do you mean by—the more you love me, the more you hate me? Or was it—the more I open up with my emotions, the more you hate me? Please elaborate."

"Why the hate?" Leitch asks.

"Just . . . I always had, like, feelings that he was seeing other women, but he rejected them and was aloof about that, and I was madly in love with him, but I wasn't sure how he felt back at me. I kind of felt like I was being played, and I wasn't sure what was going on."

"What do you mean?"

"Maybe it's just because he was in jail he was getting really passionate and emotional," she says. He had expressed loving and lustful sentiments before, but he had never come on quite so strong.

So, Leitch asks, it was the "declarations of love interspersed with requests to reach out to Crown witnesses. Is that what you mean by getting played?"

Noudga says it is.

Leitch comes to an undated letter with AGENT COYOTE written in the top right-hand corner. In it, Millard refers to Michalski as Kodiak again and to Mark Smich as Itchy. Along the top of the paper are instructions for Noudga: "reread this page, commit to memory, then *destroy this letter*."

> What Kodiak has the power to say, about what Itchy said to him, could change everything. Maybe Itchy told Kodiak that "I wasn't there" and "not involved with what went down." That Itchy had gone with two of his "boyz" and "something bad happened." That when I found out, Itchy's boyz threatened violence against Itchy's family, and my family, if either of us spoke a word about them. Itchy begged me to help him hide what had happened, and I tried to. When police arrested me, I could not help them in their investigation, because to do so would have endangered my mother, my property and Itchy's family. This is also why I have not answered questions about the case for the media. And why my mother is selling my property and her house, so that there is nothing vulnerable. And why I have not attempted bail or house arrest. I would be a sitting duck for the killers who would want to ensure I never talk. Maybe Itchy told this to Kodiak. Maybe Kodiak will tell the court. I need this kind of help to win this. Have you made contact with Kodiak? Will he help?
>
> What it is that I found out is still uncertain. And as for what happened with Itchy and his "boyz" to result in a dead guy and a stolen truck, that is uncertain too.

Maybe Itchy's boyz were somehow involved with the dead guy, or his wife.

Maybe some fluke accident occurred.

Maybe Itchy knew I was shopping for a truck, and knew that I was tiring of supporting him, so he hatched a plan to steal a truck, and sell it to me for a reduced price thereby engraciating himself with me, at the same time as scoring some cash for himself. A perfect plan in Itchy's books. He enlisted two of his boyz, who had experience with car theft and armed robbery. Itchy thought he was setting up a pleasant surprise for me, that was going to pay off for him. But something went wrong.

Maybe we'll never be certain, but what is certain is that Itchy told Kodiak that I wasn't there. Right?

destroy this letter

Also of some importance is that Dell does NOT own a gun. Itchy has Boyz who are said to own guns. Their street names are Lyle and A-pock. Maybe it's the same "boyz." Itchy's street name is Say10. Dell does not have a street name

This actually does more to help Itchy than I feel he deserves.

"Who's Agent Coyote?" asks Leitch.

"I don't know," says Noudga. "Well, maybe he was referring to me, but it was never specified."

"You knew this was an attempt at fabrication when you read this?"

"At the time I read it, I honestly believed in his innocence. . . .

He was always gentle and kind." Noudga says she never knew Millard to be aggressive. "I was in denial for a very long time."

Leitch puts one of the last of the letters from Millard on the courtroom screens and suggests to Noudga that it's essentially a script for her to follow in answering questions about Millard and Mark Smich and their strange relationship. While she claims she didn't interpret the letter that way at the time, Noudga now concedes Leitch has a point. The overall theme of the letter is that Smich was starting to get on Millard's nerves in a big way.

"Dell was complaining more and more about Mark," Millard tells Noudga, feeding her his storyline. "He said that Mark was always smoking pot, and that Mark wasn't helping at all, and that Dell felt like his time was being wasted. . . . Dell told you he was going to cut Mark off soon. The first week of May, Dell told you he had the cash together, and that he was buying a diesel truck that week."

Unfortunately for Millard, if there ever were a moment when Noudga was prepared to learn and recite her lines, it has passed. She tells the court she never heard any mention from Millard of cutting Smich off or raising cash for a truck. She also denies that Smich had access to Millard's passwords, as Millard wanted her to say. In his letter, Millard writes, "When at Maple Gate, Mark would ask to buy songs on Dell's itunes, or even ask to use Dell's eBay account. Dell would yell over that it was okay. Apparently Mark had Dell's passwords. You heard and saw this while chilling at Maple Gate. Mark had access to everything in Dell's life."

Millard was no doubt worried about his eBay account because he had used it to buy concealment holsters, including for a Walther PPK. As for Millard's iTunes account, Smich having access would explain how an iPad, obtained around the time Laura Babcock disappeared, had come to be synced to Millard's computer.

"Dell's goal was to make Mark self sufficient," his letter to Noudga continues. "Dell talked of the plan to produce a rap album with Mark. Dell would supply the equipment, and network with others to bring in musical talent. It was Mark's dream. Dell thought it would be the way to finally make Mark self sufficient." The problem, according to Millard's script for Noudga, was that Smich had started drinking too much and taking oxycodone. And as a result, Millard was no longer prepared to further Smich's rap ambitions.

In his letter to Noudga, Millard writes, "In March Mark told you that he didn't think Dell was ever going to get around to making the rap album. That he thought Dell was too busy with his grandfather's company. Mark told you that his sister had a place in Calgary, and that he was gonna move out there with Marlena, as soon as he could get enough money together to go."

According to the script, Noudga was to say she had witnessed a conversation in which Smich admitted to Millard he was torn about the Calgary plan, and that Millard told him if he wanted to stay and make the rap album, Smich would have to get off oxycodone and work hard. Noudga was to recount that she later asked Millard why he continued to support Smich. "I told you some people gave food to food banks, some people donated money to the homeless, and some people spent months in africa building homes," he writes. "Mark was all three rolled into one for me."

AS THE LAST OF the letters are read into the court record on her third day of testimony, Noudga remains as unpleasant and unforthcoming as ever. When Leitch asks her a few final questions, she is still making faces and being rude. She does, however, seem to relish the chance to deliver a line straight out of the movies when asked if she sees Dellen Millard in the courtroom. "Right over there," she says as she points across the room. Then, at Leitch's request, she does the same for Mark Smich—all with a big smile.

Out of necessity, Millard's lead lawyer, Ravin Pillay, is relatively kind in his cross-examination of Christina Noudga, who can still inflict more damage on his client, should she choose to do so.

"You are facing very serious charges," he begins.

"Alas, I am."

"Your world has been torn apart?"

"Yes."

"Life as you've known it has ceased to exist. Fair?"

"Yes."

"All your plans for the future have been put aside?"

"Yes."

"You live under constant scrutiny of the media?"

"Yes."

"You and your family have experienced significant hardship?"

"Yes."

"You appear to be very composed."

"Yeah."

"But you're scared, aren't you?"

"Terrified."

"Your primary focus is on your case?"

"Yes."

"You're not here to help Mr. Millard?"

"No."

Pillay suggests that Noudga knew from Millard's letters that he was in a steady emotional decline. "You could tell the isolation was getting to him. He was losing hope. He was desperate, depressed?"

"He didn't come off as depressed, but, yeah, being in jail, you get depressed," says Noudga, who does not have fond memories of her four months behind bars before she made bail in August 2014.

Pillay says she knew the things Millard was asking her to do were "stupid, foolish, wrong," which was why she never acted on them.

"No, I just filled him with more love and support," Noudga replies. She says she told Millard, "You're not, like, alone in here. Don't worry about it. Everything will be fine."

Pillay suggests that she didn't answer when Millard asked if he could rely on her testimony, she didn't go on Facebook to look for pictures of Smich, and she never had any contact with Michalski.

Noudga agrees.

Pillay says she kept the letters for their sentimental value and didn't destroy them because she never intended to act on what they proposed.

"Yeah," she agrees.

"You never thought they would be introduced at trial."

"I'm a little surprised they are, actually."

Pillay gets as tough as he's going to get with Noudga when he asks her how someone who fancies herself a science geek, as he puts it, could have accepted Millard's explanation that the Eliminator would be used to burn metal.

"I used the term *burning* improperly," she says, and clarifies that she meant melting. It's possible, she agrees with Pillay, that she doesn't remember very well at all the conversation she had with Millard about why he acquired an incinerator.

ONE OF THE FIRST questions Thomas Dungey asks Noudga is when she stopped loving Millard.

"When he got me arrested," she says. She describes her current feelings toward her ex-boyfriend as "contempt and a bit of loathing."

"I've been humiliated in public and by the courts for two years, so I don't necessarily like him," she says.

"Of course, your trial's coming up," says Dungey, referring to her November 2016 court date. "If Mr. Millard was to testify he told you everything, if he said you knew there was a truck in the trailer, that would hurt you?"

Yes, she says, but then he would be lying under oath.

Dungey wonders about what he calls Noudga's selective memory, and she explains that it's not that she forgets things, more that she just didn't ask questions she knew Millard wouldn't answer.

"He didn't tell you about what criminal activity he had done?"

"No, he never told me."

"Did he tell you he stole a Bobcat?"

"No."

"Did he ever tell you he was on an illegal mission with Andrew Michalski?"

"No."

Nor, according to Noudga, did Millard mention theft missions with Hagerman or Smich.

"You would have parties at Maple Gate. You'd be there with Michalski, Marlena, Hagerman," says Dungey. "And never did it ever come up about illegal missions?"

"No."

"Never?"

"If it did, I wasn't there," Noudga says. "I would have been like, What the fuck?"

"What does that mean?"

"It means, Why would you do that when you can just buy it?"

"So, nowhere along the lines did he ever tell you he was going to steal a truck?"

"No."

"Did Andrew mention it?"

"Andrew and I were not that close."

"So he kept you completely isolated from that aspect of his personality?"

"I'm kind of glad he did."

"It's kind of like we're dealing with a whole other personality."

"I'd say more secrets," says Noudga. "If he was in criminal activity, he did this to protect me."

"That's your defence in your case: it's that he didn't tell you anything?"

"Well, I didn't know anything."

Dungey asks Noudga to read some notes she made to herself under the heading "Brilliant Ideas." She had written that if she ever dated another criminal, she should blackmail him.

It was "because I had dated Dellen, who had a criminal life," she explains, adding that she has a bad and inappropriate sense of humour. She tells Dungey that those notes have nothing to do with the case. "You're misreading it. This was written in a way for me to profit off men's criminal activity for blackmail." It was simply planning for the future.

Dungey asks why she played along with Millard and his letters for so many months.

"I maintained this idea he was innocent. Maybe he had some role to play in it, but I didn't believe in him being a murderer."

"He's charged with murder and telling you he wants you to tamper with Crown witnesses."

Noudga tells Dungey what she told Leitch: that she avoided answering Millard's questions. "I didn't want to make him feel like I wasn't supporting him. That's how I did it," she says.

"At this point, do you not say, How can this guy be innocent?"

"Sometimes people can't get out of certain situations, and I thought he was trying to get out of the situation. . . . I thought, Maybe no one's going to believe the truth, so he has to come up with a story."

"It gets worse as it goes along," says Dungey about the letters.

"I think he was just getting more anxious because I had not responded."

Noudga traces many of her current problems to legal advice she claims she was given after Millard's arrest. "I got advice, and I'm sorry that I followed it," she says.

Justice Goodman tells her that it was her "constitutional right" and she doesn't have to be sorry she spoke with a lawyer. The details cannot be revealed due to solicitor–client privilege.

Noudga says her friends and family were unfairly harassed

by police and media because she was advised not to make a statement.

Dungey points out that talking to people is how the police conduct investigations and that it doesn't constitute harassment. He finds her whole attitude puzzling, he says, including the fact that when Tim Bosma was missing and Millard's trailer was in Madeleine Burns's driveway, neither Noudga nor Burns called the police.

Noudga makes a face as if to suggest Dungey is as crazy as Leitch.

"You wouldn't assume there might be evidence?" he asks.

"It was a possibility we didn't explore," she says. "We didn't explore where the person might be." As always, Noudga fails to say Tim Bosma's name. "I don't know why we didn't call the police then. We waited for legal counsel . . . and then called it in."

When Dungey asks why she wiped down the locks on the trailer, Noudga replies, "I wasn't tampering with possible evidence. I was just removing my involvement." Lawyer and witness go round in circles about whether fingerprints constitute evidence, provoking laughter in the courtroom and consternation from the judge.

As his cross-examination ends, a somewhat exasperated Dungey displays one final letter from Millard on the screen. It was written in January 2014. "You are a truly special woman," Millard signs off. "I believe we deserve each other. I deserve you, and you deserve me."

"The last line in the letter," says Dungey. "'I deserve you and you deserve me.' That's what he wrote to you?"

"Yes," says Noudga.

"Thank you," he says. "No further questions."

It takes a while for it to register with Noudga what's just happened. While Dungey didn't succeed in rattling Noudga as he did Shane Schlatman and Matt Hagerman, his last question was what CBC News later referred to "a mic drop moment."

FOURTEEN

CUTTHROAT

After Christina Noudga's five days of testimony wrapped up on May 4, the court did not sit on Friday, May 6, the third anniversary of Tim Bosma's death. This was a happenstance of scheduling as opposed to a planned day of remembrance. Then on Monday, May 9, the prosecution made it official: after more than three months of trial, it was closing its case. The time had finally come for the defending lawyers Ravin Pillay and Thomas Dungey to let it be known if they would be calling evidence and witnesses, including the accused.

The most common reason given for not calling evidence is simply that the accused does not believe the prosecution has proven its case beyond a reasonable doubt. Another reason, although defence lawyers hate to admit it, is that calling evidence might only make the situation worse.

At the Bosma trial, since it is Dellen Millard who is listed first on the indictment, it is Pillay who must make his intentions known first. "The defence elects to call no evidence," he tells the court.

In her front-row seat, Sharlene Bosma seems pleased with the news that Millard won't testify, that the trial finally appears to be winding down.

The judge asks Dungey for his client's decision. He responds that he would like a few minutes to talk to Smich. Although Dungey has known for a couple of days that Millard would likely elect not to testify, nothing is final until it is announced in court. Justice Goodman orders a brief recess. Some fifteen minutes later, when everyone is back in their seats, Goodman says, "I'm putting Mr. Smich at this time to his election."

"Mr. Smich will be calling evidence," says Dungey, who then asks for two extra days to prepare.

Unlike the prosecution, the defence has no obligation to make its witnesses known in advance. But there has been much speculation that Smich himself will take the stand, partly based on his brand-new haircut.

Two days later, on Wednesday, May 11, Dungey makes a brief opening address to the jury. He reminds them that the presumption of innocence follows an accused individual at all times, that the onus is on the Crown to prove guilt, and that his client has no obligation to testify to prove his innocence; Mark Smich does so by his own choice. "We believe that you, the jurors, should have the full picture, the absolute full picture," Dungey says. "He is going to tell you what he did and what happened on May 6 and 7."

Smich, who is dressed in a red checked shirt and ivory chinos, gets up from the table where he normally sits and walks to the witness box. He is not wearing his usual shackles, since that might prejudice the jury. He swears on the Bible to tell the truth.

Dungey asks Smich how old he was when Tim Bosma was murdered.

"I believe twenty-four," says Smich, who was in fact twenty-five and is now twenty-eight. His birthday is in August.

"Tell us about your mother," says Dungey

"My mother was diagnosed with breast cancer. It might have been a year or two prior. I was taking care of her. She needed someone there. My sisters were busy at that time with their own lives, so I decided to go and do that." His mother is sixty-eight now and retired from the aerospace company where she worked for decades.

Smich says his father wasn't much of a presence in his life after his parents divorced when he was about two years old. Along with his two older sisters, he also has a half-sister from his father's remarriage. "My family means the world to me," says Smich. "We were very close."

At the time of his arrest, Smich had only a Grade 10 education, but he completed his high school diploma while in custody at the Toronto East Detention Centre. The document is shown to the court. One of his teachers has written a letter describing Smich as "a dedicated, capable and engaged participant." Smich says he wants to continue his studies.

Jail has also been good for his health. He has given up drinking and drugs. He works out regularly.

Dungey skips as quickly as he can past his client's patchy employment record, about which Smich can recall few details. Basically, apart from a short stint washing dishes and cleaning at Woodie Wood Chuck's, a knockoff of Chuck E. Cheese's, he's never had a proper job. He handed out pamphlets for a friend who owned a Croissant Tree franchise in Mississauga and went canvassing door to door for the Heart & Stroke Foundation as part of his compulsory community service in high school. After his mother moved to Oakville, Smich says, "I did more under-the-table cash jobs, if you want to call it that."

He worked briefly at a local motorcycle shop doing renovations and painting, but mostly he earned money dealing drugs, which is how he met Dellen Millard. He puts the year they met at 2008, though a former friend of Millard remembers the connection dating back to 2006. Somebody gave Millard Smich's number, and Millard made the occasional drug purchase. Then the two fell out of touch.

A couple of years later, they renewed their acquaintance. Millard would drive Smich, who didn't have a licence, to pick up drugs. They introduced each other to their different circles of friends, and Millard would invite Smich to play video games. Smich estimates that they started getting closer in 2011. "We had similar things we liked to do," he says. "We both liked to smoke weed and hang out."

Not long after, the thieving "missions" began. The two friends spotted a big enclosed trailer that said "Corvette" on the side and saw that its hitch was facing the road. "We didn't know what was inside," says Smich, "just hitched it up and drove off. I believe we took it to Maple Gate." Inside, they found Corvette rims. On another occasion, Millard and Smich stole trees from a plant nursery, throwing them over the fence onto an open trailer.

"Were you compensated, paid?" asks Dungey.

"Yes. I wouldn't be able to recollect exactly, at this time, the amount, but there would have been cash involved."

Their missions ranged from spur-of-the-moment capers to well-planned activities. Once, when Smich and Millard were at the Wingporium restaurant eating chicken wings, Millard spotted a concrete-floor polisher in the back of a truck. "After we were done eating and having a beer, he said, 'We're going to take it.' . . . We kind of pulled it from one vehicle to another, right in the middle of a busy parking lot." Smich chuckles at the memory.

A more elaborate heist involved the theft of a wood chipper from a city equipment storage lot in Oakville. Millard and Smich "scoped out" the grounds in advance, looking for cameras and other security obstacles. "We had bolt cutters, chopped the lock, hooked up the wood chipper to the Yukon, and drove off," says Smich. Millard used licence plate covers installed by Shane Schlatman to ensure that his plates couldn't be seen. The thieves brought gloves, paint, and a change of clothes. They sanded off the Town of Oakville logo and spray-painted over it.

"Did [Millard] have a purpose for stealing these things, a need?" asks Dungey.

"Nothing that he would really tell me. He wanted it, and that's it."

Smich says he never kept any of the stolen goods, but he was paid for helping steal them. The numerous trailers they took ended up at the hangar or Millard's Riverside Drive property.

"What other jobs did you do for Dellen?" Dungey asks.

"Legal jobs?"

"Yes."

Smich says he worked on various Millard properties, painting, renovating, and digging ditches, among other things. When he and Marlena Meneses lived in Millard's basement, she would also help with painting and would keep the place clean.

Sometimes, Millard paid Smich cash, at other times it was food, marijuana, or a new pair of shoes. By 2012, their relationship had intensified to the point that Smich was building a room for himself in the basement at Riverside Drive. The plan was that he would live there and share kitchen facilities with Millard, whose apartment would be directly above.

"I felt like he was a brother to me, family," says Smich. "I invited him over for Christmas dinner with my own family." Christina Noudga attended as well. It was December 2012, less than one month after the death of Wayne Millard.

Despite their shared fondness for marijuana and other recreational drugs, Millard wanted Smich to quit drinking and smoking cigarettes. He gave him medical advice about what to do for his chronically dislocating shoulder. He also promised to build his friend a recording studio to further his rap ambitions. At first, the studio was supposed to be in the garage at Riverside, then Millard decided to locate it at the farm. The excavator was supposed to be used in its construction, but it got stuck in the swamp. "I was kind of pissed off it didn't happen," says Smich, "but what can you do, right?"

Dungey asks how much Millard knew about Smich's criminal record, which stretches back to 2003, when Smich was sixteen and convicted of breaking and entering and theft. In 2004, there was another theft conviction and a failure to comply with parole conditions. Smich says Millard was aware only of the more recent drug charges and an impaired driving infraction from 2009, as well as the graffiti incident in 2012.

"Whose idea was it to steal a truck?" Dungey asks.

"Dell's idea," says Smich. "It was a plan for quite some time. I couldn't give an exact date. It was well over a year."

Smich said it took so long because they were "scoping things out" and constantly modifying the plan. They needed to find an accessible diesel truck and then go back to get it. Smich's role would be to "keep six," which is criminal slang, derived from military communications, for being a lookout. The test-drive part of the plan was more recent, devised by Millard after their targeted trucks kept getting moved. Smich was aware that Millard had a special phone to set up the appointments.

He claims that on the test drive with Igor Tumanenko, they were concerned Tumanenko's truck might have a GPS, like the Bobcat they had stolen.

Smich confirms Marlena Meneses's testimony that she tried to talk him out of stealing the truck. "I guess women have intuition, and she might have had a bad feeling," he tells the jury. "She was telling me repeatedly it was a stupid idea and not to go."

Millard asked him to bring a change of clothes, because if they decided to steal the truck later that night, they would need to wear all black, which might have looked odd to prospective sellers. They also didn't want their clothes to give them away as the guys who were there earlier. Smich says that on May 6, they intended to check out the truck and then, if it was what they wanted, return wearing black and take it using one of a number of techniques shown to them by Shane Schlatman.

Millard and Smich parked on the side of the road near the Bosma residence and left Pedo in the Yukon. The location Smich describes in court is the field owned by Rick Bullmann's father. It's where Bullmann testified he later saw two vehicles pull out—a truck followed immediately by what looked like an SUV—when he was walking his dog. Smich remembers that as they left the field and walked up to the Bosma house, Millard was on his phone. "There was both a lady and a man standing out there," says Smich, who thinks he saw Tim Bosma come out from the garage and start talking to Millard right away.

As Smich gives his version of the last hour of Tim Bosma's life, the courtroom is tense. Hank Bosma puts his arm around his wife, who is in tears. A few seats over, Sharlene Bosma holds her head in her hands.

On a highly discordant note, after Smich has described the first moments of meeting Tim Bosma, Dungey asks him to describe his health problems.

"I was still ill from the night before, so I wasn't feeling the best," Smich says. "My shoulder was bad at that time. It actually popped out that night, so I was in pain." No explanation is provided as to why what Smich describes as the "unbearable" pain of this dislocation failed to deter him from his truck-stealing mission. He continues with his account of the theft.

"Dell gets into the vehicle. Mr. Bosma gets into the vehicle. Mr. Bosma gives Dell the keys. I proceeded into the rear. Then we proceed to leave the driveway."

Mary Bosma cannot bear to hear any more. She rushes from the courtroom, followed almost immediately by friends and a victim services worker. Hank Bosma remains in his seat, looking straight ahead. He is prepared to hear it all.

Just as the truck was about to turn out of the driveway, Millard hit the brakes and pulled out his phone. He said his fictional friend—the one who Tim Bosma believed had dropped them off—couldn't find the Tim Hortons where he was supposed to wait. He was around the corner instead. Smich says they then pulled over near where the Yukon was parked. Millard suggested Mark follow behind with the Tim Hortons friend so they wouldn't have to return to the Bosmas at the end of the test drive. Smich took the hint.

"I get out. Dell pulled a U-turn. I got into the Yukon. The keys were in the cupholder. Pedo was in the car. I started the vehicle and proceeded to follow him."

"Was this planned out?" asks Dungey.

"No. Like I said, the plan was to scope out the vehicle and come back and take it later, once the time was right."

"Then what happens?"

"I followed him," says Smich, shaking his head in a characteristic gesture. "We just kept driving until he pulls over on the side of the road and I pulled up behind him."

"Was any of this part of the plan, the scoping?"

"Dell does random things," says Smich as Millard looks on.

Smich can't remember much about the drive, how long it took, or exactly where they went after turning north on Trinity Road. He says Millard pulled over with a sudden swerve. "Dell gets out of the vehicle and he proceeds to walk toward the Yukon, and he was putting what looks to be a gun into his satchel."

"What's your reaction to this?"

Smich says he asked what was going on, to which Millard replied, "I'm taking the truck." He reached into the Yukon and grabbed a flashlight.

"As he was walking back, I proceeded to follow him, and that's when I seen a bullet hole through the window and Mr. Bosma laying head first on the dashboard," says Smich.

"I was in utter and complete shock. I'm not sure there are words I can describe it. I was in disbelief. I said, 'What the fuck is going on?' It was all crazy. Dell looked like something came over him. He didn't look like his normal self.

"He said, 'Go and get the plates from the Yukon.' They were the licence plates from his red Dodge Ram.

"I was freaking out. I said, 'This is not the plan, not how it's supposed to go down.' He just said, 'Go and get the plates.'

"He was loud and forceful. I'd never seen him like this. He looked mad, like a lunatic, like something came over him.

"I went and did as he said and got the plates. He told me to change the licence plates from one vehicle, the Bosma vehicle, with the licence plates of the red Dodge."

They had changed plates on previous thefts, says Smich. "But the way that it went down was not how it was supposed to go down."

He tells the court that nobody had ever been harmed during their previous criminal activities. Although many of the spectators know that Smich is also facing charges for the 2012 murder of Laura Babcock, the jury has not been informed of this fact, nor that her death coincided with the purchase of the Eliminator.

While they were stopped, Millard wiped off Bosma's phone and prepared to discard it. Smich says Millard told him, "Everything's going to be all right. Don't worry, just follow me."

"He was very forceful in his tone," says Smich. "It didn't change much as time went on. He was telling me to not worry, because I was panicked and I was shocked, and that was not part of the plan. At that point, I don't know, I felt like I had no choice. I was scared."

Dungey plays the video from Bobcat of Brantford, which the court has already seen. It begins with the two loud booming sounds as the vehicles enter the camera's range. Then it shows the vehicles pulling over and, twelve minutes later, leaving. It is impossible to make out any human figures, let alone what they are doing while pulled over. Apart from passing traffic, there are just a few occasional flashes of light. Smich appears nervous in the witness box as the video plays.

After they left Brantford, Smich says he followed Millard to his farm. Millard unchained the gate, and they drove around to the back of the barn.

"He gets out of the vehicle. I get out of the vehicle. He tells me to go close the gate, chain it back up, make sure no one follows. So that's what I did. I went with Pedo. I stood there for a minute. There was nobody, no cars driving around. I walked back. Then I seen Mr. Bosma laying on a sort of sheet. The passenger side of the truck was open. There was blood all over the whole left side of Mr. Bosma's head.

"Dell told me to open the barn door. He rolled Mr. Bosma up in the sheet. I opened the barn door. Then he told me to help him hitch the Eliminator, which was on the trailer, to the truck. So I took the flashlight. I went up to where the incinerator was, and he backed up the Bosma vehicle to the Eliminator and we attached it. He pulled it forward to where Mr. Bosma's body was laying, and after that he got out of the vehicle. He proceeded to open the hatch of the Eliminator. He asked me—well, I don't want to say ask—he told me to help him put Mr. Bosma into the Eliminator.

"I didn't want to go anywhere near it. I told him it was because of my shoulder. He gave a kind of little huff and puff, like he was mad."

According to Smich, Millard stepped up onto the trailer and then single-handedly lifted Bosma's body into the Eliminator, the hatch of which was four and a half feet above the trailer floor. Then Millard opened the gate, chained it back up, and proceeded to drive to the hangar. He drove the Bosma truck with the Eliminator in tow while Smich followed behind in the Yukon.

At the hangar, Millard unhooked the Eliminator and drove the truck to Shane Schlatman's work station. He ordered Smich to strip the vehicle while he went to get gas. Using an X-Acto knife, Smich cut out the carpet and seat belts. When Millard returned, he told Smich to wash the truck. While Smich hosed down the stolen vehicle, Millard turned on the Eliminator. Then together they removed the truck's seats. As Tim Bosma's remains were being incinerated, Millard and Smich stuffed garbage bags with everything they had removed from the truck, along with their gloves, the heavy-duty mechanic's paper towels they used to clean up, and spray-paint cans. Smich isn't asked what they did with their clothes. The garbage bags were put in the back of Millard's red Dodge truck, along with the Bosma truck's front seat frames. The next thing Smich remembers is pulling the incinerator into the hangar and Millard sending text messages telling his employees not to come to work.

About an hour later the pair left for Oakville and picked up Marlena Meneses in the Yukon. "She was kind of stressed out. It was also very early in the morning, so she was kind of tired," says Smich. "She was mad, if you want to put it that way. Dell said he got the truck." When Millard dropped them off at Smich's mother's house, he told Smich he would pick him up later that day to move the incinerator.

"Did you tell Marlena anything?" asks Dungey.

"No, I was so exhausted," says Smich. "I woke up—I was still in pain—got in contact with Dell. I don't recall exactly what the conversation was. I was trying to, you know, I guess play along, like everything was all right kind of thing. I don't know. I had so many thoughts going through my head at that time. I don't know how to explain it.

"He said he was coming to pick me up. I didn't want to not answer the phone. That would cause some kind of suspicion. After seeing him like that, I was just trying to pretend everything was normal."

Dungey asks if Smich went along with Millard because he had looked like a lunatic.

Smich said his behaviour was a result of being "concerned, scared, frightened. I felt threatened. I didn't know what exactly to do at that point. I was confused."

They moved the Eliminator from the Waterloo hangar back to the barn in Ayr late Tuesday night. Smich spent Wednesday in Oakville because he had a doctor's appointment for his shoulder. "I was still in pain and I wanted to get things checked out," he says. Although he and Millard had planned to burn the garbage left in the red Dodge truck that day, they postponed the job. "I might have spoken to him on the phone so as not to raise suspicion or make him think I was going to call the police on him," says Smich.

By Thursday, May 9, Millard appeared completely back to normal. "The same Dell that I've seen every day before that, which scared the shit out of me even more," says Smich.

"Where did you see him on the ninth?" asks Dungey.

Millard picked him up, says Smich, and they went to the hangar, where Shane Schlatman was removing the emblems and tail lights from Tim Bosma's truck, prepping it for painting. They swapped the Yukon for Millard's red Dodge and drove to the farm, picking up gas canisters along the way. They also brought a fire extinguisher from the hangar. "Dell was normal, talkative, telling me he wanted to paint the truck," says Smich, explaining that the original plan called for a VIN switch from Millard's red truck to the new one. "This was my knowledge from months and months prior to these events taking place." He wanted it red to match the description on the licence plates. (Smich may have meant the car's registration.)

When they finished burning the truck seats and garbage at the farm and returned to the hangar, Smich sensed something was amiss between Art Jennings and his son-in-law, Schlatman. Millard told Smich they had to move the Bosma truck. After Jennings and Schlatman left, they put it inside the trailer, hooked it to Millard's red Dodge, and left. Several hundred metres down the road, Millard realized he had forgotten the front seat frame. They returned to the hangar and put it in the trailer. Millard then dropped off Smich in Oakville.

"We heard from Marlena Meneses you said you had fucked up," says Dungey. "What did you mean?"

"Well, that I went with Dell for a test drive."

Smich says that after Millard's arrest, when he received the toolbox with the gun, he immediately thought his friend was trying to frame him. "I was very scared at that time. You know, I had lots of thoughts going through my head. I was confused. I ended up going out and burying the gun." While Smich admits he told Brendan Daly about the toolbox, he denies ever saying it was his gun inside. "I've never owned a gun," he says.

Given that Dungey has so vociferously taken other witnesses to task for not calling the police, he is obliged to put the same questions to his client. He asks why Smich had done nothing when a man was missing and his family were in agony.

"I was scared," says Smich, "because, you know, the possibility that with my criminal record . . . the police wouldn't believe me." He was already being asked for details about the crime by Meneses, who had begun following the story on the news after Millard's arrest. "I told her, Dell shot Mr. Bosma, Dell burned Mr. Bosma," he says. "I didn't really want to tell her anything, but she did press me, and I had to tell her. I felt like I had to tell somebody. I know I should have went to police."

"Mr. Millard is now arrested. He's in custody. Why don't you go to the police?"

"At the time, I was torn up. I wanted to go to my sister's wedding. I know I didn't kill Mr. Bosma, and I didn't feel like I was, you know, guilty of that part of it. At the same time, the other part of me was saying, you know, I have to do something.

"I didn't want to go straight to police. I wanted to get proper advice," he says, meaning legal advice. He was also worried about ruining his sister's wedding. "I know it's stupid, and it's not an excuse," he says. "My family means the world to me."

"Mr. Bosma meant the world to his family," says Dungey. "Did you not feel an obligation?"

"Of course. I don't know how to explain. It was just confused. I was literally confused on what to do."

THE REACTION TO SMICH'S testimony on social media and in online crime forums was overwhelmingly and surprisingly positive. *I believe him*, they proclaimed on Facebook. *His story makes sense*, they tweeted on Twitter. *Why would he run the risk of taking the stand if it weren't true?* they asked on Websleuths.

In just one day, the three months of evidence that preceded Mark Smich's testimony was all but forgotten as the accused offered up a story many people desperately wanted to hear. Never mind that his version of events was entirely self-serving and predictable. Its simplicity was part of its appeal, as was the fact that it made the unknowable appear knowable. To finally learn the truth of what happened to Tim Bosma, all you had to do was believe Smich's story.

Better yet, Smich's tale helped renew one's faith in humanity. There was, after all, a sliver of hope. Smich had never planned to kill an innocent man, merely to steal a truck. According to his account, at least one of the two accused was not a monster. He had even earned his high school diploma in jail. He was on the road to redemption.

To a certain extent, this willingness to believe Smich is a by-product of the adversarial legal system. A witness in a highly publicized trial gets on the stand and tells his story, and almost everyone believes him—until he is cross-examined, and then almost no one believes him. It's the way things work in court. It's what makes a trial real-life theatre. And it's why both the main courtroom and the overflow room were packed the day Mark Smich took the witness stand.

FIFTEEN

TEAM SMICH

Nadir Sachak's cross-examination of Mark Smich begins with the close-up photo of the Walther PPK in Smich's dirty fingers. "Please tell us," says Sachak. "Where is that gun?"

Smich shakes his head. "I don't know."

Sachak informs him that there are three detectives who worked on the case in the courtroom. "Tell them now. Where did you bury that gun?"

"Sir, I was under a lot of shock and stress. I was paranoid. I don't know where it is."

"Did you really bury that gun, or is it somewhere else right now?" Sachak asks. "Help me out. What day was it?"

"It would have been the day or night that my sister came and all the stuff happened," says Smich, who can't pinpoint the date but remembers his sister Andrea yelling at him to get his belongings out of the house. "The same day where I wasn't able to sell it."

Sachak tells him that the gun could have fingerprints, DNA from the shooter, or blood and DNA from Tim Bosma on it. "That gun you buried could have been tested by three police forces—the very gun that may have one hundred percent proof of who held it when it was fired," he says. "The jury will never get the benefit of seeing that gun, because you buried it."

Smich quickly tries to shift the blame for the gun's disappearance to his one-time friend Brendan Daly, who he says gave him the idea to bury it. Sachak responds that Smich alone bears responsibility and points out that he has refused for three years to disclose the gun's whereabouts. To make his point, he plays the video of Smich's police interrogation on May 22, 2013, the day of his arrest. It shows Smich, wearing his customary grey hoodie, huddled in a corner on a chair with a large white blanket covering one shoulder and his lap. He looks like a drug addict, a different person from the clean-cut man on the witness stand. In the video, he is being questioned by Detective Matt Kavanagh, who is playing good cop. "Where's the gun, son? Where's the gun?" Kavanagh asks. "Bring some peace to [the Bosma] family."

Smich turns away in his seat, holding his shoulder and saying nothing.

"Does someone else have to die before we get the gun back?" says Kavanagh. "Let's get it off the street, Mark."

Smich tells Sachak that he told Kavanagh he was given legal advice not to talk, but that part of the video isn't being shown.

Sachak is puzzled that Smich can't remember anything at all about where he buried the gun. "Let's just break it down step by step so the jury can really understand this shock you're suffering from."

Smich says the gun was hidden in the washing machine in the garage at his mother's house.

"The house of your mother recovering from cancer?" asks Sachak. He reminds the jury that Smich had recently told them that "family means everything."

"She had recovered already."

"Oh, so she was cancer free when you put the gun in the washing machine?"

Smich, who has a tendency to ramble, tries to explain about his mother's diagnosis, but Sachak cuts him off to ask what he did with the gun once he retrieved it from the washing machine.

Smich says he wrapped it in tape.

"I don't get it. Why do you wrap the gun with tape? Why do you do that?"

"Um, I wasn't thinking completely," says Smich. "I don't know."

No matter how much he prods, Sachak can't get Smich to explain his reason for taping the gun. In mock frustration, Sachak moves on to asking him how he buried the weapon.

Smich says he used a gardening tool.

"What gardening tool?"

"Like a spade, I think they call it."

"I live in a condo in a congested city. What's the average length of a spade?"

Smich looks confused.

"Use your hands and describe it for the jury."

Smich doesn't react, so Sachak says he will move his hands apart gradually and Smich can tell him when to stop.

"My hands are fully extended," says Sachak.

"I don't know," says Smich, looking blank.

Eventually, after much questioning, Sachak gets Smich to remember putting the taped gun into a shopping bag. Then

Sachak broaches the topic of how he got to the forest on his bike, if he carried the spade in his hand or in the bag. "Did you tape it to your head?" he asks sarcastically.

"That would be highly unlikely, but it could be possible."

"Presumably, you have a bag with a gun in your hand?"

"I wouldn't agree with that. I don't know."

"Then give us a likely scenario. . . . As you're cycling to the forest, where's the bag with the gun?"

"I don't recall," says Smich. "I couldn't sell the gun. Everyone's telling me, Get rid of all the stuff. Brendan Daly told me to bury it."

Sachak makes a show of looking at his watch and shaking his head. He asks Smich which way he turned when he cycled off from his mother's house. Smich says he doesn't recall.

"You know the roads, some of the ravines, landmarks where there's a Mac's Milk, Becker's, Costco," says Sachak, trying to jog his memory.

"I don't recall, sir," says Smich. "Those other times we just went over, I was never in that state of shock in my life, so that day was completely different. So that's why I don't recall."

"So the jury gets *the full picture*," says Sachak, alluding to the promise Dungey made in his opening remarks, "you're saying, that night, you have no idea what road you took, no idea what landmarks you may have cycled past . . . not the slightest recollection which forest you cycled to."

"That's correct," says Smich.

Sachak asks how it was possible to cycle in the dark forest on the BMX bike Smich claimed he was riding.

"I don't recall."

"Did you see any wildlife in this forest? Bears? Deer? How deep in the ground did you dig? How long were you digging?"

Smich can't remember anything, except for some reason he thinks the hole he dug would have been relatively small.

"Is this gun-burial-induced amnesia? You seem to have forgotten every detail except that it's a magical forest."

As Smich tells Millard's lawyer that he can't remember due to being in a state of shock, stress, and paranoia—three words he keeps repeating—Sachak leans on his lectern and looks at the jury in disbelief.

"Were you concerned about little kids, that they may pick up this gun and it may go off?" Sachak asks.

"Well, I buried it somewhere no one will find it."

The discussion drags on, with lawyer and witness increasingly antagonizing each other. By the end, only the truly gullible could believe Mark Smich's gun burial story.

But strangely, on the internet there was a rising tide of anger at Sachak for discrediting Smich. Sachak's quirky style and snarky questions didn't always translate well on Twitter. As much as lines about bears and taping a spade to one's head can work in the courtroom, where it's clear that Sachak is responding to the ridiculousness of what Smich has just told him, his remarks may also look childish and pointless in print without context.

In their primal need to pick a side, people all over Facebook and Websleuths were opting for Team Smich, chiming in to say that, memory is fragile, especially in times of stress. They didn't seem to recognize that while it was necessary to keep in mind the complexities of memory function, it was also critical not to forget the complexities of liars and con men.

WHEN MARK SMICH LEFT his mother's house to go into hiding at his girlfriend's sister's apartment, he took along four phones: a BlackBerry, a Samsung slider, a Sony Ericsson, and an LG Chocolate. Sachak says he finds this odd.

Smich explains that all the phones had problems, ranging from a broken tracking ball to a short-lived battery to a screen that kept going white. "What I would do," he says, "is switch the SIM cards into the different phones."

"Could you tell me how many SIM cards you possess?" asks Sachak.

Smich doesn't know.

"Was it more than five, ten?"

"No."

"Police did not find a SIM card for any of the four phones at Elizabeth's place," says Sachak, meaning Marlena Meneses's sister's apartment on Speers Road in Oakville. "What happened to the SIM cards?"

"Like I said, they're probably inside one of the other phones," says Smich.

"From the four phones seized at 30 Speers, we only have information from the BlackBerry. The other three phones we can't get any information from, because they don't have SIM cards," says Sachak. "Everything's from Dell's phone. I haven't seen much come out of your phones. Can you explain why?"

Smich can't, but he points out that there was indeed evidence on his BlackBerry. "You and your friend there just used the picture." He's referring to Ravin Pillay and another photo of the Walther PPK, which was found on the BlackBerry and shown to the court.

"The point I want to make is that there is not a phone that was active in April or May 2013," says Sachak. The last text sent or received by the BlackBerry was January 19, 2013, the same day it made its last phone call.

With the exception of a few messages retrieved from the BlackBerry and the device named "Mark's Ipad," almost all the text messages exchanged between Millard and Smich that were entered into evidence at trial came from Millard's phone. Marlena Meneses testified that she believed Smich dumped the phone he was using in May 2013. She never saw it again after Millard's arrest. Smich told her to call Rogers, the wireless service provider, and cancel the number, which was listed in her name. Smich's electronic trail was, and remains, covered far better than that of Dellen Millard.

AS MUCH AS MARK SMICH'S memory is patchy, even blank, in matters related to phones and the buried gun, there are other events he has no difficulty recalling. He is adamant, for example, that he did not speak to Christina Noudga in the hours after Millard was arrested, even though she provided detailed testimony about their conversation. "She texted my phone. After that, Marlena spoke to her," Smich says. "I told Marlena to call her and say that I'm not around." Noudga, he insists, was lying.

Smich also says that his friend Brendan Daly is confused about who owned the gun in the toolbox.

Sachak tells him, "Mr. Daly stated that you, Mark Smich, said the gun in the toolbox was yours."

Smich denies it. Conversations with Daly are a topic where his memory appears to be almost perfect.

"You're saying you never, ever told Mr. Daly that 'the gun in the toolbox is mine'?"

"No, never said that, no."

"Mr. Daly said that you had the bullets for the gun in the toolbox."

"No, he said something different to each counsel," says Smich.

This is an inaccurate characterization of Daly's testimony. On this point Smich is wrong. Even when pushed hard in cross-examination, Daly never wavered from his position that Smich told him he owned the gun in the toolbox. Smich is trying to make Daly, whose evidence was damaging to him, look bad. It is an example of Smich's cunning, and it is at odds with the image of a lovable loser on the path to reform that he and his lawyer have tried to create.

In one of the most intimidating situations anyone can face—sitting in a witness box under cross-examination for first-degree murder—Smich easily and confidently lobs accusations of lying at his fellow witnesses and former friends. Not only was Brendan Daly wrong, so was Andrew Michalski. Smich says he never asked Michalski to get "the thing," meaning the toolbox, from Matt Hagerman.

"Just like Daly might be mistaken?" asks Sachak. "It seems like everyone who's been testifying is lying, right?"

"Over time, people's memories aren't that good," says Smich. He insists he only asked Michalski for the drugs because Meneses wanted them.

Sachak shakes his head at that. "Did you tell Marlena, 'You're nuts. This guy killed some guy. Why do we need his weed? What's so important about the weed?' Did you tell her that?"

"We just didn't discuss that. She said to get the drugs, so I called Andrew to get the drugs."

"Why not tell Marlena, 'I'm not getting the drugs. I want nothing to do with that guy'? Why not just say that?"

"I don't know."

The idea that Smich would have taken directions from Meneses under these circumstances is implausible. Just as Millard exerted a lot of influence over his friends, Smich was the leader of his circle. He instructed Michalski to bring him the toolbox and the drugs. He used his friend Arthur as his unpaid errand boy to fetch the toolbox from the stairwell where Michalski and Hagerman had left it and then to store it at his mother's house. He pressured Daly to help him sell the gun. Daly and Michalski both testified that they were intimidated by Smich.

Yet for a large segment of people on social media, these facts were overlooked or forgiven as Sachak and Smich battled it out over four full days of cross-examination. For them, Smich had become the underdog fending off Dellen Millard's big bad counsel. And the social media crowd was about to get even angrier at Sachak when he suggested that clues to Smich's personality might be found in his rap music and lyrics.

"Why don't you rap for the jury?" Sachak suggests to Smich as he puts some of his lyrics up on the courtroom screens.

Smich's lawyer objects, and the judge agrees, saying, "He can read, but I don't think he has to perform it." Smich reads his rap lyrics aloud for the court:

Its me muthaphuka, so relentless

Runnin from cops outta them spots, over them fences

Im high so im half fuckin demented

But i still

gotta get away nice and splendid

Got my 9

So im runnin like its nothing . . . Till im dead, kid!

I am not unstoppable

but I like to live my life without the cops involved

Its not probable, but if it happened to me. . . . Problem solved!

Im just comin for the loot, so shoot first, i come for your new purse,
*   and wallets, I*

want some chronics, and that juice cuz ima alcoholic,

No stallin, give it to me in a quick haste, more speedy then
*   fast paced,*

Im runnin away from the police in a cash race,

First one, im never last place

The creation date for this particular lyrics file on his iPad is February 16, 2013, while the date for last modification is May 21, 2013, the day before Smich was arrested.

Sachak points out that the Walther PPK has the number nine on its side. Smich argues that it actually says "9 kurz," *kurz* being the German word for short. It takes him a while to agree to the obvious, that the number nine is indeed there.

"Thank you, sir, thank you very much," says Sachak, displaying once again his annoyance at Smich's evasiveness.

Not surprisingly, the feeling is mutual. When Sachak errs in referring to a date, Smich jumps on it. "Could be one of those brain cramps again," he says. "You're probably under a lot of stress."

It's another comment that doesn't fit with Smich's portrayal of himself as the victim of his powerful friend's crime, but it provokes laughter in the courtroom and is much remarked upon online.

"Zing," writes "meterclicks" on Websleuths. "MS is giving Sachak a taste of his own medicine this morning."

"Oh snap LOL," writes "Kamille." "MS should have been a comedian LOL."

"Interesting. I'm starting to believe that MS is not as dumb as what I first thought," says "Redheart."

"Smich is getting sassy," writes "Katpaws." "I'm still fully on the fence about MS's role, but I'm not a fan of Sachak's style at all . . . so I can't help but take a little delight in MS's quick comebacks. Clearly cleaning himself up has revealed a more clever and quick-witted guy than we initially realized."

Undeterred by Smich's retort, Sachak asks what exactly Smich modified on May 21, 2013.

Smich explains instead that adding one letter or a space would cause a file's modification date to change.

"Tell us what was modified," says Sachak. "What part was modified on May 21, 2013?"

Smich gives a lengthy account about how Meneses could have used the iPad and caused the modification. He repeats his explanation about inserting a character by mistake, adding that the file could have been opened randomly.

Sachak cuts him off. "I don't need to know how an iPad works," he says, looking at the jury. "Just tell me, What did you modify? Please help me. Please answer that question."

Smich never does.

More rap lyrics go up on the screen.

Never lonely, its just me & my chrome piece, Im holding
The cards i was dealt . . . Im never folding
The One & Only .... SAY10, its no fony ....

"'My chrome piece,'" says Sachak. "What you're saying is, 'My handgun is not a phony.' That's what you wrote."

"Uh, no, that's not in proper context."

"Okay, what do you mean by 'me and my chrome piece I'm holding'?"

"[It] would be a reference to not being lonely because I'd be holding a chrome piece."

"Let's call it for what it is. You're not lonely because you're holding a handgun," says Sachak. "Please help the jury out. Who is holding that gun, according to those lyrics?"

"No one's holding a gun. It's just lyrics."

Another set of lyrics is scrutinized.

I am muthaphuka! Get slapped with my gun hand muthaphuka!
Leave you dead, with some contraband muthaphuka!

"You know what the word *slapped* means on the street," Sachak tells Smich. "You know for a fact, sir, that 'slap' is street slang for murder and kill."

"Sir, that's not how it's written."

"What did you mean by 'slap someone with my gun hand muthaphuka'?"

Smich answers that it's just lyrics. Sachak asks him again what it means, and they go round and round. Eventually Smich says, "I'm not sure if I even wrote that one." He thinks Millard may have written it. Hundreds of lyrics were found on Smich's iPad, and he says he often wrote them with Millard.

"'Leave you dead,'" quotes Sachak.

"Like I said, I don't think I wrote that portion."

"What do you and Dellen mean by 'Leave you dead, with some contraband muthaphuka'?"

"What did I mean?"

"Yes, you."

"I didn't write it, so I don't know what he meant by it."

Sachak plays a thirty-second selfie video of Smich improvising, or freestyling. He's shirtless and shaven headed with a scraggly moustache and goatee. He appears aggressive and angry as he chants,

Yes, it's like a freestyle session with no lesson, no question
I'm killing you in possessions. It's mine
Ima killer, check my design, mountains I climb and throw
    you off too
Dangle you from the roof true motherfuckers know
I'll leave you blacked up and blue, bruised
Who's who? Blues clues
Tell the cops anything and you die on the news.
Peace, bitch. You're deceased kid
Fuck with me SAY10 the genius

"The rhyme means, I kill you and make what is yours mine," says Sachak.

"Like I said, it's just a rhyme," says Smich. "It all goes together and has nothing to do with reality."

"It's not like 'Give Peace a Chance,'" says Sachak, providing Smich with another opening, as may be his intent.

"Is that a rap song?" Smich sasses him back.

Sachak ignores him and asks again for an explanation of the lyrics.

"Like I said, it's an art form. It's just raps, rhymes."

"'Ima killer, check my design, mountains I climb and throw you off too'?"

"I've never been up a mountain before, and I've never thrown anyone off a mountain before," says Smich. "I never owned a gun."

"We'll let the jury decide that," Sachak says.

"'Peace, bitch. You're deceased kid.' Is that what you were thinking when you were killing Mr. Bosma?"

"I did not kill Mr. Bosma."

"'Fuck with me SAY10.' Is that what you said to Mr. Bosma before he died?"

"I was not with Dellen Millard when he shot and killed Mr. Bosma, then parked his truck on his mother's property," says Smich, who grabs every chance he can to put across his storyline. "I remember yesterday you asked me a question about profiting from selling Dell's gun. This is where it's confusing, because Dell was profiting from Mr. Bosma's truck. That's what happened. That's what happened, sir."

Later, Sachak revisits the topic of art and reality. He tells Smich that his rap was not mere artistic expression but "an artistic diary" of his criminality. "There are rap artists engaged in exactly the type of criminality you wrote about."

Smich brings up Stephen King and Dr. Seuss. "Just because somebody writes something a certain way does not make them a certain way," he says.

Sachak says he understands that, but there's also a unique category of artist who acts out his art. "Those rap lyrics, that video that the jury saw, are an indication of your true aspirations," he says.

He calls Smich a drug dealer who writes about drug dealing, a .380 owner who writes about .380s, a man on trial for first-degree murder who writes about killing.

"There's a lot more to it than that," says Smich. "I've written thousands [of lyrics] in my lifetime."

"Those rap lyrics are a reflection of your inner soul," says Sachak.

In keeping with this life-imitates-art theme, a Websleuths member had, back before Smich took the stand, looked anew at his "Ghozted" video, the one that spiked in popularity on the internet after he was arrested. The sleuth, whose user name was "InducedLogic," picked up on something that hadn't been noticed before and took on new meaning in the light of Marlena Meneses's testimony. Meneses had told the court that when she asked Smich what had happened to Tim Bosma, he replied he was "gone, gone." In "Ghozted," after the fictional victim has been killed and dismembered, the last words of the soundtrack are a chant of "gone, gone, gone."

That video was never shown in court.

IN A TRUE CUTTHROAT DEFENCE, both defendants would have told their version of events to the jury. But because Dellen Millard chose not to take the stand, it's Nadir Sachak who puts Millard's account of what happened the night of May 6 to Mark Smich. As Sachak tells it, after leaving the Bosma property,

Millard wanted to take the truck on the highway to see how it would drive. Tim Bosma agreed. They headed up Trinity Road past the Super Sucker camera. (This was ostensibly the mysterious truck sighting that Ravin Pillay had grilled forensic video analyst Michael Plaxton about earlier in the trial.) No sooner had they gotten onto Highway 403 eastbound when Smich purportedly pulled out the Walther PPK concealed in the pocket of his red hoodie.

"We're going to take this truck," Smich said, according to Millard.

In this scenario, Tim Bosma grabbed the gun that was pointing at him, there was a struggle, and the Walther was discharged. Bosma was struck and the window was shattered. Millard swerved onto the shoulder and stopped. He was furious and said they should call an ambulance. Smich said Tim Bosma was already dead.

Millard panicked, because his Yukon was still in the field with his dog in it. He had been seen by Sharlene Bosma and Wayne De Boer. He thought he would be blamed; it had always been his idea to look for a Dodge Ram 3500. He exited the 403 at Wilson Street, outside Hamilton, turned around, and headed back west on the 403. Travelling south on Trinity Road, as he drove to the field, he passed the Super Sucker camera once again. (This was the second video sighting brought to the court's attention by Pillay during the cross-examination of Plaxton.)

As Sachak describes Millard's version of events, Smich regularly disagrees. "Absolutely not, sir," he says. "No, sir, that did not happen." He shakes his head while craning his neck ever so slightly. It's a gesture that gives a vaguely cartoonish impression.

Sachak says that when Smich and Millard arrived back at the

field, Smich got into the Yukon and followed Millard onto the highway to Brantford.

Smich says this couldn't be true, because he doesn't know how to drive on highways. In his account, they took back roads when they set out from the Bosmas' house—Millard and Bosma leading, Smich following in the Yukon—but because he had to concentrate hard on his driving he can't remember the route. Nor does he recall hearing a shot from a gun or seeing a flash from a muzzle. After they had both stopped at the side of the road, Millard was putting the gun away in his satchel as he exited the truck.

Sachak asks if Millard shut off the vehicle, and Smich says he believes he did. If that was the case, says Sachak, how could Millard have put the truck in park, switched off the ignition, and opened the door of the vehicle, all the while holding a gun? He also says he finds the detail of Millard putting the gun into the satchel odd.

Smich appears slightly flustered. He repeats that he was scared and in shock. He describes Millard's eyes as bulging like a lunatic's. Smich just did what he was told, which was to switch the licence plates on the Bosma truck with those of Millard's red Dodge.

Sachak asks why. It makes no sense.

"We've done this before on other missions."

Sachak says that Millard was in a panic about Bosma's phone, because he thought the police might trace it. He began searching the body so that he could find the phone and get rid of it. He was concerned that the phone and the truck might have GPS, which was why he grabbed the flashlight from the Yukon to look.

At the farm, according to Sachak, both men struggled to load Tim Bosma's body into the incinerator. Then, when they got to the hangar, Millard left briefly in the Yukon. He had to get away from Smich, if only temporarily. He needed to process what had just happened. His plan had been to scope the truck that night and, if he liked it, return later to winch it into the trailer and steal it.

Smich rejects the account. Millard was so deranged that night that even Pedo, who normally stuck faithfully by his side, was scared off, he says. The dog followed Smich around the entire time they were at the hangar. Yet, by the next morning, Millard was happy again. On the drive back to Oakville, Smich borrowed his phone to contact Meneses and tell her they were coming to pick her up. Then Millard dropped them both at Smich's mother's house, where Mark Smich went to sleep.

"How many hours?" asks Sachak.

"I don't recall how long I would have slept for."

His ability to sleep would seem to require an explanation, yet Smich, who on the witness stand has over-explained many of his actions, glides right by this one. It's almost as if he doesn't realize that going to sleep after incinerating a murder victim might not be seen as a normal reaction. Nor does he explain why he would choose to put his girlfriend in the same car as an alleged lunatic killer.

Despite the numerous flaws in his story, Smich emerges from his cross-examination by Sachak with many people still convinced that he was an innocent dupe. Judging by the online chatter, they are willing to forgive and forget the gun amnesia, the suspicious cell phone behaviour, the disturbing rap videos, the wedding partying, and everything else. They want, more than anything, to believe Smich when he says, "I'm sitting here right now, taking ownership and responsibility." And they laugh when, near the end of his questioning by Sachak, Smich tells his adversary, "If you want stories, you can ask your client Walt Disney over there."

DELLEN MILLARD'S STORY is that Mark Smich killed Tim Bosma because he wanted a red Cadillac. According to this scenario, Smich would take the car, part of Carl Millard's collection, to Calgary when he moved there, which he was planning to do very soon. The move to Calgary, first raised in the Noudga letters, was not entirely a figment of Millard's imagination. Detective Kavanagh asked Smich about it in his post-arrest interview. And Smich's mother told a police officer who was present at the search of her house that Mark had said after Millard was arrested that now he would never get the car.

The Cadillac is yet another thing Smich rapped about, Sachak says, another incidence of his rhymes reflecting reality. Smich denies it, saying that at one time his sister Andrea had owned a Cadillac Escalade.

Sachak says Millard promised Smich the Cadillac, valued at about $7,000, once they pulled off the truck theft. It was to be his payment for a job well done. Meneses was getting her licence so that she could drive it. The problem for Smich was that Millard was enjoying their scoping missions a little bit too much. "As pathetic as that may sound, he got a kick out of it," says Sachak. "It's you, Mr. Smich, who got very anxious that this theft of a truck wasn't taking place."

No, answers Smich. The pressure to get the Dodge Ram 3500 diesel had nothing to do with a Cadillac. It came strictly from

Millard, who needed the truck to go to the Baja race. When he had taken his gas-fuelled red Dodge to Mexico in 2011, it had cost him a fortune. He wanted to save money on gas. "Like I said," says Smich, "Dell is cheap."

SIXTEEN

THE PLAN

Craig Fraser begins his cross-examination of Mark Smich with a blunt accusation of cold-blooded murder.

"The plan that you and Dellen Millard had was to steal, was to kill, and was to burn," Fraser declares.

"No, sir."

"Executed with chilling perfection."

"No, sir. The plan was, like I said, to steal a truck."

According to Fraser, the plan took over a year to execute, had multiple incarnations, and involved only two people, Mark Smich and Dellen Millard. Unlike Nadir Sachak, Fraser does not have a client to protect and consequently whole areas of evidence he must avoid. His goal in this cross-examination is simply to prove there was a plan to murder. To accomplish this, he says he will show repeated examples of how Smich and Millard worked together to plan and cover up their crime, and that Smich's actions weren't born out of fear, confusion, and shock, as he has maintained.

Fraser describes the video of the two men walking through the hangar in the early morning hours of May 7. "It looked more like a stroll. There was no confusion, no panic, no fear in that walk," he says. "We can see you and Mr. Millard calmly walking through that hangar going about your business. That's what it looks like, doesn't it?"

"No, sir."

"In lockstep, side by each, calmly walking."

Fraser says Smich and Millard immediately began to destroy evidence. He uses examples from Smich's testimony, starting with Smich cutting the carpet and seat belts out of the truck. "That, sir, is destruction of evidence. That's you doing something positive to destroy evidence."

"I was told—" Smich starts to say, but Fraser cuts him off. He's not interested in hearing from Smich about his motivations. He's not going to let him get under his skin, or think he's getting under his skin, as happened with Sachak.

"The second thing you do, with Mr. Millard present, you hose down the truck," says Fraser. Then, he says, Smich and Millard removed the seats from the truck, stowed the evidence in garbage bags, and put the bags in the back of Millard's red Dodge truck to burn at the farm.

"I didn't want to be involved," says Smich. "I was just pretending to go along with it."

"Excuses, justifications, rationalizations . . . I'm just pointing out the facts, what you and Mr. Millard did."

This cross-examination is the only one the Crown attorneys will do at this trial. When they were preparing for the possibility the defendants might testify, it was decided that Tony Leitch would cross-examine Millard and Fraser would take on Smich. As always, Fraser is well prepared. And, liberated to ask the leading questions permitted on cross-examination, he comes across very differently than he has before. He keeps Smich firmly under his control.

Fraser moves ahead to Tuesday night, when video evidence shows the Yukon arriving at the hangar at 9:09 P.M. and leaving with the Eliminator in tow at 11:40. Smich looks worried, not as cocky as he was with Sachak.

"I'm going to suggest that it doesn't take very long to hitch on and drive to the farm," says Fraser. "The other thing that was going on at that hangar for two and a half hours was you had to clean the Eliminator. That's when you went back and cleaned out the remains of Tim Bosma. That's what you did." The Eliminator had been too hot earlier that morning.

Smich obfuscates, saying he can't recall exact details.

Fraser treats his claim with skepticism and carries on. He says that after Smich and Millard stuck the incinerator away from "prying eyes," they took Wednesday as an unplanned day off. Smich saw a doctor about his sore shoulder and got fitted for a suit for his sister's wedding before returning on Thursday to destroy more evidence with Millard.

"Those burn sites that we see, that's where you did it," Fraser says. "Tucked away at the back of the farm. That's the spot that he chose?"

"I don't think any of this was a good plan," says Smich, dodging the question. He continues to insist that all he set out to do was steal a truck.

"The plan was to steal, the plan was to kill, and the plan was to burn," Fraser corrects him. He reminds Smich that he and Millard even brought along a fire extinguisher from the hangar.

The devil was in the details as the two partners—"just the two of you," Fraser repeats—spent several hours at the farm destroying evidence.

Unfortunately for Smich and Millard, when they returned to the hangar later Thursday afternoon, they learned there was a problem. "Things are getting a little hot, a little uncertain, a little worrisome because of Art and Shane," says Fraser. Millard realized that he needed to get the truck out of the hangar.

"I don't think you explained exactly what you knew about where that truck was going," Fraser says to Smich. "You must have discussed it with him. 'What are you going to do with the truck, Dell?'"

"No, sir, I didn't want to be involved."

"Whether you wanted to be or not, logically you would say, 'Where are you taking that truck, Dell?'"

"No, sir. He seemed very in control of everything. He told me not to worry."

"You know for a stone-cold fact that trailer was going in his mother's driveway and you two discussed it."

Smich denies it. He also says he doesn't recall talking to Millard on the phone shortly after the police left the hangar on Friday afternoon, May 10.

"You're Canada's most wanted at this point," says Fraser in disbelief. "You don't recall? You don't remember the words he said to you?"

"The exact words, no."

Millard told Smich things were not looking good, says Fraser.

"I won't agree, because I don't remember."

After the police visit, Millard was under surveillance. Police followed him as he and Schlatman stashed Millard's red truck nearby at a house owned by a friend of Schlatman's. Millard then visited his bank in Kitchener before stopping on his way home to see Smich for fifty minutes at Meneses's sister's apartment.

Smich claims not to remember what they discussed at that meeting, but somehow he recalls without a doubt that Brendan Daly was present and let Millard into the building.

"I don't remember Brendan Daly saying that," says Fraser. "I remember you saying that." Then, having set the record straight, he moves on.

"Mr. Millard needs to talk to you, Mr. Smich, because you have to come up with a plan. Because he knows the jig is up."

"It's very difficult to remember a verbal conversation," says Smich.

"No it's not. It's not difficult, Mr. Smich, when you're in the predicament you're in. . . . Mr. Millard turned to you, his partner in crime, to talk to you about what to do when he got arrested."

CRAIG FRASER INSISTS that Millard and Smich's "mission" was never just to steal a truck. A truck would have been easy for them, given their success with Bobcats, trees, motorbikes, trailers, and wood chippers. "The difference with this plan is you needed a target to kill, and you needed a target to incinerate, and that's why it took as long as it did," he says. "That's why it took you over a year."

The elements of the plan were the 3500 diesel truck, the gun, and the Eliminator, "so chillingly referred to as the barbecue, [which] was the last piece of the puzzle," says Fraser. "The truck, the gun, the incinerator, the plan. That's how it went down."

Fraser next displays a text on the courtroom screens from February 29, 2012, more than a year before the Bosma murder. It was sent from Millard to Smich. "Next on the list is: getting you a G1, sound equipment for recording, nab a dodge 3500, sell the green jeep, nab a nacra 18 sailboat."

Two more texts, from March 14, 2012, are shown to illustrate the closeness between Millard and Smich. "I love you my kneegrow," says Millard. Mi Negro is one of the contact names he used for Smich and a term of endearment in Spanish. Smich responds, "I love you a whole lot like large. Big huge monstrously massive . . . You're really the brother I never had."

"Like I said," Smich tells Fraser, "I treated him like family."

"Remember Miss Meneses's description? She said you were in love with him," says Fraser. "Right up until the events of May 2013, you were as tight as ever."

"Our bond was stronger," Smich agrees.

Fraser points out some more texts from early 2012. Millard was messaging Smich about how big missions would lead to way bigger payoffs. "I think we can grab that truck I need before I go to the states next, they are common enough it doesn't have to be that one, it just has to be a dodge 3500, red's just a bonus," he writes on March 24.

"Yea we need a proper plan tho so lets work on that," Smich replies. "We can't make any mistakes."

He tells Fraser that they floated many ideas on how to steal the Dodge Ram 3500.

"But you know, Mr. Smich, we heard your evidence that Schlatman showed you how to do it. It's not hard. It doesn't take fifteen months to execute the theft of a truck."

Fraser brings up the gun, which he says introduced an element of lethal force into the plan. He shows an April 2012 text Millard sent Smich from Las Vegas, a photo of bullets, with the message "five fingered you some practice ammo."

"A little bit of ammo gun talk between you and Dellen Millard. You're cool with it," says Fraser. "That suggests you had a comfort level with firearms and ammunition?"

"Yes, sir."

The ammo text conversation took place about a month after Smich had photographed Millard's newly acquired Walther PPK.

"Some people would think that that's a glorification of violence," Fraser tells Smich.

"I didn't think that at the time."

"It shows that you, as well, Mark Smich, were good with it. You were helping him find ammo for the Walther that he bought from your good buddy Iisho." Fraser's referring to Matthew Ward-Jackson, the alleged gun dealer.

"I wasn't against it. I thought it was interesting. It wasn't meant to harm anybody. I don't know."

Fraser points out that Smich's gun fascination was still going strong six months later, when he took another photo of the Walther with his newly acquired iPad.

"Do you think that's a suggestion that you're okay with violence?" Fraser asks.

"Just me being foolish," says Smich.

"You see the photo there, Mr. Smich, of those bullets? Was one of those used to kill Tim Bosma?"

"I don't know, sir."

"Maybe," says Fraser. He pauses for effect before showing a text sent from Smich to Millard in May 2012: "I'm fuckin hungry now for a mission too and I know I've been slackin on that lately."

"Your hunger for a mission," says Fraser, "I take it would be in furtherance of stealing a Dodge 3500?"

"No, I was broke and I needed money."

"Again, it's this mission, it's this Dodge 3500?"

"No, there are lots of other missions."

By May 2012, Fraser tells the court, the homemade incinerator project was well underway. Schlatman's handiwork—the rocket ship–like device he created from fifty-gallon steel drums— was ready for testing. Millard texts Smich, "We go do incinerator, cool?"

"Yo I'm down bro I would even say come sooner than that. We can chill and talk about other shit as well."

Fraser asks where they were going to see the homemade incinerator, at the farm or the hangar.

"Uh, I assume it would be at the hangar," says Smich. "I'm not sure of the events that happened that day."

"You had the truck, you had the gun, and you had the bullets, but you didn't have the incinerator. And you're starting to get that phase of the plan in place . . . to check things out to see if you can execute your plan."

"No, sir, it was for garbage."

"So you're good leaving your house at ten o'clock at night to go to the incinerator to burn garbage?"

Fraser shows a text from June 6. Smich has been researching incinerators. "I'm lookin at a mobile one right now. Some chopping wood [sic] be necessary," he tells Millard.

"So you're putting your two cents' worth in on this homemade incineration device," says Fraser. "You don't have an interest in an incineration device because it burns garbage."

Smich says he worked for Millard, the implication being he did his friend's and boss's bidding.

"Mr. Smich, it's just another phase of the plan . . . and that's why you showed a keen interest."

Fraser asks what he meant when he said chopping would be necessary. "Dismemberment?"

"No, sir."

The text messages now skip ahead two months to August 20, 2012.

Millard texts Smich "35," short for 3500, and "I want a cop bicycle."

"Done. I think I know a spot," says Smich.

"No more money bro, we take what we want from the source."

Okay, replied Smich. He told Millard he would be seeing Ward-Jackson the following night. "We will get everything done. I got 35 stuff already here with me."

"Things are happening," says Fraser. "The 3500 is being scoped and potentially taken."

He asks Smich what he means by "35 stuff," to which Smich answers, "Stuff for scoping."

"What did you need to scope, besides a pair of eyes?" asks Fraser. "What is the other 35 stuff?"

"Probably bolt cutters, change of clothes."

Fraser asks Smich if he was Millard's connection to Matthew Ward-Jackson.

"Yes, I introduced them through drugs."

"But you'll agree with me, we're not talking drugs here. We're talking about stealing a 3500."

Smich agrees.

Late summer 2012 is also when the newly bought incinerator was moved from the hangar to its permanent home at the farm. On September 5, Millard texts Smich, "Let's reach Waterloo, pick up your girlfriend, move the BBQ into the barn (need some things from home depot for that) and do more equipment painting, then scope 35 at night."

"Mr. Smich," says Fraser, "things are happening, plans are being made. . . . Part of that plan is the incineration of the man you target for the theft of the truck."

Smich says, no, the incinerator had to be moved because people were coming to look at the hangar.

"I want to ask you some questions about that Eliminator," says Fraser. "This is a $22,000 killing machine, isn't it?"

Smich says Millard told him he bought the incinerator to get into the pet cremation business with his uncle.

Fraser reminds him that Millard's uncle, Robert Burns, testified that he wanted nothing to do with his nephew. "He made that one hundred percent clear to everyone in this room. And you're saying you just took that explanation at face value?"

Fraser has more questions about how they got Tim Bosma's body into the incinerator, given that the burn chamber opening was four feet six inches above the trailer floor and its opening was eighteen inches by twenty-four.

"Mr. Smich, it's a two-man job. Tim Bosma was six feet tall, a hundred and seventy pounds. The two of you put Mr. Bosma together in the Eliminator."

Sharlene Bosma covers her face with her hands.

ON OCTOBER 1, 2012, Smich texted Millard a photo of a pickup truck with the caption "3500 Tow truck."

"We're now in October, and the two good thieves are having a lot of trouble stealing a 3500," says Fraser. "My suggestion is it's because this was planned with a difference. Because the plan with a difference was the killing of a human being and the incineration of a human being."

Smich insists that it's simply because they hadn't found the right truck.

On October 8, he texted Millard, "It's all about me, you, myself and my greed get TXDeed. we be taking anything we need that means everything, indeed."

"Nice rhyme," replies his friend.

Fraser asks why they needed so many plans and ideas to steal a truck. "It's pretty darn simple to put your mind to stealing a truck if you want to steal a truck. It's not that complicated."

"I'd agree with that," says Smich. He explains that their target trucks kept being moved or getting locked up.

"You never had that problem with the Bobcat, the trailer, floor polisher," Fraser says. "The common denominator is it was done and you didn't get caught. So on that score, if you want to say it, you were pretty good at thieving, and Dellen Millard was pretty good at thieving."

Smich bobs his head in agreement in his cartoonish way.

"You know, Mr. Smich, you're very quick to pin everything on Dell," Fraser continues. "But you were chiming in with your suggestions. You were all in on this."

"Well, I knew what I wanted."

"You're not Dellen Millard's patsy, Mr. Smich. You're his partner in crime."

Fraser shows a text exchange from April 6, 2013. "Reminds me," writes Millard. "Shane's starting modification on the white van for search and capture missions."

"I love search and destroy," Smich messages back. "Lol."

Fraser points out that this was the white Millardair company van, the one Millard gave to Villada when he took the red truck.

"Search and destroy is part of a video game," says Smich. "The one where you plant a bomb."

"There is nothing in that message that even hints at a video game," says Fraser. "Real-life Shane, real-life white van, real-life search and capture. You're not responding with a video reference."

Fraser shows another text, this one from April 16. "They chose to call me MARK at birth, but they should've called me MERK. All I do is put in work, no fun and games, til someones hurt."

"MERK" means kill in street slang, says Fraser. The rhyme is "a clear expression of violence . . . wanting to hurt people."

"No, it's an art form," says Smich.

Fraser points out that Smich was aware things had moved beyond that. "Your good friend Iisho [Ward-Jackson] selling a handgun to your best friend, Dellen Millard," he says. "What did you think your best friend, Dellen Millard, was doing when he bought a handgun and ammunition, and you helped him?"

"I'm not sure what I thought at that time."

"You didn't ask him because you knew."

"When Dell had a question, I would research things. It's just I did what he wanted. I didn't question him. . . . Like I said, I'd been in the drug game for a little while. I don't know how to explain it."

Fraser shows a text sent from Smich to Millard on April 26, 2013: "its almost mission time. ;)"

He brushes off the anticipated objections from Smich. "Yes, there were many missions. I know there are many missions, Mr. Smich, but at this time the only one you are referring to is the 3500. What other mission were you running at this time?"

Smich begins a rambling explanation that there were lots of missions: big missions, small missions. It was just a word. The jury has heard this from him many times already.

"It has nothing to do with the 3500, is that your evidence?" asks Fraser. "You were able to tell us about many of your missions with some detail. If it's not the Dodge 3500 you're talking about . . . what is it?"

"I can't be specific. We've done so much stuff together. Like I said, 'mission' was a very common thing between us."

Fraser shows texts from April 27. "Headed to Waterloo, figure out BBQ situation for this week," Millard tells Smich.

Smich contends that this refers to a real barbecue Millard would be hosting.

"No, it doesn't, Mr. Smich."

"As you can see, there's a comma there," says Smich, referring to the comma after "Waterloo" in Millard's text. The man who regularly says "I seen" is using a punctuation excuse. He explains that the comma is separating two different ideas: a trip to Waterloo and a genuine poolside barbecue. Earlier in the trial, Ravin Pillay had questioned Andrew Michalski about a barbecue his client had indeed hosted at his Maple Gate home on May 1.

Fraser bats away Smich's excuses. "He is telling you, Mr. Smich, his partner in crime, 'We've got to figure out this incinerator.'"

At the same time he's communicating with Smich, Millard is also texting Schlatman about the incinerator. "Where's the big generator?" he asks him. "Unless you remember putting it back on the BBQ, it should be at the hangar."

"Last I saw generator was in corner by incinerator in the barn," says Schlatman. Then he texts later, "Just remembered generator is out with excavator. Using it to run air compressor."

Fraser points out that a generator is not needed for a backyard barbecue. He shows texts from May 2 after Millard's party. "I gotta be in Waterloo tomorrow morning, planning on checking you before 4 pm, work on the mission," Millard writes.

Fraser says this is the 3500 mission slated for the upcoming weekend.

Smich denies it.

Fraser shows a text from Smich: "Ok it's fireworks tomoro night."

"'Fireworks' meaning running your mission with Mr. Millard," says Fraser.

Smich claims he meant actual fireworks with his friend Alex and Alex's girlfriend, Liz.

"May 2 or May 3 is not known as a traditional fireworks weekend in this country," says Fraser. "Let's look at the next day, Friday, May 3."

"Can Marlena reach and chill with Pedo," Smich texts Millard. "Can you bring me gloves and tape and maybe an orange guy?"

Smich says he needed gloves and tape because he was painting at the time, and explains that an "orange guy" is an oxycodone pill.

Then the 3500 mission gets bumped, first from Friday to Saturday, then to Sunday, and finally to Monday.

Fraser describes the scene at Maple Gate over the weekend

as Smich and Millard scan online ads. "You are targeting people and their trucks. That's what you're doing," he says. "Do you remember if you targeted [Tim Bosma] or if Millard targeted him, or if you both happened to find the same ad?"

"I don't want to use your words 'targeting him.' We were looking for a vehicle to steal," Smich replies.

"I am going to use the word, Mr. Smich," says Fraser. "He didn't know you two guys were going to walk up his driveway, and that was the last time he would be seen or heard from. It was just the two of you working together on May 6 when all this happened. Somewhere along the way, someone got shot, killed, and burned. Executed with chilling perfection, Mr. Smich, by the two of you working together. Isn't that what happened, Mr. Smich? It sure looks like it."

Smich looks very nervous as Fraser displays texts from Saturday, May 4. Millard writes, "change of plans, meet up with you tomorrow [Sunday] at noon. We've got 2 appointments to make." Then Millard leaves to switch vehicles with Javier Villada at the shopping mall.

Fraser says a Saturday test drive wasn't convenient for Tim Bosma, who had weekend plans.

Smich replies that it was Millard in control of the burner phone, setting up appointments. He insists the plan was just to go and scope out vehicles.

Sunday began with a text from Millard reading, "yeaow, you up negro? Mission day." It was followed in short order by another text: "reaching you now, eta 20 mins, bring change of clothes."

"The plan wasn't just to scope. The plan was to steal, to kill, and to burn," says Fraser. "It would have been Igor, but he was a little too much six foot four, a little too much Israeli army, for your liking. So then you picked the nice guy, Mr. Tim Bosma, on the sixth."

Fraser tells Smich he's skeptical about the explanation he gave Thomas Dungey concerning the need for a change of clothes. "It would look a little funny if we showed up in black," is what he recalls Smich saying. But Fraser argues that it makes no sense to show up as Dellen Millard and Mark Smich, scope Igor Tumanenko's truck, and then, if they like it, change into black clothes and take it later on.

Instead of providing an explanation, Smich digresses about the need to check for GPS tracking devices and coming back to scope the truck again a few days later. He appears not to realize that this plan would eliminate the need for a change of clothes.

Fraser says the reason Smich and Millard weren't shy about showing their faces was that Tumanenko was intended as their victim that Sunday. He would be dead, unable to identify them.

Smich continues to protest as Fraser explains, "A change of clothes is necessary because there's going to be a bloody mess. And that's what happened."

CRAIG FRASER REMINDS the court of some testimony from almost four months earlier in the trial. According to Sharlene Bosma, her husband was concerned about the test drive before it even began. The buyer was two hours late, and it was getting dark out. Tim asked Sharlene, "When they come, should I go with them?"

"Yes, you should," she said, "because we want the truck to come back."

Fraser says, "It is clear he was on high alert and suspicious." Smich's sketchy behaviour would have added to the anxiety. Fraser asks him what excuse Millard used to get Smich out of the Dodge truck and into the driver's seat of the Yukon, still parked in the field with its lights out. Smich can only recall the ruse about the fictional friend who couldn't find Tim Hortons.

After suggesting that Bosma was likely made uneasy by the Yukon parked in the dark field, Fraser brings up the testimony of Rick Bullmann, the neighbour who saw two vehicles pull out in quick succession from his father's field. He says Bullmann did not observe a U-turn being made, only two trucks leaving the field at the same time.

As he dissects Smich's story about the fictional friend in the field and where exactly the two vehicles were in relation to each other, Fraser finally reveals the prosecution's theory: that the murder took place in the field adjacent to the Bosma home. "That's where you and Mr. Millard shot and killed Mr. Bosma," he declares. "That's what happened, Mr. Smich."

Fraser implies that the story Smich has told the jury, of a thirty-eight-minute test drive to Bobcat of Brantford, is absurd. "Nobody goes for a test drive for over an hour to another city," he says.

"There never was a test drive. Mr. Bosma was killed in that field. The two of you had to do some repositioning of the body at Bobcat of Brantford."

Smich adamantly denies Fraser's version of events.

"You followed [Millard] because that was part of the plan. It was the incineration phase of the killing of Mr. Bosma."

If Smich had wanted to get away, says Fraser, it would have been easy for him. It was Millard who had the dead man in his truck. "You don't follow lunatic Dell for twenty-three kilometres" to a dark farm, says Fraser.

"No, sir, in that situation, like I said, I was terrified. I didn't know what to do."

"They're explanations, they're excuses, they're not actions. Unless it's a plan, you don't follow him, you don't go to a hangar," says Fraser. "Unless it's a plan."

"I felt threatened, sir. I felt scared. I did what he told me to do—that's it."

Smich powered down his phone at 9:20 P.M., almost exactly the same time Millard turned off the burner phone. "You know you're being tracked and that you killed Mr. Bosma, and you don't want to be followed," Fraser says.

Smich denies it, insisting his battery went dead. He may even be telling the truth. But it's hard to know, given that he is, after all, the man with four cell phones and multiple missing SIM cards.

FRASER TELLS THE COURT there was no indication in the days following Tim Bosma's murder that Smich was truly scared of Millard. On the contrary, he says to Smich, "there is a comfort level between you two that is consistent from day one to day four. No fear, no distancing" is revealed in Smich's texts.

"I couldn't come to terms with the reality of the situation at the time."

"These are words, justifications, excuses," says Fraser. He shows a text from Millard to Smich sent at 11 A.M. on May 7, about half a day after the shooting. It's about their plan to return to the hangar that evening.

"Changed my mind bro, after 7pm," Millard writes.

"Oh snap," says Smich at 1:55 P.M. "Well in that case, I should go back to bed at some point, and she cant reach with us bcuz she work early next day. Link me when you're awake."

Fraser asks Smich to explain the garbled text.

"I believe [Millard] was asking Marlena to come with us," he says. "I don't think I discussed that with her."

"How about, 'Never in a million years would I have that conversation with Marlena, because that's a horrendous situation'?"

On Wednesday, having towed the incinerator back to the farm the night before and possibly cleaned it out, Smich and Millard split up. But Smich both called and texted Millard that day. Millard was heading out to Oakville to see Smich when he changed his mind. "Bro Im so tired, not going to have the energy to drive you home, I'll link you tomorrow."

"What's the dealio?" Smich texts back, and then later: "Get some sleep."

Millard tells him he almost fell asleep driving home.

"This is what I would describe as a very comfortable conversation between you and Mr. Millard," says Fraser.

At 3 A.M. on Thursday morning, Smich texts Millard asking him to come and get him at lunchtime that day.

Fraser says, "That's you on board, all in: 'Come get me.'"

Two minutes later, Smich asks, "you awake?" He tells his friend he's thinking of getting an X-ray for his shoulder.

"Yo holla," he texts, followed by a phone call to Millard. Not long after, Smich texts, "You wanna chill for a bit today?"

Fraser translates this as, "I, Mark Smich, want to spend a little time with lunatic Dell today."

"Yes, sir, like I said, I didn't know what to do at the time. I was trying to keep everything normal between us."

As the texts pile up, Smich continues to insist he really was stressed, shocked, paranoid, and that no one was supposed to die.

THURSDAY, MAY 9, WAS A very busy day for Millard and Smich, says Fraser. They had a lot of work to do to cover their tracks, including picking up Millard's red Dodge, burning evidence at the farm, and getting the Bosma truck out of the hangar to take to Kleinburg. Millard was driving his red truck and towing the trailer containing the stolen truck when he dropped Smich off at his mother's house in Oakville at 10 P.M. and then continued on to pick up Christina Noudga.

Fraser asks Smich who removed the DVR from the hangar, which Millard gave to Noudga that evening and which was eventually found in her closet. Smich doesn't recall, nor does he remember calling Millard that night at about 11 P.M., shortly after he'd been dropped off.

"What up bro, yo, link me back," Smich texted his friend very early Friday morning.

"You just wanted to get a progress report," says Fraser. "It's a comfort, it's an ease you have with each other. You're reaching out to him at 1:20 in the morning."

Some three hours later, Millard responded, "Retooled for stormy weather, all clear, getting some sleep now, 7am accounting meeting."

Smich knew exactly what that meant, says Fraser: Millard had gotten rid of the murder weapon.

Smich disagrees.

Fraser cites another Friday text from Smich to Millard in which he implies that Matthew Ward-Jackson can help get rid of the gun.

Fraser asks Smich why Millard called him at 3:43 P.M., after the Hamilton Police left the hangar. He suggests it was to say, "Mark, it's looking bad, the police were here, we gotta meet."

"You are the last person he spoke to in person before he was arrested on Cawthra Road," says Fraser. "The two of you had business to discuss: What do we do with the murder weapon, and what would we do with the stuff at Maple Gate?"

Smich insists the conversation couldn't have been detailed, because Brendan Daly was present. Fraser reminds Smich that Daly never said that.

"You can't remember a single thing about the conversation you had with Mr. Millard?" he asks.

Smich concedes that they probably would have talked about the police coming and that Millard was going to see a lawyer.

"There is no way you did not discuss with Mr. Millard exactly what you did in the hours following his arrest to get the murder weapon you destroyed and to get the drugs out of the house. You can agree or disagree, your call."

"Disagree."

Fraser shows an extraction report taken from Marlena Meneses's phone. There are several calls to and from Andrew Michalski.

"The conversation would have been me telling him Dell was arrested, get all the drugs out of the house, the police are probably coming there next," says Smich, adding that he would have later asked for the drugs because Meneses wanted them.

"He does exactly what you ask him to do," Fraser says of Michalski.

"He doesn't do exactly what I asked him to do. He contacted Matt Hagerman, which I did not ask him to do."

Fraser reminds Smich of Michalski's testimony. Michalski said Smich "wanted me to meet up with Hagerman, and he wanted whatever I had, and Hagerman had, brought to him the next day."

The phone logs show that as soon as Michalski got off the call during which Smich gave him these instructions, he phoned Hagerman. At 10:53 P.M., he also texted Hagerman "call me asap."

"Coincidence or plan, Mr. Smich?" Fraser tells Smich that getting the drugs and murder weapon from Michalski and Hagerman was all part of the plan he and Millard devised when they knew the police were closing in.

Smich counters that Michalski and Hagerman contradicted each other in court, that Hagerman said Michalski told him Dell wanted Smich to have the toolbox, that they lied to police.

Fraser cuts him off. "We'll let the jury decide who to believe, Mr. Smich. That's their function, not yours."

Smich tries again to discredit Michalski and Hagerman.

When he wants to proclaim his version of events to the jury, Smich is assertive, even aggressive, a far cry from the shell-shocked patsy he has portrayed himself as being in May 2013. Fraser asks him if he can at least concede that his ex-girlfriend Marlena Meneses was honest. Smich does. The video of him and Millard picking Meneses up on the morning of May 7 is played for the jury.

Fraser plays back the recording of the relevant portion of Meneses's evidence, where she described the mood in the truck that morning. "Very happy. They're just really happy, saying they wanted to celebrate," she testified. "They just said that their mission went well."

Fraser plays it again. "This is honest Marlena Meneses expressing clearly a celebration on the part of Dellen Millard and Mark Smich for the theft, the killing, and the incineration of Tim Bosma."

"No, sir. I believe she says also that Dell was happy that he got the truck. She was asked that by Mr. Sachak."

Fraser has come prepared. He reads from the transcripts of Meneses's cross-examination by Sachak and Thomas Dungey.

"You can just tell that they were happy," she tells Sachak. "You can tell when a normal person was happy."

Dungey asks her about her police statement given on May 22, 2013. "Dell told you he got the truck?"

"Yes," says Meneses. "They both told me that they, that the mission went well."

Fraser looks at Smich. "Mission accomplished. Right, Mr. Smich?"

"I don't know where she got this 'celebratory mood' from," says Smich.

"From you and Dellen Millard, right in that truck," says Fraser, as he ends his cross-examination, "celebrating the death of another human being."

SEVENTEEN

THE VERDICT

The closing arguments begin on May 31, 2016, after four long months of trial. Ravin Pillay appears first, followed by Thomas Dungey and then Tony Leitch. Each lawyer will take almost a full day to present his case. In a nutshell, Pillay's argument is that Dellen Millard couldn't have killed Tim Bosma because it makes no sense. Dungey's argument is that Mark Smich told the truth about a situation that makes no sense. And Leitch's argument is that while none of this makes sense, it is exactly what happened: Millard and Smich plotted for more than a year to steal a Dodge Ram 3500 and kill and incinerate its owner.

Pillay's and Dungey's closing arguments are in keeping with their style throughout the trial. Cool, calm, and methodical, Pillay has a high-tech presentation complete with audio and video and timed right down to the minute. Dungey, who says it's not his habit to rehearse, works with handwritten notes and leans so heavily on the lectern that it tilts. He looks at times as if he might keel over.

Throughout the closing arguments, the lawyers' lectern is positioned to face the jury, allowing them to talk directly to the six men and seven women, twelve of whom will decide this case. Even when they are seated and watching their colleagues, counsel will often turn their chairs so that they can see and be seen by the jurors, who now number one fewer than at the start of trial. In mid-May a jury member was dismissed after her brother died and the judge decided she would be too distracted to continue to serve.

Pillay tells the thirteen remaining jurors that in May 2013 Mark Smich was in desperate need of money. He wanted to move to Calgary, and Millard had promised him a Cadillac. He was ready to leave, but his friend felt no sense of urgency. Smich was worried that once again "Mr. Millard's overly cautious attitude would result in him backing out of the scoping mission." He was tired of living on the scraps Millard tossed him, so he brought "his chrome piece, his .380," says Pillay, quoting Smich's rap lyrics. "It was on the highway Smich pulled the gun," Pillay tells the jury. "[He] fucked up," as he later said to Marlena Meneses and Brendan Daly, and Tim Bosma died. It was an accident, not intentional. "Nobody kills somebody for a truck," says Pillay, "not even Mr. Smich."

Despite what he describes as the "sea of evidence" presented during four months of trial, Pillay maintains that none of it proves the Crown's theory that Dellen Millard and Mark Smich planned for a year to steal a truck and to kill and incinerate its owner. In fact, he says, it shows just the opposite, that there was *no* intention to kill, *no* planning and deliberation.

That night in May 2013 when he showed up in the Bosmas' driveway, Dellen Millard made eye contact with their tenant,

Wayne De Boer. Similarly, he made no secret of the fact that he wanted to get a truck, texting Lisa Whidden about it and even going so far as to tell Andrew Michalski he would steal it.

He hid neither his incriminating internet browser history nor his tattoos. The week of May 6, Millard arranged business meetings with colleagues and breakfasts with ex-girlfriends. "Why would he plan to have breakfast with Jenn [Spafford] on Thursday if he's planning to commit murder on Monday?" Pillay asks.

Millard never attempted to hide the Bosma truck. Waterloo Airport security came and looked through the Millardair windows and saw it sitting on the hangar floor. "What kind of plan is this?" says Pillay.

Millard even took Pedo along with him when he drove down to Ancaster for the test drive with Tim Bosma. "Why would anyone bring their dog on a planned and deliberate murder?" asks Pillay. "It makes no sense."

Everything Dellen Millard did was in reaction to an unforeseeable and unforeseen event. "The murder-for-a-truck allegation is simply absurd," he says.

"Consider what must have been racing through [Millard's] mind when Mr. Smich pulled a firearm," Pillay prompts the jury, attempting to explain why Millard helped incinerate Tim Bosma's body. Because there was never any plan other than to scope and steal, Millard left "a body of evidence that could identify him. He couldn't just dump the Bosma truck and run." He was trapped, and as a result "he dug a deeper and deeper hole for himself," says Pillay. "He involved others that he cared about," including his mother and Christina Noudga.

Pillay says the Super Sucker video shows that Smich is a liar. He argues that the mystery truck that drove past at 9:05 P.M. and again at 9:15 has to be the Bosma vehicle. The video corroborates Millard's version of events, and the anomalies in the timing can be accounted for by human error. Video analyst Michael Plaxton erred in not pointing out the complete story of the truck's travels, he says, and the police officer who collected the video did not follow proper procedure and failed to adequately verify the times. "The Super Sucker video establishes Mr. Smich lied to you under oath," Pillay tells the jury. "Mr. Smich's lie was designed to fit the Crown case as he knew it."

Pillay rejects the prosecution's theory that Tim Bosma was killed in the Bullmann field. A shot would have been heard. Pedo and the dog being walked by Rick Bullmann would have reacted. "Where is the glass?" he asks. "Where is the bullet?"

Millard's lawyer warns the jury not to put too much stock in the testimony of Marlena Meneses, whom he calls a proven liar. In her original statement to the police, she told them she didn't know about the incinerator and did not admit to cancelling Smich's phone almost immediately after Millard's arrest. "Relying on her evidence is very dangerous," says Pillay, who needs to discredit Meneses's testimony about Millard and Smich being in a celebratory mood the morning after the murder.

While Pillay concedes that Millard was involved in scoping out the truck to be stolen, that is as far as he is prepared to go. "There was no motive, no plan, no deliberation, no intention to kill, no attempt to conceal his identity," he says. "Mr. Millard is not guilty."

By the time he wraps up, precisely on schedule, Pillay has done almost everything a clever lawyer with a very weak case can do. The sentiment of many in the courtroom is that Pillay might well have succeeded in raising reasonable doubt for other people, *but he didn't fool me.*

AS HE BEGINS HIS closing arguments, Thomas Dungey stresses a point he will make repeatedly throughout the day. Sworn testimony is evidence, but theories floated by lawyers are not. This means that Mark Smich's version of events, given under oath, constitutes evidence. But, he says, the scenario of what happened on Highway 403, brought forth first by Nadir Sachak in his cross-examination of Smich and then by Ravin Pillay in closing arguments—in which Smich was alleged to have shot Bosma from the back seat of the truck while Millard drove—is nothing more than speculation, or "smoke and mirrors." Smich subjected himself to cross-examination and never wavered through more than a week of questioning by highly experienced defence and Crown lawyers, Dungey says. No part of the 403 scenario was ever tested in any way. "Millard's lawyers didn't call any evidence to support it," he stresses to the jury.

"Mr. Smich was not lying, and when you don't lie, you cannot break a person," he says. (Indeed, on social media, Smich's ability to stand firm was often fallaciously cited as a reason that his testimony must be true even though it was an obviously self-serving version of events.)

Dungey cannot provide an explanation of what happened in the truck that night or why. "We will never know why, as my client termed him, Lunatic Millard shot Mr. Bosma," he says. "All we know is that a man was killed for a truck for no reason. All we can know is a man flipped out, for whatever reason."

On a few points, Dungey actually agrees with Ravin Pillay. "It doesn't make any sense that there was planning and deliberation for over a year to steal, kill, and burn an individual. That theory is nonsense," says Dungey, *nonsense* being one of his favourite words. "All the evidence the Crown put forward was evidence to steal a truck, not to murder someone."

The motive of killing someone just for the thrill of it makes no sense to Dungey, he says, and he doesn't buy the prosecution's theory that Igor Tumanenko survived partly because of his size. "A gun kills anyone," he says. "Mr. Bosma was not a small man."

While Pillay tried to discredit Marlena Meneses's testimony by billing her as a liar out to protect Smich, Dungey takes a different tack. She has a "frail mind" and isn't the "fastest kid in town," he tells the jury. She may well have used the word *celebrate* to describe Smich's and Millard's behaviour after Bosma died because she was confused.

The red Cadillac is a red herring, Dungey goes on to say. The Super Sucker video can't corroborate a highway killing, because there is no evidence of a shooting on the 403. And Smich's raps are artistic expressions, nothing more.

He puts a photo of one of Millard's tattoos on the courtroom screens. It is large and located on his inner left forearm, the same arm with the small "ambition" tattoo on the outer wrist. The tattoo reads "I am heaven sent."

"'I am heaven sent.' 'I am Millard. I can do anything. I can kill with impunity.' That's the Millard before this court," Dungey blares.

Then, in a much softer voice, he concedes to the jurors that Mark Smich "is no choirboy" and that, yes, he failed to go to the police. He suggests that all his client may be guilty of is being an accessory after the fact to murder. But because that is not an option the jury can consider at this trial, Dungey tells them, "I am asking you to return the verdict that Mark Smich is not guilty."

TONY LEITCH'S CLOSING ARGUMENTS for the Crown begin in the same place that Craig Fraser's cross-examination of Mark Smich left off, with Smich's and Millard's buoyant mood after the completion of their "mission."

"Their celebration tells you everything you need to know about this case," says Leitch. "Marlena Meneses was honest and clearly now understands what she was involved in and deeply regrets her failure to do something when she should have. She is correcting that wrong here, telling the truth about everything, including Mark Smich's and Dellen Millard's celebration."

Before outlining the evidence, Leitch tells the jury he will review some legal principles crucial to their decisions. They will be covered in more detail by Justice Goodman in his charge to the jury, but Leitch wants the jurors to understand that this case is not about who fired the shot that killed Tim Bosma. They are not required to prove what happened or determine who did what inside Bosma's truck. What they are here to decide is whether Millard and Smich were in it together, whether they both knowingly participated in a murder in a way that helped or encouraged the other. "If you are spending your time trying to decide who did what, you are missing the point," says Leitch. "So long as they planned to murder Tim Bosma and one helped the other carry out the plan, they are both equally guilty in the eyes of our law."

Leitch raises the question of motive, the issue that has troubled so many since the week Tim Bosma disappeared. "Don't be left in doubt because you want to rationalize their murderous actions," he says. "Just follow the evidence that shows what they did, that shows they intended to kill him in their carefully planned mission.

"The fact is, sometimes people are just killers."

Throughout his closing, as Leitch recaps much of the evidence presented in court, he tries to explain questions raised not just by the defence lawyers but also by members of the public confused by the actions of the accused. He suggests, for example, that Dellen Millard showed his face to Sharlene Bosma and Wayne De Boer because that's the kind of guy he is. "He takes chances. He is over-confident. He thinks he's untouchable."

When Leitch raises the subject of why it took so long for Millard and Smich to carry out their plan, he faces a severe handicap. He cannot mention the death of Laura Babcock, who police believe was incinerated shortly after the purchase of the Eliminator in the summer of 2012. Nor can he mention the alleged murder of Wayne Millard five months later. Leitch can only point to the texts that show the 3500 mission had been in the works for more than a year, interrupted by Bobcat heists, Millardair official business, and cash flow woes.

As for why Millard showed people the Eliminator and informed them of his plans to steal a truck, Leitch says that he is a man who surrounds himself with a special type of person. Shane Schlatman and Christina Noudga didn't ask questions. Andrew Michalski was a trusted confidant and a member of the Millard missions team, who lived in his house. Lisa Whidden was still batting her eyes at her accused murderer ex-boyfriend from the witness box. "In his mind, Dellen Millard believed he could control all these people," says Leitch. Similarly, he expected Smich to be able to keep Meneses silent.

Leitch also believes the plan went wrong and that Tim Bosma was never meant to be killed inside his truck. This explains why Millard had meetings and dates set up for the week ahead.

He thought the cleanup would be quick and that the incineration could be done at the farm, using the generator he had prepared in late April. But when things didn't go as planned, Millard and Smich needed electricity and light and water to clean the truck, so the Eliminator was moved to the hangar. Millard's "all-nighter" turned into an unplanned "three-dayer."

Leitch says the Crown can't prove definitively that Tim Bosma was killed in the field, as he and Craig Fraser believe. He has no explanation for the Super Sucker truck sightings. There are only two people left who know the truth about what happened, and they are keeping it to themselves. "We don't have all the answers," he tells the jury. "You don't need to know exactly how it happened."

The Noudga letters, Leitch reminds the jury, show Millard desperately scrambling for a story that will get him out of jail. In them, Millard states that he won't know what defence he should use until he sees more from the Crown's disclosure and learns what exactly the police have on him. At first, Millard is obsessed with getting Michalski to change his story and say Millard wanted to buy, not steal, a truck. Then he begins fabricating tales of fictitious killers named Itchy and his "boyz." At the trial, he tests the we-were-only-going-to-scope-it defence, followed by the Smich-shot-him-on-the-highway version, which emerged in the final days of testimony.

According to Leitch, Mark Smich's evidence is not reliable. "It is a lie," he says. "And it was designed by him to shift the blame for a joint crime he and Millard committed." His vagueness and memory failure was to avoid being pinned down and tested in cross-examination. "He was weaving a story to fit the evidence, a story he hopes will cause you to doubt his guilt."

Leitch says Thomas Dungey repeatedly failed to put critical parts of Smich's story to key trial witnesses. Igor Tumanenko was never asked if the GPS features of his truck were discussed on the test drive. Shane Schlatman was never asked if he showed Millard and Smich how to hotwire cars. Brendan Daly was never asked if he was present at the meeting between Millard and Smich that took place at 30 Speers Road just before Millard's arrest. Rick Bullmann was never asked if he saw a vehicle do a U-turn. Marlena Meneses was never asked if she spoke with Christina Noudga the night of Millard's arrest.

Smich's evidence also conflicts with the testimony of many reliable witnesses, says Leitch. Not to mention that it makes no sense to shoot somebody in a moving vehicle while you are driving, as Smich implies Millard must have done. It wouldn't be easy, Leitch points out, to get a good shot with one hand on the wheel and the other on a gun that your intended victim could grab at any moment when your attention was on the road. The notion is "ridiculous," he concludes. "It never happened."

In the three and a half days following the murder, Millard and Smich were in contact by phone sixty-eight times outside the hours they were actually together, strong evidence of their continuing partnership, says Leitch. Reminding the jurors of the nicknames the two friends gave each other, he describes them as "the Millard and Smich team—Dellen the Felon and Sayio."

He asks the jury not to forget the victim when they retire to consider their verdict. "Let the evidence guide you to the only just result for their crime: convictions for both of them for the first-degree murder of Tim Bosma."

JUDGES' CHARGES TO JURIES are not easy to sit through, especially when they last almost two entire days. The purpose of the charge is to instruct the jurors, who are the so-called triers of facts, on how to apply the law to the facts of the case.

At this charge, one of the first orders of business is the dismissal of another juror over family matters. As a result, there is no need, with the number already down to the required twelve, to draw straws before the jury can retire. The original jury of six men and eight women is now composed of six men and six women.

Jury charges consist in part of boilerplate instructions familiar to viewers of TV legal dramas. Among other things, the jurors are reminded that the accused are innocent until proven guilty; that if a defendant chose not to testify, his decision should not be held against him; and that though a defendant may have done bad things on other occasions, it doesn't make him guilty of the crime with which he stands charged.

The judge will also summarize the evidence in the case and instruct on the specific legal issues that are relevant. Pedagogically, the exercise is a nightmare. The legal points can be arcane and intricate. Listening to a person talk for hours is exhausting. And everyone—jurors, court officers, spectators—is locked in the courtroom, forbidden to leave while the judge is speaking. Journalists at the Bosma trial tweet, on at least one occasion, about the sounds of snoring emanating from the audience.

On day two of the charge, when the judge gives the jury handouts of four decision trees they will be asked to use, there is mass confusion among those following the case online. A decision tree is a schematic tree-shaped diagram, like a flow chart, used to outline potential courses of action. In a complicated murder case, unless you are a savant, you have to look at the trees to make any sense of them (and even then, there are no guarantees), but only the jury gets hard copies. In this case, the decision trees are supposed to help guide jurors through the decision-making process, whether the decision being contemplated has to do with first-degree murder, second-degree murder, manslaughter, or aiding and abetting. Among the non-lawyers, the charge gives rise to jokes and eye-rolling about not seeing the decision forest for the decision trees.

Finally, late in the afternoon of June 13, the jurors are sent off to make their deliberations. Until they reach a verdict, they will be sequestered at the courthouse from 9:30 A.M. to 8:30 P.M. and then in a hotel at night. Although, from the time they are selected, jurors are ordered to refrain from reading and watching media reports about the case, it is only during deliberations that they are actually monitored and physically cut off from media. There is no TV in their hotel rooms, their phones are taken away, and court constables patrol the hallways.

THE MOMENT THE JURY is sequestered at a major trial, reporters publish what have come to be known as What the Jury Didn't Hear stories. These articles, which reveal information about the accused deemed inadmissible as evidence at trial, frequently provoke indignation and outrage about how the rights of the accused trump those of victims and prevent police and prosecutors from doing their jobs. (In the Bosma case, however, much of the inadmissible material remained withheld after the trial and is subject to an ongoing temporary publication ban.

This is because Justice Goodman ruled that releasing it could prejudice the fair trial rights of Millard and Smich, who also face first-degree murder charges in the death of Laura Babcock. That trial is scheduled to begin in Toronto in February 2017. Only when the jury is sequestered in the Babcock case will all the details of what wasn't heard at the Bosma trial become known. And in fall 2017, Millard alone is set to stand trial for the murder of his father. Millard has said he plans to represent himself and plead not guilty at both those trials. Smich will also plead not guilty to the murder of Laura Babcock.)

After the jury retired to deliberate, Justice Goodman did allow the following revelations to be published, however.

Robert Burns, Dellen's uncle, had told the police that his nephew was a "sick, twisted prick," but he was instructed not to make similar comments in court. That kind of character evidence is frequently considered too prejudicial. Despite having his testimony seriously constrained, Burns made it clear from his body language that he loathed Millard.

Along with Christina Noudga, Shane Schlatman also received letters written in jail by Millard and delivered by Madeleine Burns. He destroyed the letters, which he said were about cars and which violated the court order forbidding Millard to contact him.

Schlatman's father-in-law, Art Jennings, was not allowed to tell the jury about a secret compartment he and Schlatman were building in one of Millard's trailers, possibly to smuggle drugs into Canada after Millard attended the 2013 Baja race in Mexico.

Millard wanted Marlena Meneses to wear a fake pregnancy belly to bring bullets into Canada from the United States. She tried it on but never went through with the proposed plan, as both she and Smich thought it was a bad idea.

There was far more drug use in Millard's circle than the judge wanted revealed at trial. Although he originally tried to restrict the drug evidence to marijuana, by the end of the trial the jury had heard about narcotics in the toolbox, cocaine use, and Smich's oxycodone habit. But the jury did not hear about incidents involving heroin and steroids.

Millard owned a second gun, a Smith & Wesson Bodyguard .380, but the judge did not want it mentioned at trial. Goodman's rationale for restricting gun evidence remains unclear.

THE JURY SPENDS ALMOST four days deliberating. The Bosma family and friends stay either at the courthouse or nearby, prepared to be called back to hear a verdict within an hour's notice. The "Bosma Army," as the family's many supporters have come to be known, can often be spotted at the park across the street from the courthouse, where television crews are staked out and members of the family's Christian Reformed Church have set up a makeshift "prayer wall" complete with brightly coloured Post-it Notes. Sharlene and her sister try their hand at Jenga, the block-stacking game, while others sit in the sun and chat. Inside, on the sixth floor of the courthouse, there are card games, knitting, snacks, and full meals.

The jury makes two requests during its sequestration. On Monday evening, just hours after deliberations began, they ask when Tim Bosma went for gas. The answer is that there was no testimony about a trip for gas. A day later, the jurors say they want to listen again to portions of the testimony of Millard's friend Matt Hagerman. Not long after they enter the court-room to hear the testimony on Wednesday morning, one juror blanches. He is taken away for emergency medical attention and given a shot for what turns out to be a migraine. Soon he is ready to proceed, and everyone is ushered back into the courtroom to resume listening.

THE JURY IS NOT heard from again until Friday, just after 2 P.M., when court officials begin spreading the word that the verdict will be delivered in one hour. Within minutes, a long line has formed outside Courtroom 600. Sharlene Bosma, with her sister at her side, rushes back from outside. She looks as if she is about to break down in tears.

As a security measure, the front row, which is usually occupied by the Bosmas and journalists, is filled with police. Everyone else is bumped one row back. There is no sign of Smich's mother, but court officers make room for his sister. The blond mystery woman who is friends with Millard is in her regular seat. One of the dismissed jurors has come back to hear her fellow jury members' verdict. She is placed in the front row, next to police. Sharlene's head is bowed. Mary and Hank Bosma look straight ahead.

The atmosphere in the courtroom is extremely tense. In a four-month trial with two defendants and more than ninety witnesses, three and a half days is not a long time to deliber-ate. This jury was a conscientious one. Many members took notes throughout the trial. Others would decline to ride in the courthouse elevators not just with the lawyers on the case but also with the press. The general feeling is that a relatively quick decision is good news for the prosecution, although juries can always surprise. As they enter the room for the final time, most of the jury members avoid meeting anyone's eye. One or two cast a glance at the accused.

Millard and Smich are in the prisoner's box for the first time since jury selection. Smich appears nervous, while Millard is unreadable. In the last few weeks of the trial, Millard has been far less animated than he was at the beginning, but he has continued to smirk and regularly look Smich up and down even as his co-accused ignored him.

"I am informed that the jury has arrived at their verdict," says the judge. The jury foreman, who is an older man, hands an envelope to a court officer to pass to the judge, who opens it, looks at the contents, and nods. The envelope is returned to the foreman.

The lawyers for the two accused stand beside them next to the prisoner's box.

Millard is told to stand. The court registrar asks the foreman for the verdict.

"Guilty of first-degree murder," he says.

Now comes the verdict for the second defendant, the one who many observers believe—or fear—has a reasonable chance of a second degree conviction.

Smich is told to stand.

"Guilty of first-degree murder," says the foreman.

Ravin Pillay and Thomas Dungey ask for the jurors to be polled individually. One by one, they stand and say they agree with the verdict for Dellen Millard and then they rise again to voice their agreement with the verdict for Mark Smich.

As they absorb the news, the Bosmas are smiling broadly and

crying. One of Tim's sisters, who until now has always been calm on the surface, is half sobbing, half laughing. The dismissed juror looks quietly pleased. The overwhelmingly delighted audience was warned before the verdict to maintain order no matter what the result.

The judge endorses the indictment and enters first-degree murder convictions. He reminds the jurors that according to Canadian law everything that happened during their deliberations must be kept secret. "You are now all discharged," he says. "Goodbye, and thank you." Tony Leitch says the Bosma family does not wish to make victim impact statements for the purpose of sentencing. Because the penalty for first-degree murder is an automatic twenty-five years to life, no sentencing hearing is required. "We're asking they be sentenced immediately," says Leitch.

Justice Goodman is caught by surprise by this request and says he needs time to prepare some comments. Sentencing will take place at 4:30 P.M. As the courtroom clears, loud cheers can be heard in the hallways as spectators applaud the exiting Bosma family, the Crown attorneys, and the homicide detectives in charge of the case. It's a moment that might not make sense unless you're present, in which case it seems like the most natural reaction in the world. There's a giant wave of relief that justice has been done and the trial is finally over.

Outside the courtroom, people are hugging each other, from the top OPP officer on the case to the young woman who cleans the courthouse bathrooms. The only person who appears unhappy is Millard's blond mystery friend. She is talking on her phone, visibly distraught and more animated than she has ever been.

WHEN COURT RESUMES FOR the sentencing, Millard and Smich are asked if they have anything to say. Both decline to comment. Justice Goodman calls their crime "incomprehensible and unimaginable" and praises the Bosma family for its strength of character. Despite the despicable and callous actions of Millard and Smich, he says, Tim Bosma's memory and spirit cannot be taken away. Then he turns to the two convicted men.

"You are both sentenced to an automatic mandatory term of imprisonment for life, or at least until 2038."

Millard had tried to make eye contact with Sharlene Bosma as he entered the courtroom for sentencing, prompting jeers from onlookers. But on his way out for the last time, he keeps his eyes straight ahead. Smich bows his head, something he has never done before.

A few minutes later, in the park across the street, Sharlene Bosma, surrounded by microphones and cameras, reads from a statement she has prepared. It is a hot, humid, late spring day, and she is wearing a long white eyelet skirt and black blouson T-shirt. She is glad that the trial is done, that this chapter is over, that she no longer has to sit in the same room and breathe the same air as Millard and Smich. "For Tim's murderers, their life sentence begins now," she says. "Ours began over three years ago when they murdered Tim."

As Sharlene speaks, with Hank and Mary Bosma, Tim's sisters, and her own family behind her, passing cars honk in support and a crowd gathers to watch. Although the pain of losing Tim will never go away, Tim's friends and family have learned to laugh again and to enjoy what they still have, she says. Later that night, they will celebrate, drink champagne, and remember Tim.

The next day, *The Hamilton Spectator* publishes a revelatory interview with Hank and Mary Bosma. Mary uses an expression few would have dared utter in her presence when she tells journalist Susan Clairmont that Tim's murder was a "thrill kill" and that his killers were "upping their game." Hank reveals that he was not always as composed as he looked. There were times, he says, when he wanted "to jump out and kick the living daylights out of" Millard and Smich.

At first, when the Bosmas contemplated their son's death, they were haunted by horrific possibilities. "That was the hardest part," says Mary. "Not knowing his last moments, how he died. Did he suffer? Did they torture him? Did they burn him alive?" When they eventually learned the Crown's theory, that Tim was shot in his truck shortly after leaving his house, "the weight just went off our shoulders," says Hank.

The Bosmas, like so many of the strangers who have followed their case, still ponder the question of what turned Millard and Smich into thrill killers, what toxic combination of nature and nurture produced two young men whose ambition in life was to target, murder, and incinerate a fellow human being. While more facts are bound to be revealed at the Laura Babcock and Wayne Millard trials, the full truth may never be known. Those with genuine insights into Millard's and Smich's backgrounds may choose, as they have until now, not to share their knowledge. How the two friends became monsters may remain as unknowable as what happened inside Tim Bosma's truck.

What can be known, and what this book has told, is the story of just some of the people—family, friends, police officers, lawyers, expert witnesses, jurors, and judge—who all did their part to ensure that justice was done for Tim Bosma.

ACKNOWLEDGMENTS

Starting at the very beginning, I'd like to thank Kevin Libin at the *National Post* for publishing my first article on the Millard family and Millardair. The *Post*'s crime reporter Adrian Humphreys generously provided his insights and input.

It goes without saying that I am grateful to everyone who talked and wrote to me to share their knowledge of events and how they unfolded. Some of those many people are named in this book. Others preferred to remain unnamed. All were a big help and should not be blamed for any mistakes or inaccuracies. Those are all on me.

Special thanks to kickass researchers Sylvia Nowak and Lynn Wiegard; photographer Mike Burgess, a man of many skills; and "Ms. Sherlock," an online sleuth whose breadth of knowledge covers everything from airport regulation to dairy barns to mojito making. "Civilians" James Andrew and Ron Verbeek put together trial documents and Tweet sheets that were an invaluable public resource, and that I relied on time and again in pulling everything together.

The staff at the Hamilton courthouse deserve a huge shout out for being so efficient and helpful in providing the media with trial exhibits almost daily. My colleagues in the press corps always had each other's backs. Extra thanks to Alex Pierson and

Sam Pazzano for the many rides and rush-hour conversations en route back to Toronto, and to Nicole Lampa and Molly Hayes for favours rendered.

At Penguin Random House Canada, assistant editor Justin Stoller was a huge help at deadline time. And it was a pleasure to work with publishing director Diane Turbide for the first time since the old *McGill Daily* days. Alex Schultz was the best copy editor ever, solving my tense problems and so much more.

Thanks, too, to Tycho Manson for introducing me to Iain MacKinnon, who is always soothing, supportive, and succinct with his legal advice.

I am grateful as always to my family and friends for their patience and encouragement as I worked on this project.

And finally, I am in awe of the Bosma family for the inspirational manner in which they coped with an unimaginable crime. If you would like to know more, please visit the website for TimsTribute.ca, the charity founded by Sharlene Bosma after her husband was murdered.

INDEX

Note: See pages xi–xiii for a list of individuals grouped by category.
See pages viii–x for a timeline of events.